SUSTAINABLE BUSINESS MODELS

ENTREPRENEURIAL BEHAVIOUR

Series Editors:

Dr Andrea Caputo, University of Trento, Italy

Dr Massimiliano M. Pellegrini, University of Rome Tor Vergata, Italy

This series is dedicated to communicating innovative and multi-disciplinary new research that advances theory and practice in *Entrepreneurial Behaviour*. The series is focused on expanding the scope of *Entrepreneurial Behaviour* theory and analysis and enriching practice by encouraging multi-theoretical, multi-cultural, and multi-disciplinary approaches.

Key issues explored in *Entrepreneurial Behaviour* include cognition, decision-making, organizational behaviors, and identifying, creating, and exploiting opportunities concerning new products, services, processes, innovations, or ventures from entrepreneurial perspective.

The primary focus will be on the study of entrepreneurs, small and medium enterprises, and family businesses, with a secondary focus on entrepreneurial and innovative behaviors in other forms of organizations, such as non-profit corporations, and public administration.

SUSTAINABLE BUSINESS MODELS

Insights from the Tourism, Cultural and Creative Sectors

EDITED BY

MARIA DELLA LUCIA
University of Trento, Italy

ERICA SANTINI
University of Trento, Italy

ANDREA CAPUTO
University of Trento, Italy

AND

FABRIZIO PANOZZO
Ca' Foscari University of Venice, Italy

United Kingdom – North America – Japan – India
Malaysia – China

Emerald Publishing Limited
Emerald Publishing, Floor 5, Northspring, 21-23 Wellington Street, Leeds LS1 4DL

First edition 2026

Editorial matter and selection © 2026 Maria Della Lucia, Erica Santini, Andrea Caputo, and Fabrizio Panozzo.
Individual chapters © 2026 The authors.
Published by Emerald Publishing Limited.

Reprints and permissions service
Contact: www.copyright.com

British Library Cataloguing in Publication Data
A catalog record for this book is available from the British Library

ISBN: 978-1-80592-674-0 (Print)
ISBN: 978-1-80592-671-9 (Online)
ISBN: 978-1-80592-673-3 (Epub)

INVESTOR IN PEOPLE

CONTENTS

LIST OF FIGURES AND TABLES

FIGURES

TABLES

ABOUT THE EDITORS

Maria Della Lucia is Professor of Tourism and Business Management at the University of Trento, Italy, and Coordinator of the Research Task "Sustainable Business Models," iNEST Spoke 6. She holds a PhD in Economics and Management. Her research focuses on heterodox approaches to systems development and management, culture-based urban regeneration, creative cities and creative tourism, humanistic tourism, destination management and governance, and digital and social media marketing. She has authored and co-authored articles in leading journals such as *Tourism Management, Journal of Sustainable Tourism, Cities, International Journal of Tourism Research, Tourism Geographies, and European Planning Studies.*

Erica Santini is Associate Professor of Innovation at the Department of Economics and Management and at the School of Innovation of the University of Trento. She holds a PhD in Economics from the University of Florence, Italy, and researches technological transformation and sustainable transition in both manufacturing and service industries. Her work has been published in *Regional Studies, Entrepreneurship & Regional Development, Small Business Economics, Journal of Cultural Economics*, and other international journals.

Andrea Caputo is Associate Professor in Management at the University of Trento, Italy, and Professor of Strategy & Negotiation at the University of Lincoln, UK. He holds a PhD in Management from the University of Rome Tor Vergata, Italy. His research focuses on entrepreneurial decision-making, negotiation, digitalization and sustainability, internationalization, and the strategic management of SMEs. He has published over 100 academic contributions in these areas. His achievements include being recognized on the World's Top 2% Scientists List of outstanding researchers by Elsevier BV, Stanford University (USA) in 2021, 2022, and 2023.

Fabrizio Panozzo is Associate Professor of Management at the Venice School of Management, Ca' Foscari University of Venice, Italy, and Scientific Coordinator of iNEST Spoke 6. He holds a PhD in Business Administration and researches the interplay between business economics, artistic practices, and cultural production. He introduced Critical Management Studies to Italy and has explored how art-based approaches can foster innovation and sustainable economic models. He currently chairs Aiku, Ca' Foscari's research center for culture, creativity, and entrepreneurship.

ABOUT THE CONTRIBUTORS

Matteo Baldan is Research Fellow with a Msc in Chemistry from the University of Padova, Italy. His research activities focus on the revalorization of waste materials and their transformation into new products, with an emphasis on sustainability and environmental impact. He is currently affiliated with Ca' Foscari University of Venice.

Bob Bastian is Assistant Professor of Management at the University of Trento, Italy. He received his PhD from the University of Bergamo, Italy, and has had academic experiences at the Rijksuniversiteit Groningen in the Netherlands and IAE Lyon in France. His current research focuses on entrepreneurial decision-making, uncertainty, and sustainability and has published in journals such as in Harvard Business Review and Entrepreneurship Theory and Practice.

Valentina Beghetto is Associate Professor at the Department of Molecular Sciences and Nanosystems, Ca' Foscari University of Venice, Italy. She holds a PhD in Chemistry and is an expert in polymer chemistry, biomass-derived plastics, and leather chemistry. Her research focuses on the development of eco-sustainable materials and processes for the manufacturing industry, with applications supporting circular economy principles. She has authored over 150 publications and patents. Since 2014, she has been the Founder and Scientific Coordinator of Crossing Srl, leading more than 20 national, regional, and European Union-funded projects on sustainable materials and green technologies.

Maurizio Busacca is Associate Professor of Economic Sociology at Ca' Foscari University of Venice, Italy. His research focuses on welfare systems, social innovation, and the organizational dynamics of economic processes. He has published widely on the intersections between economic practices, institutional frameworks, and collective action.

Margherita De Luca is Research fellow at the Venice School of Management, Ca' Foscari University of Venice. Her work focuses on the intersection of cultural entrepreneurship, artistic practices, and sustainable tourism in heritage cities. She has contributed to iNEST – Spoke 6, focusing on art-based business models and their role in reimagining tourist destinations, particularly in the context of overtourism in Venice. She is currently involved in the Young Researchers project "Sustainable Business Models for Tourism with a Culture-based Approach."

Rossana Demurtas is a former Research Assistant at the Department of Engineering at the Free University of Bozen-Bolzano, where she contributed to the Interconnected Nord-Est Innovation Ecosystem project, focusing on compliance with accessibility regulations in the tourism sector to promote sustainability. She holds a Master's degree in Law and Economics from the University of Bologna and currently works in the renewable energy field.

Chiara Carolina Donelli is Assistant Professor at the Venice School of Management, Ca' Foscari University of Venice, Italy. She holds a PhD in Innovation and Sustainability Economics and Management from the Universities of Parma and Ferrara, Italy. Her research focuses on sustainability in the arts, particularly its social and environmental dimensions, and the role of art in sustainable tourism. She has been a visiting scholar at the University of South Australia, Adelaide. She is the Principal Investigator of the iNEST Young Researchers project "Sustainable Business Models for Tourism with a Culture-based Approach.".

Giulia Dore is Assistant Professor in Private Comparative Law at the University of Trento, Italy. She holds a PhD in European and Comparative Legal Studies. Her research focuses on the interplay of social norms in the context of intellectual property rights, legal geography, IP and managerial implications on the digitization of cultural heritage, and the broader development of open culture. She has published in journals such as *IIC – International Review of Intellectual Property and Competition Law*, *European Intellectual Property Review*, and *Queen Mary Journal of Intellectual Property*.

Stefania Denise Escobar is Postdoctoral Researcher at the Faculty of Economics and Management and is affiliated with the Competence Center for Mountain Innovation Ecosystems of the Free University of Bozen-Bolzano, Italy. She holds a PhD in Management and Economics from the Free University of Bozen-Bolzano. Her research focuses on sustainable innovation, smart business ecosystems, tourism management, and public sector management.

She has published in international journals such as *Journal of Knowledge Management, Cities and Current Issues in Tourism.*

Camilla Ferri is Postdoc at Copenhagen Business School, Department of Business Humanities and Law, Denmark, and part of the Rethinking Entrepreneurship project. She holds a PhD focused on the role of the materiality of the past in organizing for the future. Her research examines business history and entrepreneurship, particularly in the context of tourism and culture. She studies long-standing organizations and creative entrepreneurs, exploring the relationship between change and continuity and the role of temporality in business and society. Her qualitative approach includes visual and textual data as well as historical sources. She is currently involved in projects on uses of the past, organizational categories, and craft entrepreneurship from a historical perspective.

Muhammad Junaid Shahid Hasni is Postdoctoral Researcher with a PhD in Economics and Management from the University of Trento, Italy. His research focuses on consumer behavior, food-related consumption patterns, branding, and digital marketing. He has published in leading journals such as the *Journal of Business Ethics* and *the European Journal of Marketing*. Alongside international academic collaborations, he brings professional experience from the textile and telecom sectors to his research and teaching.

Stefan Lazic is a Research fellow at the Department of Economics and Management of the University of Trento, Italy where he obtained his PhD in Sustainability: Economics, Environment, Management and Society (SUSTEEMS) programme from the same University. His research focuses on regenerative development, regenerative tourism, community-led enterprises, more-than-human ethics, and heterodox approaches to the economy. In addition to his academic work, he has professional experience as a practitioner in these fields.

Maria Lusiani is Associate Professor of Accounting and Business Administration at the University of Bologna, Italy. Her research explores management and accounting practices in public and nonprofit organizations, particularly in cultural and creative sectors, using qualitative methodologies including case studies, ethnography, historical analysis, and discourse analysis. She previously was a postdoctoral fellow at HEC Montréal and held faculty positions at Ca' Foscari University of Venice, where she directed the master's degree and research center in Arts and Cultural Management.

Chiara Massacesi is Postdoctoral Researcher at the Free University of Bozen-Bolzano, Italy. She holds a PhD in Tourism and Food Heritage Tourism from the University of Otago, New Zealand. Her research focuses on tourism and authenticity in mountain areas, combining rural sociology and cultural studies. She has published articles and book chapters on cheese and gastronomic tourism, emphasizing collaboration among diverse stakeholders. Beyond academia, she has worked as a Consultant for NGOs and currently advises food-producing small businesses and Destination Management Organizations on sustainable gastronomic tourism development to promote local heritage and sustainable practices.

Maria Menendez-Blanco is Assistant Professor at the Faculty of Engineering of the Free University of Bozen/Bolzano, Italy. She holds a PhD in Information and Communication Technologies. Her primary research interest lies in human–computer interaction for societal engagement, specifically exploring how technologies can enable or hinder democratic processes of participation. Her work has been published in top international journals such as *ACM Transactions on Computer-Human Interaction* and *International Journal of Human-Computer Studies.*

Stefano Micelli is full Professor of Business Economics and Management at Ca' Foscari University of Venice, Italy, and Director of the Manager's Development Programme. His research focuses on the transformation of the Italian economic system, particularly the evolution of the manufacturing sector and the role of craftsmanship in innovation. He is Executive President of Upskill 4.0, a spin-off of Ca' Foscari University; a Member of the Advisory Board Italy and Advisory Board Nord Est of UniCredit; and a Member of the Scientific Committee of Symbola. He is the author of influential books, including *Futuro Artigiano* (Marsilio, 2011) and *Fare è Innovare. Il nuovo lavoro artigiano* (Il Mulino, 2016).

Sofia Mizzan is Research Fellow at Ca' Foscari University of Venice, Italy, working on models for regenerating the social and economic fabric of Venice. She holds a dual degree in International Management from Ca' Foscari University and SKEMA Business School, France. Her research focuses on the role of SMEs in fostering sustainable business models, cultural enterprises, and territorial revitalization. She has organized workshops, seminars, and training programs to promote entrepreneurship and innovation and collaborates with Upskill 4.0 on digital transformation projects and strategic consulting for SMEs.

Linda Osti is Senior Lecturer in Tourism Management at Bangor University, where she leads the Tourism, Destinations, and Place Engagement research group. Her research focuses on sustainable tourism, with particular emphasis on its socio-cultural aspects and the behavior of green tourists. Her academic and applied research projects aim to enhance the well-being of local communities as key actors in fostering equitable forms of tourism.

Marina Clerici Rasini is an Artist, Farmer, and Philanthropist. Together with her daughters Sofia, Olivia, and Thea Rasini, she manages the activities of the Castel Campo estate and operates the organic agricultural farm "Castel Campo," Italy. She also oversees the limited company "Il Campo s.r.l." and actively contributes to initiatives promoted by the non-profit organization "Associazione Campo Base Onlus."

Paola Rovelli is Associate Professor at the Faculty of Economics and Management of the Free University of Bozen-Bolzano, Italy. She is a Member of the Entrepreneurship, Innovation and Management Cluster and the Competence Centre for Mountain Innovation Ecosystems. She holds a PhD summa cum laude in Management, Economics, and Industrial Engineering from Politecnico di Milano, Italy. Her research focuses on organizational design, individual characteristics, and family business. She has published in leading journals such as *Journal of Management Studies, Human Relations, Strategic Entrepreneurship Journal,* and *The Leadership Quarterly.*

Silvia Sacchetti is Professor of Political Economy in the Department of Sociology and Social Research of the University of Trento, Italy, where she also coordinates the research unit on Economic Institutions and the Common Good (Cives). Her research explores the interconnections between human motivations, organizational governance, and production systems, including the role of civil society in fostering personal capabilities, identifying publics, and generating shared value for communities. Recent applications include the cultural and welfare sectors.

Olga Tzatzadaki is Research Fellow at Ca' Foscari University of Venice, Italy. She holds a PhD in Urban Planning and Public Policies from the University IUAV of Venice. Her research focuses on sustainable business models and social innovation in tourism, with emphasis on community-based approaches and participatory governance models. Additional research areas include the valorization of non-conventional narratives for socio-spatial analysis.

Federica Viganò is Senior Researcher at the Faculty of Education of the Free University of Bozen-Bolzano, Italy, and is affiliated with the Competence

Center for Mountain Innovation Ecosystems and the Competence Center for Sustainability. Her transdisciplinary research focuses on sustainability and eco-social transitions across sectors, including energy, agriculture, and creative industries, with particular attention to rural areas. Her work has been published in journals such as *Journal of Rural Studies*, *Sociologia Urbana e Rurale*, and *City, Culture and Society*.

ABOUT THE iNEST PROJECT

Under Italy's National Recovery and Resilience Plan (PNRR), funded by the NextGeneration EU program, Innovation Ecosystems are a national initiative designed to foster innovation, drive technology transfer, and support sustainable economic development across Italy. These ecosystems represent a cornerstone of Italy's broader strategy to build a resilient, green, and knowledge-based economy grounded in regional potential and inter-institutional collaboration. Each Innovation Ecosystem is a network of universities, public research institutions, territorial bodies, and companies strategically distributed throughout the country to leverage and enhance regional strengths. These networks focus on specific domains of excellence that reflect the unique economic, industrial, and research vocations of each region. The goal is to align innovation initiatives with regional needs and capabilities. To ensure strategic coherence and value creation while engaging diverse domains of excellence and stakeholders, each ecosystem follows a "hub-and-spoke" organizational model. A leading institution (the Hub) coordinates activities with a network of regional partners (the Spokes), ensuring both central guidance and localized action.

The iNEST Project – Interconnected Nord-Est Innovation Ecosystem is the ecosystem located in the North-East of Italy aimed at accelerating digital and ecological transitions across the northeastern regions of Italy, that is, Friuli-Venezia Giulia, Veneto, and the Autonomous Provinces of Trento and Bolzano. This area makes a significant contributor to the Italian economy, accounting for only 2% of the national population but producing 14% of Italy's GDP and 20% of its exports. It is marked by strong territorial identity and a diverse array of productive specializations reflected in the iNEST Project's nine domains of excellence (Spokes). These thematic networks bring together 24 partners, including 9 universities, 3 public research institutions, and 12 private entities under the coordination of the University of Padua, which serves as the Hub. Far beyond a funding mechanism, iNEST represents a strategic effort to drive regional transformation through innovation that is place-sensitive, socially embedded, and intersectorally collaborative.

Within this ecosystem, the Tourism, Culture, and Creative Industries network (Spoke 6) contributes both structurally and thematically to the overarching objectives of the iNEST project. Led by Ca' Foscari University of Venice, iNEST involves collaborative participation from the Free University of Bozen-Bolzano, the University of Trento, and the University of Verona. Spoke 6 adopts a multidisciplinary approach that integrates management, economics, STEM disciplines, the arts, and the humanities to analyze tourism, culture, and the creative industries through an ecosystem lens. Its mission is to foster and strengthen the interconnections among these sectors, reduce fragmentation, and promote the development of a diversified, culturally rich, and sustainable innovation landscape.

To achieve these goals, Spoke 6 is organized into four coordinated research tracks and designed as an integrated learning and innovation system. Digital Technologies (RT1) integrate domain expertise in tourism, culture, and creative industries with advanced technologies such as Artificial Intelligence, Blockchain, IoT, and Extended Reality. Data Analytics (RT2) analyze big data from heterogeneous sources to inform more sustainable public policies and destination marketing strategies. Sustainable Business Models (RT3) transform business models in the tourism, cultural, and creative sectors toward sustainability. Finally, narratives and communication strategies (RT4) develop new tools to challenge stereotypes and reframe tourism communication through inclusivity and sustainability.

This book concludes at a crucial moment in the NEST trajectory, documenting the main outcomes of the research track on Sustainable Business Models (RT3). It is edited by the leaders of the four key research lines within RT3, all of whom share the overarching goal of promoting the sustainable transformation of business models in the tourism, culture, and creative industries. This transformation covers a range of innovative approaches applied at different levels, including circular and inclusive business models, integrating sustainability and equality into the design of services, products, and experiences; art-based business models, leveraging the creative contributions of artists and cultural entrepreneurs to enhance authenticity and value; participatory business models, which create shared value by reconciling the needs and interests of businesses, communities, and visitors; and regenerative business models, reimagining the use of places and spaces by innovating their original functions and cultural heritage to improve living conditions, accessibility, inclusion, and user experience.

ACKNOWLEDGMENTS

An edited collection is never a solitary endeavor; it is a collaborative tapestry woven by many hands. First and foremost, we must acknowledge the exceptional dedication of Bob Bastian (Assistant Professor of Management at the University of Trento) as Coordinator of this Book project. Bob was instrumental in liaising between the editorial team, the diverse group of authors, and the publishing house. His ability to streamline communication and his keen eye for detail ensured that this book is not just a collection of chapters, but a cohesive and relevant contribution to the field. We are also grateful for the capable support provided by Giulia Dore (Assistant Professor in Private Comparative Law at the University of Trento) and Muhammad Junaid Shahid Hasni (Postdoctoral Researcher in Management at the University of Trento) in assisting with these coordination efforts.

We extend our sincere thanks to the contributing authors, whose insights and scholarship form the core of this book. We appreciate your responsiveness and willingness to engage in the editorial dialog. We also thank the reviewers who generously gave their time to read early drafts; your feedback was invaluable.

To the team at Emerald Publishing and Book Series Editors Andrea Caputo and Massimiliano M. Pellegrini, thank you for shepherding this project from proposal to print. We also acknowledge our home institutions for their academic and administrative support.

RETHINKING SUSTAINABLE BUSINESS MODELS IN TOURISM, CULTURAL, AND CREATIVE SECTORS

MARIA DELLA LUCIA[a], ERICA SANTINI[a], ANDREA CAPUTO[a]
AND FABRIZIO PANOZZO[b]

[a]University of Trento, Italy
[b]Ca' Foscari University of Venice, Italy

ABSTRACT

This introductory chapter positions the edited volume at the forefront of current scholarly debates on sustainable business models (SBMs) in tourism, cultural, and creative industries. It critically examines the conceptual fragmentation and sector-specific challenges that have limited the effectiveness of existing SBM frameworks in these fields. In response, the chapter introduces the volume's multidimensional, context-sensitive, and participatory approach, which challenges conventional models that prioritize economic outcomes at the expense of social and environmental value. Building on recent advances in sustainability, innovation, and cultural entrepreneurship research, the chapter presents four interrelated thematic pillars – circular economy and inclusivity, art-based interventions and authenticity, participatory value creation, and regenerative place-making – that collectively inform a more nuanced, empirically grounded, and actionable understanding of SBMs. Ultimately, the chapter establishes the volume as a timely resource for scholars, practitioners, and policymakers seeking to foster innovation, resilience, and inclusive development within tourism, cultural, and creative ecosystems.

Keywords: Sustainable business models; tourism; cultural and creative industries; circular and inclusive models; art-based models; participatory models; regenerative models

INTRODUCTION

Tourism, cultural, and creative industries (CCIs) face increasing pressures to reconcile economic viability with social inclusion, environmental stewardship, and cultural integrity. Global crises – including the COVID-19 pandemic, climate change, and socio-political instability – have exposed the systemic vulnerabilities of these sectors, underscoring the urgency for new business models that transcend narrow, profit-driven logics (Rocca & Zielinski, 2022). As industries deeply rooted in place, identity, and social capital, tourism and CCIs offer fertile ground for reimagining SBMs that embed social, cultural, and ecological value at their core.

This chapter situates the volume within evolving scholarship on SBMs for tourism, cultural, and creative sectors, critically engaging with persistent conceptual fragmentation and myths that undermine progress. Drawing on advances in SBM theory and practice, the chapter responds to growing calls for context-sensitive, interdisciplinary, and participatory approaches to sustainability research (Bocken et al., 2014; Geissdoerfer et al., 2018; Sandberg & Alvesson, 2011). It exposes the limitations of prevailing frameworks in capturing the dynamic, value-driven realities of cultural and tourism enterprises (Schiuma & Lerro, 2017) and demonstrates the need for models grounded in inclusivity, adaptability, and resilience (Budeanu et al., 2016; Coles et al., 2021).

The chapter introduces the book's four thematic pillars – circular economy and inclusivity, art-based interventions and authenticity, participatory value creation, and regenerative place-making – and explains how contributions within each pillar collectively foster a richer, empirically informed, and theoretically robust understanding of SBMs in these fields. By blending theoretical advancement with practical insights, the volume offers a timely resource for scholars, practitioners, and policymakers committed to fostering sustainable transformation in tourism, cultural, and creative ecosystems (Bastian & Caputo, 2024; Della Lucia & Pashkevich, 2023; Peredo & Chrisman, 2006).

GAPS AND CHALLENGES IN SBMs

Despite increasing attention, SBM research remains fragmented, particularly within tourism, cultural, and creative domains. Many existing models, such as the Business Model Canvas (Osterwalder & Pigneur, 2010) and archetypes for sustainable innovation (Bocken et al., 2014), often overlook the complex, relational, and place-based dynamics that characterize these sectors (Bellandi & Santini, 2019; Boons & Lüdeke-Freund, 2013; Kirchherr, 2022). This misalignment fosters conceptual ambiguity and limits the relevance of SBM frameworks for practitioners operating in socially embedded, culturally diverse, and ecologically sensitive environments (Rosato et al., 2021), as tourism, CCIs.

Additionally, the literature often treats the economic, social, and environmental dimensions of sustainability as isolated goals rather than adopting an integrated, systemic perspective (Geissdoerfer et al., 2018). Much existing research is firm-centric, overlooking broader ecosystem dynamics, stakeholder co-creation processes, and the influence of informal economies, social capital, and cultural values. These limitations are especially problematic in tourism and CCIs, where sectoral heterogeneity, from micro-enterprises to public institutions, and the intangible, place-specific nature of value creation complicate standardized approaches (Rocca & Zielinski, 2022). This heterogeneity is mirrored in a scholarly landscape characterized by siloed perspectives. Scholars increasingly question whether conventional tools, including the Business Model Canvas, can adequately capture the fluid, hybrid, and adaptive characteristics of creative and cultural enterprises, particularly those operating in heritage and tourism contexts (Herman et al., 2023; Osterwalder & Pigneur, 2010; Schiuma & Lerro, 2017; Zott & Amit, 2010). These debates reflect a field in transition, moving toward more critical, context-sensitive, and collaborative approaches to SBM research, better suited to the complexity, fluidity, and place-specificity of sustainable value creation in tourism and CCIs ecosystems.

Furthermore, traditional business model frameworks often assume stable hierarchies, linear growth, and clearly defined organizational boundaries, neglecting the hybrid nature and the adaptive and improvisational strategies that characterize many cultural and creative enterprises which frequently prioritize artistic integrity and social mission over growth or scalability (Cacciatore & Panozzo, 2021; Foss & Saebi, 2018; Teece, 2010). Recent research highlights the role of "bricolage" – the creative recombination of limited resources – as a strategic response to uncertainty, resource constraints, and systemic instability (Baker & Nelson, 2005; Glasbeek, 2025). Rather than viewing *bricolage* as an organizational weakness, scholars increasingly frame it as an essential capability for cultural entrepreneurs, particularly in knowledge-intensive, uncertain environments such as heritage cities or fragile tourism economies (Lumpkin et al., 2018). This perspective challenges dominant assumptions about stability, scalability, and formal organizational structures, calling instead for SBM frameworks that reflect the fluid, project-based, and relational nature of cultural production.

Addressing these conceptual and practical gaps requires more interdisciplinary, reflexive, and inclusive approaches to SBM research. These approaches can engage with complexity, embrace place-based innovation, and reconceptualize value creation beyond conventional, profit-driven paradigms (Bellandi & Santini, 2019; Buratti et al., 2022; Cajaiba-Santana, 2014). Methodological pluralism, participatory research, and context sensitivity are critical for generating insights that reflect the intertwined social, cultural, and environmental goals of tourism and CCIs enterprises (Courage et al., 2021; Lazic & Della Lucia, 2024).

A further critical barrier lies in the persistence of binary thinking, which constrains both academic inquiry and practical innovation by reinforcing simplistic oppositions. Tourism and cultural enterprises are frequently framed through dichotomies such as mass tourism versus sustainability, economic growth versus community well-being, or market-driven models versus mission-led practices (Bastian & Zucchella, 2023; Budeanu, 2007). While these binaries may help clarify competing priorities, they risk oversimplifying the complex, negotiated realities faced by organizations operating at the intersection of tourism, culture, economy, and place (Schiuma & Lerro, 2017). In practice, many tourism and cultural organizations operate within hybrid spaces of integration, rather than opposition. As Schiuma and Lerro (2017) demonstrate, cultural organizations frequently embed social and cultural missions into their core operations, redefining value creation beyond purely economic metrics. This embeddedness enables them to act as platforms for community engagement, cultural expression, and inclusive development, while also maintaining economic viability.

Moving beyond binary thinking necessitates analytical frameworks that embrace plurality, contextual nuance, and relational interdependence (Cajaiba-Santana, 2014; Courage et al., 2021). It also requires rethinking sustainability not as a trade-off between competing goals but as a multidimensional, co-created process embedded in local realities. This paradigm shift reflects a transition from merely minimizing negative impacts to actively restoring and enhancing social–ecological systems. Regenerative approaches unfold through various culture-based and biodiversity-stewarding activities, such as agriculture, handicrafts, hospitality, and education, by emphasizing co-evolutionary relationships among social, cultural, environmental, and economic forms of capital within bioregional development models grounded in mutual care (Bellato et al., 2022, 2023).

Emerging research on regenerative development highlights how places themselves can become active stakeholders in sustainable transformation, with communities and individuals serving as custodians of place-based knowledge and cultural heritage (Lazic & Della Lucia, 2024). In this sense, tourism, cultural, and creative enterprises can function as living laboratories for experimenting with integrative, place-based, and resilient business models that reflect the complexity of sustainable development and advance ecosystem regeneration.

RETHINKING SBMs

The edited volume *Sustainable Business Models: Managing Tourism, Cultural and Creative Enterprises, Organizations, and Ecosystems* seeks to advance scholarly and practical conversations on SBMs by addressing persistent fragmentation in research and challenging dominant frameworks that often prioritize economic outcomes at the expense of social, cultural, and environmental dimensions (Geissdoerfer et al., 2018; Lazic & Della Lucia, 2024). By critically interrogating conventional models, the volume moves beyond rigid binaries that frame tourism and cultural and creative enterprises as being in tension with sustainability and advocating for context-sensitive, place-based innovations that reflect the multidimensional nature of value creation (Budeanu et al., 2016). Tourism and CCIs represent ideal domains for rethinking how value is generated, distributed, and sustained. These sectors are inherently embedded within complex socio-ecological systems where economic imperatives intersect with cultural heritage, community well-being, and environmental stewardship (Cajaiba-Santana, 2014; Rocca & Zielinski, 2022). Furthermore, they reflect both bioregional and digital ecosystems characterized by high levels of fluidity, stakeholder diversity, and place-based identity (Gretzel et al., 2015; Ritchie & Crouch, 2003).

The volume responds to current challenges by promoting innovative, research-informed, and practice-oriented approaches to SBMs that can address sector vulnerabilities, enhance resilience, and empower communities (Lumpkin et al., 2018; Romolini et al., 2017). Specifically, the book introduces four interrelated thematic pillars designed to push business models beyond a narrow focus on profitability toward more inclusive, participatory, and regenerative frameworks for sustainable development.

PILLAR 1: CIRCULAR ECONOMY AND INCLUSIVITY

The first pillar explores how SBMs can be reimagined through the integration of *circular economy* principles and *inclusive practices* to promote both resource efficiency and social equity (Bocken et al., 2014; Kirchherr, 2022). Circular economy approaches prioritize the minimization of waste, the optimization of resource flows, and the design of services and products that generate educational, experiential, and environmental value (Geissdoerfer et al., 2018). Inclusive approaches – particularly addressing the needs of vulnerable or marginalized groups – meaningfully engage a broad range of stakeholders toward socially embedded innovation (de Assunção Mendes et al., 2024). By addressing the intersection of environmental responsibility, social equity, and participatory engagement, pillar demonstrates how responsible service and experience design can be leveraged as a strategic tool to create meaningful, low-impact encounters that are economically viable, socially inclusive, and environmentally regenerative. Through this lens, the book envisions business models that not only sustain but actively revitalize resources, ecosystems, fostering opportunities for full participation in cultural, social, and economic life.

PILLAR 2: ART-BASED BUSINESS MODELS AND PLACE AUTHENTICITY

The second pillar focuses on the potential of *art-based* business models to generate sustainable value by embedding the authenticity of place at the heart of organizational design (Schiuma & Lerro, 2017). These models leverage cultural heritage, craftsmanship, and artistic expression to create immersive, meaningful experiences that reflect the distinct identity and socio-cultural fabric of a place. Through active community participation and co-creation processes, art-based models foster creative ecosystems where artistic innovation is interwoven with inclusive, place-based development (De Luca et al., 2023). They promote social inclusion, equitable value distribution, and enhanced visitor–host relationships, particularly in areas beyond mainstream tourist circuits. Their focus on small-scale, context-sensitive projects also meets the growing demand for responsible, authentic travel. These models must navigate the delicate balance between cultural preservation and market exposure to avoid risks of over-commercialization or reducing artists to mere service providers (Herman et al., 2023). This pillar contributes to the book's overarching vision by demonstrating how context-sensitive and creativity-driven models can catalyze sustainable development that is grounded in cultural authenticity, community empowerment, and long-term environmental stewardship.

PILLAR 3: PARTICIPATORY BUSINESS MODELS AND SHARED VALUE CREATION

The third pillar highlights the critical role of participatory business models that prioritize collaboration, inclusive decision-making, and active stakeholder engagement to co-create shared value (Cajaiba-Santana, 2014; Defourny & Nyssens, 2010). Such models recognize that sustainable development and shared value creation are most effective when rooted in community agency, collective ownership, and distributed leadership (Bastian & Zucchella, 2023). Community-based enterprises and social innovation networks exemplify how participatory approaches foster trust, resilience, and social cohesion, especially in vulnerable or transitional territories (Buratti et al., 2022; Lumpkin et al., 2018). These models are shown to strengthen organizational adaptability and local development by embedding social, environmental, and cultural objectives at their core (Rocca & Zielinski, 2022; Romolini et al., 2017). Special emphasis is placed on strategies that promote accessibility, inclusivity, and long-term community engagement as key mechanisms for building more equitable, collaborative, and resilient tourism and cultural ecosystems. Through this lens, the book advances SBMs as tools for building more just, resilient, and collaborative tourism ecosystems, where value is co-created and shared.

PILLAR 4: REGENERATIVE BUSINESS MODELS

The final pillar of the book explores *regenerative business models* as tools to revitalize places and spaces affected by marginalization, economic decline, or cultural erosion (Della Lucia & Pashkevich, 2023). These places include not only creative cities and urban environments, but also rural, peripheral, and transitional areas. These models transcend restoration or conservation by adopting a holistic approach to renewing the social, cultural, and ecological vitality of communities, emphasizing the dynamic interplay between institutional settings (Palthe, 2014), cultural regeneration processes (Della Lucia & Trunfio, 2018), and enabling factors (Della Lucia & Pashkevich, 2023). Regeneration is understood not as a return to a fixed past but as a dynamic, forward-looking process grounded in living cultural and natural heritage (Lazic & Della Lucia, 2024). Drawing on bioregional and participatory approaches, these models promote inclusive and creative placemaking, reconciling tradition with innovation. Through inclusive and adaptive governance, regenerative models support both cultural resilience and foster vibrant cultural, tourist, and economic ecosystems (Bellato et al., 2022). Through this lens, the book positions SBMs as catalysts for ecosystem restoration, social empowerment, and the reimagining of places as vibrant, creative, and inclusive spaces.

SBMs PRACTICE IN NORTHEAST ITALY

This volume rethinks SBMs by applying four thematic perspectives across the tourism and CCIs, cultural, and creative sectors, offering nuanced contributions that bridge multidisciplinary academic discourse with practical application, with a particular focus on Northeast Italy. Multidisciplinary brings together distinct disciplinary perspectives, while preserving their distinct epistemologies, methodologies, and conceptual boundaries. This broadens the analytical lens on sustainability challenges and solutions, fostering critical engagement with the complex socio-environmental dynamics these sectors face. Methodologically, practice-oriented approaches are central to the analysis, combining participatory action research with art-based inquiry (Cacciatore & Panozzo, 2024). This hybrid approach responds to Boons and Lüdeke-Freund's (2013) call for methodological diversity in the study of sustainable innovation, enabling both analytical rigor and contextual relevance. While participatory action research is iterative, inclusive, and geared toward real-world change, art-based research blends creative expression with qualitative inquiry to explore lived experiences, cultural narratives, and place-based identities. Together, these methods support the co-creation of knowledge, deepen researcher-community engagement, and offer innovative tools to understand and enhance the resilience, inclusivity, and competitiveness of local cultural, creative, and tourism ecosystems.

Chapter 1, "The Relevance of Debunking Sustainable Myths for Theory and Practice" by Bob Bastian, Andrea Caputo, and Maria Della Lucia, lays the theoretical foundation for rethinking business models through the four perspectives explored in this volume. It calls for a critical problematization of SBMs by exposing persistent myths that continue to shape sustainability research and practice. The authors advocate for myth-busting as an essential methodological approach to challenge taken-for-granted assumptions within SBM discourse and to foster a more reflective, critical stance toward knowledge production. By highlighting the importance of embracing uncertainty and cultivating intellectual humility, the chapter positions ignorance as a generative space for innovation and more effective, context-sensitive sustainability solutions. In doing so, it introduces the core challenges and tensions in the field and sets the stage for addressing them through the lens of the volume's four thematic pillars.

Part I, "Business Models Incorporating the Principles of Circular Economy and Inclusivity," features two chapters united by a shared focus on advancing environmental responsibility and social inclusion within business models. Chapter 2, "Circular Economy in the Hospitality and Tourism Sector: the Case of Waste Cooking Oil" by Matteo Baldan, Muhammad Junaid Shahid Hasni, and Valentina Beghetto, illustrates how circular economy principles can repurpose food-processing by-products into valuable resources. It shows how recycling innovations can be integrated into hospitality operations, reducing environmental impact while creating new value streams and enhancing organizational sustainability. Chapter 3, "Inclusive Tourism Design: Bridging the Information Gap Faced by People with Disabilities" by Rossana Demurtas, Maria Menendez-Blanco, and Erica Santini, examines the digital accessibility barriers that prevent people with disabilities from fully participating in tourism experiences. The research identifies major shortcomings in information provision across tourism platforms, revealing how traditional business models often overlook the needs of diverse user groups. By addressing these gaps, the chapter underscores the importance of inclusive design in developing truly sustainable, accessible, and socially just business models. Together, these chapters reveal that embedding circular practices and inclusive design within business models is not merely an ethical imperative but a source of innovation, resilience, and value creation. By tackling overlooked resources and underserved populations, the chapters advocate for business models that are both regenerative and equitable.

Part II, "Art-based Business Models Incorporating the Authenticity of Places," explores how artistic interventions offer innovative frameworks for sustainable value creation grounded in cultural authenticity and place-based identity. Chapter 4, "Authenticity as Weaving Coherence Across Time and Place: Insights from Craft" by Camilla Ferri and Maria Lusiani, introduces the metaphor of "weaving coherence" to illustrate how authenticity is an evolving, socially constructed process embedded in craft practices. The authors identify six modes through which craft makers integrate temporal dimensions (the past, present, future) with place-based identities, revealing authenticity as an active, living practice rather than a fixed outcome. This perspective shifts the analytical focus from audience perceptions or market-driven narratives of authenticity to the practices, skills, and embodied knowledge of makers themselves, linking their creative processes to cultural heritage, social relations, and environmental contexts. Chapter 5, "Rethinking Cultural Business Models Through Artistic Interventions in Tourism-related Contexts" by Margherita De Luca, Chiara Carolina Donelli, and Fabrizio Panozzo, examines how artistic interventions within tourism-driven urban settings can catalyze transformations in cultural business models toward sustainability. Drawing on case studies from Venice, the chapter identifies three interrelated dynamics: a pragmatic turn toward market orientation in response to tourism pressures, the predominance of fragmented, project-based organizational structures, and the strategic deployment of *bricolage* – the creative recombination of available resources – to sustain cultural initiatives. These dynamics challenge conventional business model assumptions by favoring flexibility, informality, and creative autonomy over linear growth and organizational stability. Together, these chapters reveal how authenticity and artistic interventions can anchor SBMs in cultural and creative contexts. They underscore the value of time- and place-based connections, collaborative and adaptive structures, and context-sensitive strategies. These insights provide valuable guidance for cultural producers and policymakers seeking to balance creative integrity with economic viability, while enriching the vitality of the communities, cultural ecosystems, and environments in which they operate.

Part III, "Participatory Business Models for Creating Shared Value," explores how community-driven and network-based approaches can advance more sustainable, equitable business models by embedding social purpose at the core of organizational strategy. Chapter 6, "Community-based Enterprises as a Sustainable Business Model for Tourism Destination Regeneration" by Stefania Denise Escobar, Chiara Massacesi, Linda Osti, Paola Rovelli, and Federica ViganÒ, explores how community-based enterprises (CBEs) can foster sustainability and regeneration in tourism destinations facing depopulation, economic decline, and shrinking public services. Drawing on the case of the *Cooperativa di Comunità Valle del Vanoi* in Trentino-Alto Adige, the chapter shows how CBEs emerge as grassroots responses to complex socioeconomic challenges in peripheral and marginal areas. Rather than prioritizing tourist demands, successful CBEs focus on the needs of local residents, positioning tourism as a complementary – rather than dominant – development strategy. This approach marks a significant departure from conventional tourism models by asserting that community well-being, social cohesion, and local livelihoods must take precedence over visitor-driven growth. Chapter 7, "Social Innovation and Networking in Tourism: Insights from Case Studies in Northeast Italy" by Maurizio Busacca, Silvia Sacchetti, and Olga Tzatzadaki, investigates how social innovation and collaborative networks foster more resilient and inclusive tourism ecosystems. Through in-depth case studies from Northeast Italy, the chapter explores how participatory organizational forms and social innovation practices enable tourism stakeholders to navigate volatility, co-create value, and enhance benefits for local communities. These alternative organizational forms highlight the potential of tourism to strengthen both economic sustainability and social cohesion when embedded in participatory and collaborative frameworks. Together, these chapters offer compelling evidence that community-centered and networked business models offer viable alternatives to conventional structures that often separate commercial success from social impact. By embedding social objectives within their organizational design, these business models can become powerful levers for sustainability, particularly when they are locally grounded, responsive to community needs, and intentionally designed to distribute value equitably across diverse stakeholders.

Part IV, "Regenerative Business Models for Sustainable Place Development," focuses on models that blend tradition with innovation to revitalize places affected by marginalization, socio-economic decline, or cultural commodification. Chapter 8, "Rethinking Cultural Heritage in Placemaking: From Preservation to Regenerative Development in Castel Campo" by Maria Della Lucia, Giulia Dore, Stefan Lazic, and Marina Clerici Rasini, presents the case of Castel Campo, a historic, family-run, and women-led estate in rural Trentino. The research traces the estate's transformation from a traditional model of heritage preservation to a dynamic, multidimensional enterprise that integrates living heritage, regenerative agriculture, and community-based social care. Guided by female leadership and a deep respect for time, place, and community, the Rasini family's management model demonstrates how cultural heritage can serve as both a bridge between historical continuity and contemporary innovation and as a catalyst for inclusive, regenerative placemaking. The case highlights that cultural heritage, when managed as a living force, can foster shared responsibility, democratic participation, and cross-sector collaboration. Chapter 9, "Craft-based Experiences to Revitalize Touristic Urban Centers: The Venetian Case Study" by Stefano Micelli and Sofia Mizzan, offers a complementary urban perspective. Through three case studies from Venice's historic center, the chapter explores how traditional craftsmanship and artisanal practices can serve as catalysts for urban revitalization. Craft-based enterprises are portrayed not only as economic actors but also as cultural intermediaries capable of resisting the commodification of tourism by offering authentic, educational, and personalized experiences. These businesses create meaningful connections between visitors and local culture while contributing to community well-being and urban regeneration. The chapter further underscores that the regenerative potential of such enterprises can be significantly enhanced through strategic management support, policy alignment, and integration within broader urban ecosystems and cultural networks. Together, these chapters underscore the versatility and transformative power of regenerative business models across rural and urban contexts.

Finally, in Chapter 10, "Sustaining Impact: Looking Ahead in Tourism, Cultural, and Creative Sectors," the book editors synthesize the key patterns and insights emerging across the volume's four thematic pillars. They trace the transformational journey of SBMs, highlighting how they evolve as context-sensitive, adaptive ecosystems. The concluding chapter outlines multilevel implications for advancing SBMs' long-term impact and proposes future research directions to strengthen their role in fostering resilience, equity, and sustainability across tourism, cultural, and creative sectors.

CONCLUDING REMARKS

The four perspectives for rethinking SBMs offer a comprehensive and flexible lens for designing, managing, and evolving SMBs in ways that address fragmentation, challenge conventional managerial thinking, and facilitate the integration of economic, social, and environmental objectives. By combining theoretical advancements with empirical insights drawn from diverse geographic and institutional contexts within Northeastern Italy, the contributions illustrate how enterprises and ecosystems in tourism, cultural, and creative sectors navigate uncertainty while prioritizing place-based specificity. In so doing, they provide a roadmap for scholars and practitioners seeking to balance scalability with authenticity, profit with purpose, and global trends with bio-regional contexts. This integrated approach advances the conceptualization of SBMs as dynamic, evolving ecosystems – responsive to external pressures, stakeholder needs, and the distinct social, cultural, and environmental characteristics of each place.

REFERENCES

Baker, T., & Nelson, R. E. (2005). Creating something from nothing: Resource construction through entrepreneurial bricolage. *Administrative Science Quarterly, 50*(3), 329–366.

Bastian, B., & Caputo, A. (2024). Sustainable business models: Researchers as design thinkers for problem-driven research. *Strategic Change*, *33*(3), 129–138.

Bastian, B., & Zucchella, A. (2023). Nascent entrepreneurs during start-up competitions: Between beauty contests and co-created problematization. *Journal of Business Venturing Insights*, *20*, e00391.

Bellandi, M., & Santini, E. (2019). Territorial servitization and new local productive configurations: The case of the textile industrial district of Prato. *Regional Studies*, *53*(3), 356–365.

Bellato, L., Frantzeskaki, N., & Nygaard, C. A. (2023). Regenerative tourism: A conceptual framework leveraging theory and practice. *Tourism Geographies*, *25*(4), 1026–1046.

Bellato, L., Frantzeskaki, N., Briceño Fiebig, C., Pollock, A., Dens, E., & Reed, B. (2022). Transformative roles in tourism: adopting living systems' thinking for regenerative futures. *Journal of Tourism Futures*, *8*(3), 312–329.

Bocken, N. M. P., Short, S. W., Rana, P., & Evans, S. (2014). A literature and practice review to develop sustainable business model archetypes. *Journal of Cleaner Production*, *65*, 42–56.

Boons, F., & Lüdeke-Freund, F. (2013). Business models for sustainable innovation: State-of-the-art and steps towards a research agenda. *Journal of Cleaner Production*, *45*, 9–19.

Budeanu, A. (2007). Sustainable tourist behaviour: A discussion of opportunities for change. *International Journal of Consumer Studies*, *31*(5), 499–508.

Budeanu, A., Miller, G., Moscardo, G., & Ooi, C. S. (2016). Sustainable tourism, progress, challenges and opportunities: An introduction. *Journal of Cleaner Production*, *111*, 285–294.

Buratti, N., Sillig, C., & Albanese, M. (2022). Community enterprise, community entrepreneurship and local development: A literature review on three decades of empirical studies and theorizations. *Entrepreneurship & Regional Development*, *34*(5–6), 376–401.

Cacciatore, S., & Panozzo, F. (2021). Models for art–business cooperation. *Journal of Cultural Management and Cultural Policy*, *7*(2), 179–207.

Cacciatore, S., & Panozzo, F. (2024). Rethinking research through artistic experimentation. *European Journal of Cultural Management and Policy*, *14*, 1–20.

Cajaiba-Santana, G. (2014). Social innovation: Moving the field forward. A conceptual framework. *Technological Forecasting and Social Change, 82,* 42–51.

Coles, T., Zschiegner, A.-K., & Dinan, C. (2021). Climate change mitigation in tourism: Progress, challenges and opportunities. *Journal of Sustainable Tourism, 29*(2–3), 241–260.

Courage, C., Bason, C., & Hillgren, P.-A. (2021). Co-design and the new landscapes of design. *She Ji: The Journal of Design, Economics, and Innovation, 7*(2), 178–197.

de Assunção Mendes, H. J., de Paiva, T. M. D., Felgueira, T., Alves, C. A., & Costa, A. (2024). The need for business models in accessible, inclusive and sustainable tourism. *International Journal of Professional Business Review, 9*(4), 1–10.

De Luca, M., Gatto, C., Liaci, S., Corchia, L., & Trunfio, M. (2023). Participatory art-based practices for place-based development: Co-creation and community empowerment in creative heritage projects. *Journal of Cultural Heritage Management and Sustainable Development, 13*(2), 151–170.

Defourny, J., & Nyssens, M. (2010). Conceptions of social enterprise and social entrepreneurship in Europe and the United States: Convergences and divergences. *Journal of Social Entrepreneurship, 1*(1), 32–53.

Della Lucia, M., & Pashkevich, A. (2023). A sustainable afterlife for post-industrial sites: Balancing conservation, regeneration, and heritage tourism. *European Planning Studies, 31*(3), 641–661.

Della Lucia, M., & Trunfio, M. (2018). The role of the private actor in cultural regeneration: Hybridizing cultural heritage with creativity in the city. *Cities, 82,* 35–44.

Foss, N. J., & Saebi, T. (2018). Business models and business model innovation: Between wicked and paradigmatic problems. *Long Range Planning, 51*(1), 9–21.

Geissdoerfer, M., Savaget, P., Bocken, N. M. P., & Hultink, E. J. (2018). The circular economy: A new sustainability paradigm? *Journal of Cleaner Production, 143,* 757–768.

Glasbeek, L. (2025). Bricolage and its strategic connotations: A study of Greek social entrepreneurs in times of crisis. *British Journal of Management, 36*(3), 1003–1022.

Gretzel, U., Sigala, M., Xiang, Z., & Koo, C. (2015). Smart tourism: Foundations and developments. *Electronic Markets*, *25*(3), 179–188.

Herman, K., Szromek, A., & Naramski, M. (2023). Examining the utility of a sustainable business model for postindustrial tourism attractions: The case of the European Route of Industrial Heritage. *Journal of Heritage Tourism*, *18*(1), 36–55.

Kirchherr, J. (2022). The circular economy: A new sustainability paradigm or just empty rhetoric? *Resources, Conservation and Recycling*, *176*, 105965.

Lazic, S., & Della Lucia, M. (2024). A holistic and pluralistic perspective for justice through tourism: A regenerative approach. *Tourism Geographies*, 1–18.

Lumpkin, G. T., Bacq, S., & Pidduck, R. J. (2018). Where change happens: Community-level phenomena in social entrepreneurship research. *Journal of Small Business Management*, *56*(1), 24–50.

Osterwalder, A., & Pigneur, Y. (2010). *Business model generation: A handbook for visionaries, game changers, and challengers*. John Wiley & Sons.

Palthe, J. (2014). Regulative, normative, and cognitive elements of organizations: Implications for managing change. *Management and Organizational Studies*, *1*(2), 59–68.

Peredo, A. M., & Chrisman, J. J. (2006). Toward a theory of community-based enterprise. *Academy of Management Review*, *31*(2), 309–328.

Ritchie, B. W., & Crouch, G. I. (2003). *The competitive destination: A sustainable tourism perspective*. CABI.

Rocca, M., & Zielinski, S. (2022). Rethinking tourism business models for sustainability: A research agenda. *Journal of Sustainable Tourism*, *30*(11), 2501–2520.

Romolini, M., Brinkley, W., & Wolf, K. L. (2017). What is urban social-ecological stewardship? Constructing a practitioner-derived framework. *Urban Ecosystems*, *20*(4), 889–904.

Rosato, P. F., Caputo, A., Valente, D., & Pizzi, S. (2021). 2030 Agenda and sustainable business models in tourism: A bibliometric analysis. *Ecological Indicators*, *121*, 106978.

Sandberg, J., & Alvesson, M. (2011). Ways of constructing research questions: Gap-spotting or problematization? *Organization*, *18*(1), 23–44.

Schiuma, G., & Lerro, A. (2017). The business model prism: Managing and innovating business models of arts and cultural organisations. *Journal of Open Innovation: Technology, Market, and Complexity*, 3(3), 1–13.

Teece, D. J. (2010). Business models, business strategy and innovation. *Long Range Planning*, 43(2–3), 172–194.

Zott, C., & Amit, R. (2010). Business model design: An activity system perspective. *Long Range Planning*, 43(2–3), 216–226.

1

THE RELEVANCE OF DEBUNKING SUSTAINABLE MYTHS FOR THEORY AND PRACTICE

BOB BASTIAN, ANDREA CAPUTO AND MARIA DELLA LUCIA

University of Trento, Italy

ABSTRACT

Research on sustainable business models has expanded considerably, reflecting the growing need to align organizational strategies with sustainability goals. However, the theoretical fragmentation within this field has led to unchallenged assumptions in which existing paradigms are reinforced rather than questioned. This chapter introduces myth-busting as an approach for researchers and practitioners to debunk taken-for-granted assumptions in sustainable tourism management. By actively dismantling myths, both researchers and practitioners can improve deeper critical thinking and strengthen multidisciplinary collaboration. Embracing a myth-buster mindset enables researchers and practitioners to think better, ask more relevant questions, and make smarter decisions in research, policy, and practice.

Keywords: Sustainability; sustainable business models; problematization; myths; ignorance; problem-based research; multidisciplinary

INTRODUCTION

Studies into the relationship between organizational strategies and sustainability have increased substantially in recent years (e.g., Bocken & Geradts, 2020; Geissdoerfer et al., 2018; Ringvold et al., 2023). To achieve the Sustainable Development Goals, organizations are on a challenging road to reevaluating how they create, deliver, capture, and exchange value with their stakeholders. One popular avenue for researchers has been the study of sustainable business models since it has explanatory power about how economic, environmental, and societal value are produced and how negative impact can be reduced (e.g., Bocken et al., 2014; Geissdoerfer et al., 2016). A rich scope of special issues (e.g., Boons et al., 2013; Dentchev et al., 2018; Pinkse et al., 2023; Schaltegger et al., 2016) and literature reviews have emerged in the last decade to provide insights on sustainability progress (Evans et al., 2017), indicating that the area is promising and emerging. Nevertheless, transitioning to these new models presents significant challenges, both for practitioners and researchers.

The presence of at least 14 different notions and frameworks of sustainable business models in the literature reflects a general lack of consensus on what a sustainable business model is or should be and what does not (Geissdoerfer et al., 2018). However, this fragmentation appears to be part of the ongoing (mostly theoretical) discussion that has also embodied the concept of sustainability (Lüdeke-Freund & Dembek, 2017). Definitional and conceptual issues are, at the same time, a result of the popularity of the field, and in this way, sustainable business models may have become victims of their own success. Yet, sustainability paradigms rely on distinct assumptions, implying that the way they address solutions contains different problems and ways forward. Hence, the relevance of distinguishing sustainable problems (Foss & Saebi, 2017; Sharma et al., 2022).

A different breed of problems is related to assumptions of the underlying literature (Matthews et al., 2016; Reuber, 2016). Problems related to the latter go beyond definitional and conceptual issues (Hasenzagl et al., 2018; Matthews et al., 2016; Reuber, 2016). They are, in a sense, taken for granted (Alvesson, 2013) and in the domain of dominant knowledge. Identifying what these underlying assumptions are and how they could be challenged is not a method researchers commonly employ. Instead, most contributions build on existing literature and spot gaps to find an issue (Colquitt & Zapata-Phelan, 2007; Pratt, 2009). When assumptions remain largely unchallenged, they tend to be underproblematized and reinforce existing knowledge (Alvesson & Sandberg, 2011).

In this way, dominant assumptions of sustainable business models may turn persistent over time and become sustainable myths. These myths arise when the status-quo is maintained (Burmeister & Schade, 2007; Hannan & Freeman, 1984), when assumptions go unchallenged and are reconfirmed (Klayman, 1995), when critical thinking is lacking (Kennedy et al., 2013), and when the wrong type of questions are asked (Foucault, 2013). Understanding what sustainable myths are, where they come from, and how they can be dismantled is relevant to nurturing critical thinking to address the root cause of sustainable problems.

In this chapter, we propose myth-busting as a way forward to question taken-for-granted sustainable assumptions. Myth-busters debunk myths, rather than confirming them, problematize, rather than spotting gaps (Sandberg & Alvesson, 2011), and reframe problems between researchers and practitioners jointly (Dimov, 2020; Hyytinen, 2021; Ringvold et al., 2023) with a multi-disciplinary lens. This is important as organizations cannot solve complex sustainability issues in isolation (Bastian & Caputo, 2024; Fobbe & Hilletofth, 2021). However, taking on the myth-buster role is challenging. It implies acknowledging and embracing one's (own) ignorance (Alvesson et al., 2022; Alvesson & Spicer, 2016). The more myths we bust, the more unknowns we reveal, leading to greater nuance, understanding, and new unknowns. Acknowledging one's ignorance through myth-busting has surprising positive effects for creativity, imagination, and innovation (Firestein, 2012).

Myth-busting, however, is not just a tool for researchers. Practitioners, too, should increasingly become myth-busters. Myth-busting for practitioners implies seeking evidence-based knowledge rather than relying on self-declared experts (Chavda et al., 2022), influencers (Petrocelli et al., 2023), and populist leaders (Bergmann, 2020). By distinguishing facts from misinformation (Vasist & Krishnan, 2023) and informed decisions from conspiracy theories (Douglas et al., 2019; Sunstein, 2014), myth-busting opens space for better thinking, more relevant questions, and smarter decisions, in research, policy, and practice.

The remainder of this chapter is organized in the following way. First, we explain what myth-busting is and exemplify how myth-busting can help to debunk assumptions. Second, we theorize that researchers need to question and reassess their assumptions within sustainable business model practices and that researchers and practitioners need joint alignment to frame sustainable solutions jointly. Third, we argue that both approaches require multidisciplinary approaches to avoid box thinking. In the last section of the chapter, we propose a way forward for theory and practice with concluding thoughts.

SUSTAINABLE BUSINESS MODELS AND SUSTAINABLE MYTHS

Sustainable business models integrate components of both traditional organizational frameworks and corporate sustainability (e.g., Bocken et al., 2014; Osterwalder & Pigneur, 2010; Teece, 2010). By addressing social, environmental, and business considerations concurrently, these models require collaboration and coordination with a wide array of stakeholders, including communities, customers, investors, shareholders, employees, suppliers, partners, NGOs, and governments (Antikainen & Valkokari, 2016; Schaltegger et al., 2016).

Given their interest in empirical and theoretical research, the sustainable business model field is expected to continue to evolve (Ringvold et al., 2023; Rosato et al., 2021). For example, Geissdoerfer et al. (2018) hypothesize that sustainable business models might substitute "traditional" ones to the same extent as sustainable competitive advantage might replace "simple" competitive advantage. Yet, as business models are concerned with strategy, pricing, market positioning, value chain integration, and value creation, it is more likely that sustainability is becoming a core part of business models, rather than entirely replacing it. A realistic transition toward a sustainable economy requires the reevaluation and redesign of business models, a challenging task that often appears to be taken for granted (Montiel et al., 2020).

Amid the overplus of proposed definitions (Bocken et al., 2014; Schaltegger et al., 2016), sustainable business models can be defined as a "simplified representation of the elements, the interrelationship between these elements, and the interactions with its stakeholders that an organizational unit uses to create, deliver, capture, and exchange sustainable value" (Geissdoerfer et al., 2016, p. 2). Yet, many other definitions exist (see Geissdoerfer et al., 2018), and sustainable business models have been described as architectural blueprints, as attributes of organizations, as conceptual representations, and as cognitive schemas in which actors make sense of their logics in order to create value (Bastian & Caputo, 2024; Massa et al., 2017).

The peril of the variety of descriptions and conceptualizations is that sustainable business models risk becoming an umbrella term, a concept that encompasses various meanings and ideas under the same label (e.g., Glavič & Lukman, 2007). In addition, sustainable business models have been called out to lack critical reflection on trade-offs (Prescott & Filatotchev, 2021), on problems, construct clarity (Suddaby, 2010), and ambiguity of how sustainable business models are operationalized in practice (Fobbe & Hilletofth, 2021). In the long term, this may lead to the emergence of myths.

When the wrong kind of questions are asked and assumptions are no longer questioned, what sustainable business models imply for theory and practice becomes increasingly problematic (Alvesson, 2013; Sandberg & Alvesson, 2011). For example, typical sustainable business model myths that are already persistent are that sustainability is good for everyone, that certain types of sustainable interventions are, and will stay, too expensive, that sustainable transitions imply sacrificing comfort and convenience, or that it conflicts with economic growth (Leal Filho, 2000; Mwampamba et al., 2013; Sorman, 2023).

MYTH-BUSTING

Despite being a promising and rapidly expanding field, research on sustainable business models frequently lacks diverse perspectives to compare and contrast the theory with alternative approaches (Alvesson & Sandberg, 2011; Hardy & Grant, 2012; Laguerre, 2023). This is problematic as it may lead researchers to be over reliant on dominant literature streams while ignoring important consequences and trade-offs of the studied phenomenon (Sabaruddin et al., 2023). For example, there is ongoing confusion about how to operationalize sustainable business models, sustainable business model solutions are framed as effective in any context while ineffective solutions are not considered, and assumptions that sustainable business models always bring benefits indicate that they may be misleading (e.g., Fobbe & Hilletofth, 2021; Susur & Karakaya, 2021). When researchers do not critically examine and expose the underlying assumptions of their theories, widely used and overexploited scientific concepts evolve into dominant, ambiguous concepts and constructs with indistinct boundaries (Alvesson & Blom, 2021), with the sustainable business model field might risk becoming a business buzzword (Dzhengiz et al., 2023).

Consequently, a step beyond moderate critical analysis is necessary that questions how new knowledge, and not only current dominant logic, can be detected and questioned. We propose myth-busting as a way forward to question sustainable beliefs that are persistent and largely taken for granted. Myth-busting is crucial to comprehend the nature of sustainable myths, their origins, and the methods to address them. It implies that (1) researchers need to question and reassess their assumptions in order to create impactful theories on sustainability within sustainable business model practices (Alvesson & Sandberg, 2013); (2) researchers and practitioners better align and co-create more concretely how they interpret and refine their knowledge to frame sustainable solutions jointly (Berglund et al., 2018); and (3) a multidisciplinary approach to avoid box thinking (Alvesson & Sandberg, 2014).

PROBLEMATIZING MYTHS

Problematization as a methodology (Alvesson & Sandberg, 2011) deliberately guides researchers to identify and challenge dominant assumptions
that are underlying the sustainable business model literature. Problematizing
implies that researchers disconfirm some (but not all) of the assumptions held
by their audience (Bartunek et al., 2006) to ask more interesting questions
and generate reviews that go beyond systemization. Rather than identifying
"gaps" within the literature, problematizing helps researchers to detach from
familiar perspectives and critique the assumptions of others for the purpose
of challenging underlying assumptions. In this way, problematizing seeks to
question prevailing assumptions to broaden perspectives and reconsider our
understanding past a descriptive level (Alegre et al., 2023; Breslin et al., 2020)
that are often overlooked or accepted as given (Patriotta, 2017).

Sustainable business model researchers that chose to problematize may
start with the foundational literature and significant works that consti-
tute the core of the field, identify the major assumptions that underlie the
sustainable business model field, and develop alternative assumptions
based on more broader readings and a constant process of reflexivity (see
Alvesson & Sandberg, 2020). When these alternative assumptions are developed, researchers may ask themselves if these have the potential to produce
theories that are compelling. For example, one assumption that may be challenged is the nature of sustainable problems, which may emerge from the
sustainable business model literature as often well-structured with a single
solution for a clearly framed problem. Problematizing these assumptions
may lead researchers in the direction of ill-defined problems and uncertainty
(Foss & Saebi, 2017, Ho, 2001) or see sustainable problems as subjective
mental models (Björkdahl et al., 2022) that requires a reframing process in
which problems and solutions are part of a dynamic, instead of a static, sense-
making process (Bastian & Caputo, 2024).

PROBLEM-BASED RESEARCH BETWEEN ACADEMICS
AND PRACTITIONERS

While most researchers aim to impact their research with practical applications, only a small proportion perceive themselves as successful in doing
so (Rynes et al., 2018). This highlights a research-practice gap between
researchers who tackle and resolve sustainable issues and those who study
these practices as a focus of their research (Sharma & Bansal, 2020). For
much published or publishable research, a significant reason why researchers

study a phenomenon can be attributed to the need to publish, for example, to secure tenure or achieve promotion (Pfleegor et al., 2019). However, the value of researching impactful problems lies in its potential to influence future studies and other researchers. This apparent gap between research and practice may reduce when researchers and practitioners collaborate more closely in addressing a meaningful problem to develop sustainable solutions collectively (Berglund et al., 2018; Ellis & Levy, 2008; Volkema, 1983).

Recent academic discussions regarding key stakeholders to be included within a broader spectrum of this process emphasize the critical role of researchers and practitioners jointly (e.g., Bastian & Zucchella, 2023; Sharma & Bansal, 2020). Including practitioners in research settings leads to collaborative efforts that can stimulate the co-creation and alignment of propositions and joint knowledge development (Rynes et al., 2001). A co-creation process between practitioners and academics may also uncover epistemic differences as stakeholders contribute varying perspectives on the defined problem (Shams & Kaufman, 2016). This process may encourage the co-creation of research and knowledge or uncover epistemic distinctions as stakeholders contribute varying perspectives on the defined problem.

These collaborative interactions are essential for addressing the research-practice gap. For example, when practitioners and researchers venture together, they may decompose sustainable problems and generate new heuristics about different problem–solution combinations. Identifying and redefining problems may then facilitate the creation of alternative hypothetical "what-if" scenarios (Dorst, 2011). Thus, while practitioners can aid researchers in contextualizing sustainable business model problems, researchers can contribute by leveraging their expertise to deconstruct and reframe these problems (Bastian & Caputo, 2024; Ho, 2001).

MULTIDISCIPLINARY APPROACHES

Successful myth busting can be achieved through questioning and reassessing assumptions, and through problem-based research in which a careful problem statement is the starting point for academics and practitioners to jointly understand what can be done about it. However, a common denominator between problematization and joint problem-based research is that both approaches require multidisciplinary. Multidisciplinary research involves collaboration among two or more disciplines to undertake a research project, with each discipline preserving its distinct boundaries, epistemologies, methodologies, and core values (Okumus & van Niekerk, 2015).

For problematization, multidisciplinary approaches matter as researchers are stimulated to look beyond meaningless gaps and the usual suspects (Alvesson & Sandberg, 2024). For example, when reviewing sustainable business model literature, problematizing researchers may consider reading and including multidisciplinary sustainability journals (Dzhengiz et al., 2023), as using journal rankings and impact factors can be misleading and lead to excessive emphasis on research of lesser significance simply because it is published in prestigious outlets (Elbanna & Child, 2023).

For problem-based research between academics and practitioners, multidisciplinarity matters because it is essential to extend perspectives beyond the organization to generate lasting value for all stakeholders. For instance, "researchers and practitioners can investigate complex social problems by collaborating across the basic stages of the research process, including formulating problems, building theory, designing research, and solving problems" (Bansal et al., 2012, p. 74), to decrease the research-practice gap. Thus, acknowledging the importance of the multidisciplinary character of different stakeholders within the business model is important for collective views on the value-creation processes (Alvarez et al., 2020).

Multi-disciplinarity can also help research on sustainable business models to adopt the so-called "outside view" (Kahneman et al., 2011; Lovallo & Kahneman, 2003). The inside view is an approach that typically happens when same-minded researchers work on sustainable problems together. When researchers use their inside view, they concentrate narrowly on the problem at hand which may lead to overoptimistic judgments. The outside view, on the other hand, ignores information at hand and instead examines a broad set of problems outside the narrow scope of what comes to mind first. Multidisciplinary approaches help researchers to obtain an outside view as different fields and expertise bring different perspectives on sustainable problems and solutions for their sustainable business model design (Geissdoerfer et al., 2016).

Understanding these underlying cognitive processes (Bastian et al., 2025) matter as they may positively impact the quality of idea-generation processes (Frederiks et al., 2019). However, including a broader range of stakeholders may simultaneously create novel challenges. When stakeholders have different expectations, developing a common pathway becomes more complicated (Scheyvens et al., 2016). This may happen when stakeholders do not see a clear direction in the future (Aldrich & Fiol, 1994) or question the plausibility that problems are addressed correctly (Suchman, 1995). Thus, it is evident that collaborations should be aligned, with stakeholders committed and motivated to common goals that represent shared values (Bastian & Zucchella, 2023; Lindenberg & Foss, 2011). This also involves a mutual understanding of roles and potential perceptual differences between stakeholders and what they know (Huber & Lewis, 2010).

CONCLUSION

In conclusion, this chapter highlights the significance of myth-busting as a crucial tool for challenging long-standing assumptions in sustainable management. By critically examining prevailing beliefs, both researchers and industry professionals can move beyond conventional approaches to encourage deeper insights and drive meaningful transformation. Debunking myths not only strengthens evidence-based decision-making but also promotes innovation and multidisciplinary collaboration, leading to more sustainable tourism practices. Future myth-busters will enable organizations to ask more relevant questions, make more informed choices, and make smarter decisions across research, policy, and practice.

REFERENCES

Alegre, J., Callahan, J., & Iszatt-White, M. (2023). Innovative conceptual contributions – Raising the game for theory-driven reviews. *International Journal of Management Review*, *25*, 233–239.

Aldrich, H. E., & Fiol, C. M. (1994). Fools rush in? The institutional context of industry creation. *Academy of Management Review*, *19*(4), 645–670.

Alvarez, S. A., Young, S. L., & Woolley, J. L. (2020). Creating the world's deadliest catch: The process of enrolling stakeholders in an uncertain endeavor. *Business & Society*, *59*(2), 287–321.

Alvesson, M. (2013). Do we have something to say? From re-search to roi-search and back again. *Organization*, *20*(1), 79–90.

Alvesson, M., & Blom, M. (2021). The hegemonic ambiguity of big concepts in organization studies. *Human Relations*, *75*, 58–86.

Alvesson, M., Einola, K., & Schaefer, S. M. (2022). Dynamics of wilful ignorance in organizations. *The British Journal of Sociology*, *73*(4), 839–858.

Alvesson, M., & Sandberg, J. (2011). Generating research questions through problematization. *Academy of Management Review*, *36*(2), 247–271.

Alvesson, M., & Sandberg, J. (2013). *Constructing research questions: Doing interesting research*. Sage.

Alvesson, M., & Sandberg, J. (2014). Habitat and habitus: Boxed-in versus box-breaking research. *Organization Studies*, *35*(7), 967–987.

Alvesson, M., & Sandberg, J. (2020). The problematizing review: A counterpoint to Elsbach and Van Knippenberg's argument for integrative reviews. *Journal of Management Studies*, *57*(6), 1290–1304.

Alvesson, M., & Sandberg, J. (2024). The art of phenomena construction: A framework for coming up with research phenomena beyond 'the usual suspects'. *Journal of Management Studies*, *61*(5), 1737–1765.

Alvesson, M., & Spicer, A. (2016). *The stupidity paradox: The power and pitfalls of functional stupidity at work*. Profile.

Antikainen, M., & Valkokari, K. (2016). A framework for sustainable circular business model innovation. *Technology Innovation Management Review*, *6*, 5–12.

Bansal, P., Bertels, S., Ewart, T., MacConnachie, P., & O'Brien, J. (2012). Bridging the research–practice gap. In *Academy of Management Perspectives*, *26, 1*, Symposium.

Bartunek, J. M., Rynes, S. L., & Ireland, R. D. (2006). What makes management research interesting, and why does it matter? *Academy of Management Journal*, *49*(1), 9–15.

Bastian, B., & Caputo, A. (2024). Sustainable business models: Researchers as design thinkers for problem-driven research. *Strategic Change*, *33*(3), 129–138.

Bastian, B., Hjelle, M., & Shepherd, D. (2025). Systemizing entrepreneurial Metacognition: Thinking about the past and future. *Entrepreneurship Theory and Practice*, 10422587251315664.

Bastian, B., & Zucchella, A. (2023). Nascent entrepreneurs during start-up competitions: Between beauty contests and co-created problematization. *Journal of Business Venturing Insights*, *20*, e00391.

Berglund, H., Dimov, D., & Wennberg, K. (2018). Beyond bridging rigor and relevance: The three-body problem in entrepreneurship. *Journal of Business Venturing Insights*, *9*, 87–91.

Bergmann, E. (2020). Populism and the politics of misinformation. *Safundi*, *21*(3), 251–265.

Björkdahl, J., Fallahi, S., & Holmén, M. (2022). Explaining business model innovation processes: A problem formulation and problem solving perspective. *Industrial Marketing Management*, *105*, 223–239.

Bocken, N. M. P., & Geradts, T. H. J. (2020). Barriers and drivers to sustainable business model innovation: Organization design and dynamic capabilities. *Long Range Planning*, *53*(4), 101950.

Bocken, N. M. P., Short, S. W., Rana, P., & Evans, S. (2014). A literature and practice review to develop sustainable business model archetypes. *Journal of Cleaner Production*, *65*, 42–56.

Boons, F., Montalvo, C., Quist, J. N., & Wagner, M. (2013). Sustainable innovation, business models and economic performance: An overview. *Journal of Cleaner Production*, *45*, 1–8.

Breslin, D., Gatrell, C., & Bailey, K. (2020). Developing insights through reviews: Reflecting on the 20th anniversary of the International Journal of Management Reviews. *International Journal of Management Reviews*, *22*, 3–9.

Burmeister, K., & Schade, C. (2007). Are entrepreneurs' decisions more biased? An experimental investigation of the susceptibility to status quo bias. *Journal of Business Venturing*, *22*(3), 340–362.

Chavda, V. P., Sonak, S. S., Munshi, N. K., & Dhamade, P. N. (2022). Pseudoscience and fraudulent products for COVID-19 management. *Environmental Science and Pollution Research*, *29*(42), 62887–62912.

Colquitt, J. A., & Zapata-Phelan, C. P. (2007). Trends in theory building and theory testing: A five-decade study of the Academy of Management Journal. *Academy of Management Journal*, *50*(6), 1281–1303.

Dentchev, N., Rauter, R., Jóhannsdóttir, L., Snihur, Y., Rosano, M., Baumgartner, R., & Nyberg, T. (2018). Embracing the variety of sustainable business models: A prolific field of research and a future research agenda. *Journal of Cleaner Production*, *194*, 695–703.

Dimov, D. (2020). Opportunities, language, and time. *Academy of Management Perspectives*, *34*(3), 333–351.

Dorst, K. (2011). The core of "design thinking" and its application. *Design Studies*, *32*(6), 521–532.

Douglas, K. M., Uscinski, J. E., Sutton, R. M., Cichocka, A., Nefes, T., Ang, C. S., & Deravi, F. (2019). Understanding conspiracy theories. *Political Psychology*, *40*(S1), 3–35.

Dzhengiz, T., Miller, E. M., Ovaska, J. P., & Patala, S. (2023). Unpacking the circular economy: A problematizing review. *International Journal of Management Reviews*, *25*(2), 270–296.

Elbanna, S., & Child, J. (2023). From 'publish or perish' to 'publish for purpose'. *European Management Review*, *20*(4), 614–618.

Ellis, T. J., & Levy, Y. (2008). Framework of problem-based research: A guide for novice researchers on the development of a research-worthy problem. *Informing Science*, *11*, 17–33.

Evans, S., Vladimirova, D., Holgado, M., Van Fossen, K., Yang, M., Silva, E. A., & Barlow, C. Y. (2017). Business model innovation for sustainability: Towards a unified perspective for creation of sustainable business models. *Business Strategy and the Environment*, *26*(5), 597–608.

Firestein, S. (2012). *Ignorance: How it drives science*. Oxford University Press.

Fobbe, L., & Hilletofth, P. (2021). The role of stakeholder interaction in sustainable business models: A systematic literature review. *Journal of Cleaner Production*, *327*, 129510.

Foss, N., & Saebi, T. (2017). Business models and business model innovation: Between wicked and paradigmatic problems. *Long Range Planning*, *51*(1), 9–21.

Foucault, M. (2013). Archaeology of knowledge. In A. M. Sheridan Smith (Ed.), Routledge.

Frederiks, A. J., Englis, B. G., Ehrenhard, M. L., & Groen, A. J. (2019). Entrepreneurial cognition and the quality of new venture ideas: An experimental approach to comparing future-oriented cognitive processes. *Journal of Business Venturing*, *34*(2), 327–347.

Geissdoerfer, M., Bocken, N. M. P., & Hultink, E. J. (2016). Design thinking to enhance the sustainable business modelling process – A workshop based on a value mapping process. *Journal of Cleaner Production*, *135*, 1218–1232.

Geissdoerfer, M., Vladimirova, D., & Evans, S. (2018). Sustainable business model innovation: A review. *Journal of Cleaner Production*, *198*, 401–416.

Glavič, P., & Lukman, R. (2007). Review of sustainability terms and their definitions. *Journal of Cleaner Production*, *15*(18), 1875–1885.

Hannan, M. T., & Freeman, J. (1984). Structural inertia and organizational change. *American Sociological Review*, *49*(2), 149–164.

Hardy, C., & Grant, D. (2012). Readers beware: Provocation, problematization and... problems. *Human Relations*, 65(5), 547–566.

Hasenzagl, R., Hatak, I., & Frank, H. (2018). Problematizing socioemotional wealth in family firms: A systems-theoretical reframing. *Entrepreneurship & Regional Development*, 30(1–2), 199–223.

Ho, C. H. (2001). Some phenomena of problem decomposition strategy for design thinking: Differences between novices and experts. *Design Studies*, 22(1), 27–45.

Huber, G. P., & Lewis, K. (2010). Cross-understanding: Implications for group cognition and performance. *Academy of Management Review*, 35(1), 6–26.

Hyytinen, A. (2021). Shared problem solving and design thinking in entrepreneurship research. *Journal of Business Venturing Insights*, 16, e00254.

Kahneman, D., Lovallo, D., & Sibony, O. (2011). Before you make that big decision. *Harvard Business Review*, 89(6), 50–60.

Kennedy, M., Fisher, M. B., & Ennis, R. H. (2013). Critical thinking: Literature review and needed research. In J. A. Bellanca (Ed.), *Educational values and cognitive instruction* (pp. 11–40). Routledge.

Klayman, J. (1995). Varieties of confirmation bias. *Psychology of Learning and Motivation*, 32, 385–418.

Laguerre, R. (2023). Challenging assumptions in research and practice using problematization principles. *Industrial and Organizational Psychology*, 16(1), 101–104.

Leal Filho, W. (2000). Dealing with misconceptions on the concept of sustainability. *International Journal of Sustainability in Higher Education*, 1(1), 9–19.

Lindenberg, S., & Foss, N. J. (2011). Managing joint production motivation: The role of goal framing and governance mechanisms. *Academy of Management Review*, 36(3), 500–525.

Lovallo, D., & Kahneman, D. (2003). Delusions of success. *Harvard Business Review*, 81(7), 56–63.

Lüdeke-Freund, F., & Dembek, K. (2017). Sustainable business model research and practice: Emerging field or passing fancy? *Journal of Cleaner Production*, 168, 1668–1678.

Massa, L., Tucci, C. L., & Afuah, A. (2017). A critical assessment of business model research. *Academy of Management Annals, 11*(1), 73–104.

Matthews, L., Power, D., Touboulic, A., & Marques, L. (2016). Building bridges: Toward alternative theory of sustainable supply chain management. *Journal of Supply Chain Management, 52*(1), 82–94.

Montiel, I., Gallo, P. J., & Antolin-Lopez, R. (2020). What on Earth should managers learn about corporate sustainability? A threshold concept approach. *Journal of Business Ethics, 162*(4), 857–880.

Mwampamba, T. H., Ghilardi, A., Sander, K., & Chaix, K. J. (2013). Dispelling common misconceptions to improve attitudes and policy outlook on charcoal in developing countries. *Energy for Sustainable Development, 17*(2), 75–85.

Okumus, F., & van Niekerk, M. (2015). Multidisciplinarity, tourism. In J. J. Liburd & D. Edwards (Eds.), *Encyclopedia of tourism* (pp. 1–3). Springer.

Osterwalder, A., & Pigneur, Y. (2010). *Business model generation: A handbook for visionaries, game changers, and challengers.* John Wiley & Sons.

Patriotta, G. (2017). Crafting papers for publication: Novelty and convention in academic writing. *Journal of Management Studies, 54*(6), 747–759.

Petrocelli, J. V., Seta, C. E., & Seta, J. J. (2023). Lies and bullshit: The negative effects of misinformation grow stronger over time. *Applied Cognitive Psychology, 37*(2), 409–418.

Pfleegor, A. G., Katz, M., & Bowers, M. T. (2019). Publish, perish, or salami slice? Authorship ethics in an emerging field. *Journal of Business Ethics, 156*(1), 189–208.

Pinkse, J., Lüdeke-Freund, F., Laasch, O., Snihur, Y., & Bohnsack, R. (2023). The organizational dynamics of business models for sustainability: Discursive and cognitive pathways for change. *Organization & Environment, 36*(2), 211–227.

Pratt, M. G. (2009). From the editors: For the lack of a boilerplate: Tips on writing up (and reviewing) qualitative research. *Academy of Management Journal, 52*(5), 856–862.

Prescott, J. E., & Filatotchev, I. (2021). The business model phenomenon: Towards theoretical relevance. *Journal of Management Studies, 58*(3), 517–527.

Reuber, A. R. (2016). An assemblage–theoretic perspective on the internationalization processes of family firms. *Entrepreneurship Theory and Practice*, 40(6), 1269–1286.

Ringvold, K., Saebi, T., & Foss, N. (2023). Developing sustainable business models: A microfoundational perspective. *Organization & Environment*, 36(2), 315–348.

Rosato, P. F., Caputo, A., Valente, D., & Pizzi, S. (2021). 2030 agenda and sustainable business models in tourism: A bibliometric analysis. *Ecological Indicators*, 121, 106978.

Rynes, S. L., Bartunek, J. M., & Daft, R. L. (2001). Across the great divide: Knowledge creation and transfer between practitioners and academics. *Academy of Management Journal*, 44(2), 340–355.

Rynes, S. L., Colbert, A. E., & O'Boyle, E. H. (2018). When the "best available evidence" doesn't win: How doubts about science and scientists threaten the future of evidence-based management. *Journal of Management*, 44(8), 2995–3010.

Sabaruddin, L. O., MacBryde, J., & D'Ippolito, B. (2023). The dark side of business model innovation. *International Journal of Management Reviews*, 25(1), 130–151.

Sandberg, J., & Alvesson, M. (2011). Ways of constructing research questions: Gap-spotting or problematization? *Organization*, 18(1), 23–44.

Schaltegger, S., Hansen, E. G., & Lüdeke-Freund, F. (2016). Business models for sustainability: Origins, present research, and future avenues. *Organization & Environment*, 29(1), 3–10.

Scheyvens, R., Banks, G., & Hughes, E. (2016). The private sector and the SDGs: The need to move beyond 'business as usual'. *Sustainable Development*, 24(6), 371–382.

Shams, S., & Kaufman, A. (2016). Entrepreneurial co-creation: A research vision to be materialized. *Management Decision*, 54(6), 1250–1268.

Sharma, G., & Bansal, P. T. (2020). Partnering up: Including managers as research partners in systematic reviews. *Organizational Research Methods*, 24(4), 817–846.

Sharma, G., Greco, A., Grewatsch, S., & Bansal, P. (2022). Cocreating forward: How researchers and managers can address wicked problems together. *Academy of Management Learning & Education*.

Sorman, A. H. (2023). Deceitful decoupling: Misconceptions of a persistent myth. In F. Demaria, J. Martinez-Alier, & D. Temper (Eds.), *The Barcelona school of ecological economics and political ecology: A companion in honour of Joan Martinez-Alier* (pp. 165–177). Springer.

Suchman, M. C. (1995). Managing legitimacy: Strategic and institutional approaches. *Academy of Management Review, 20*(3), 571–610.

Suddaby, R. (Ed.). (2010). Editor's comments: Construct clarity in theories of management and organization. *Academy of Management Review, 35*(3), 346–357.

Sunstein, C. R. (2014). *Conspiracy theories and other dangerous ideas.* Simon and Schuster.

Susur, F., & Karakaya, E. (2021). A reflexive perspective for sustainability assumptions in transition studies. *Environmental Innovation and Societal Transitions, 39*, 34–54.

Teece, D. J. (2010). Business models, business strategy and innovation. *Long Range Planning, 43*(2–3), 172–194.

Vasist, P. N., & Krishnan, S. (2023). Fake news and sustainability-focused innovations: A review of the literature and an agenda for future research. *Journal of Cleaner Production, 388*, 135933.

Volkema, R. J. (1983). Problem formulation in planning and design. *Management Science, 29*(6), 639–652.

Part I

BUSINESS MODELS INCORPORATING THE PRINCIPLES OF CIRCULAR ECONOMY AND INCLUSIVITY

2

CIRCULAR ECONOMY IN THE HOSPITALITY AND TOURISM SECTOR: THE CASE OF WASTE COOKING OIL

MATTEO BALDAN[a], MUHAMMAD JUNAID SHAHID HASNI[b] AND VALENTINA BEGHETTO[a]

[a]Ca' Foscari University of Venice, Italy
[b]University of Trento, Italy

ABSTRACT

The hospitality sector, one of the fastest-growing global industries, significantly contributes to economic development but is simultaneously responsible for substantial environmental impacts, particularly waste generation. Waste cooking oil (WCO) emerges as a critical environmental and economic issue within this industry, presenting challenges and opportunities. This chapter explores the transformative role of circular economy (CE) principles in hospitality through the reutilization of WCO, showcasing its conversion from an environmental burden into valuable industrial resources, such as biofuels, polymers, and industrial additives. It further examines regulatory frameworks, innovative recycling pathways, and sustainable business models that leverage WCO within regional hospitality contexts.

Keywords: Circular economy; waste generation; sustainable environment; sustainable business models; waste cooking oil; tourism and hospitality sector

INTRODUCTION

Industrial progress in the 20th century brought substantial economic and social benefits, but simultaneously created pressing environmental challenges, including resource depletion, pollution, and climate change (Geels et al., 2015). Among the industries significantly contributing to these environmental burdens, hospitality stands out due to its high resource consumption and waste generation (Jones & Wynn, 2019). Within this sector, WCO represents a critical yet often neglected waste stream. Recognizing the potential for resource recovery, recent scholarly and industrial interest has focused on integrating CE strategies into hospitality management, aiming to transform WCO into valuable products and reduce environmental impacts (Amicarelli et al., 2023).

This chapter discusses the theoretical and practical dimensions of the CE related to WCO in hospitality. It outlines current regulatory contexts, explores innovative recycling technologies, and examines case studies demonstrating sustainable business models leveraging WCO as a strategic resource.

CE IN HOSPITALITY: A PARADIGM SHIFT

CE strategies emphasize resource recovery, waste reduction, and sustainability through systematic reuse and recycling. Despite initial adoption in manufacturing and agriculture, these principles remain underutilized in hospitality due to fragmented supply chains, seasonal demands, and stakeholder diversity (Jones & Wynn, 2019). However, given the industry's scale and waste generation profile, embedding circular strategies can significantly enhance sustainability outcomes.

The hospitality and tourism sector ranks among the most prominent global industries, fueling substantial economic growth and employment opportunities in developed and developing regions. This industry encompasses various activities from accommodations and food services to transportation, entertainment, and leisure, ultimately catering to a diverse and ever-expanding customer base. Despite its economic significance, it is also widely recognized for its negative externalities, including environmental degradation, resource overconsumption, and disruptions to local communities and cultures. These impacts have prompted calls for sustainable development within the sector, as underscored by scholars (Boley, 2011) who highlight the urgency of addressing ecological and social challenges. Nevertheless, achieving sustainability in such a multifaceted domain remains an intricate task (Jones & Wynn, 2019), whose research underscores the persistent struggles in integrating environmental responsibility into business models and day-to-day operations.

Recent scholarly work indicates that formal research on the CE in hospitality and tourism began gaining traction around 2018. However, a few earlier studies did emerge periodically (Bux et al., 2025). Before this period, farm-to-fork perspectives and sustainability considerations within hospitality's food and service segments saw rising interest between 2017 and 2018. Such attention has frequently revolved around waste management, reflecting a consistent theme in the literature from 2013 through 2021. This demonstrates the centrality of waste reduction and recycling to CE approaches, particularly in industries that deal heavily with consumable resources.

Despite the growing recognition of sustainability's importance, embedding CE principles into tourism and hospitality remains an ongoing challenge for academics, policymakers, and industry practitioners. While CE strategies have seen broader adoption in agriculture, manufacturing, and construction (Pattanaro & Gente, 2017), the acceptance within tourism has been more limited, often hindered by split supply chains, seasonal fluctuations in demand, and the diverse array of stakeholders involved. Consequently, scholars have increasingly focused on understanding how circular models might be adapted to the unique characteristics of tourism destinations and hospitality services.

Literature exploring CE within tourism frequently examines farm-to-fork strategies (Dolnicar et al., 2020), sustainable waste management programs (de Grosbois & Fennell, 2021), and eco-innovations tailored to hospitality operations (Kim & Hall, 2019). Scholars have recommended that increased government intervention, green procurement, and energy-saving initiatives highlight the vital role that policymakers and local authorities play in guiding sustainable transformations (Zhang et al., 2018). Scheepens et al. (2016) examined sustainable water recreation in Friesland (Netherlands), identifying strategic pathways toward reduced environmental footprints. However, the study also revealed that insufficient customer recognition of eco-friendly efforts can reduce market competitiveness, underscoring the importance of consumer education and stakeholder collaboration in supporting sustainable business models. In many tourism businesses, circular practices, such as reusing cooking oil from waste, are being adopted. However, customer value recognition remains uncertain. One of the most significant risks of these initiatives is their invisibility, as eco-innovations are often invisible to customers. A lack of transparency in communication can lead to customers undervaluing sustainability initiatives, lowering their impact on brand loyalty and willingness to pay. In addition, some people may question greenwashing's authenticity due to skepticism. Therefore, it is essential to develop communication strategies that are transparent, credible, and contextually relevant for circular business models to be seen and appreciated.

When it comes to hospitality-specific contexts, academic inquiries remain comparatively scarce. The alignment of CE principles with hospitality operations can accelerate business growth while fostering a more sustainable experience for patrons and communities (Zaki & Farrag, 2024). However, beyond isolated studies estimating the financial and environmental benefits of waste reduction and recycling in hotels, the literature still lacks robust frameworks tailored explicitly for hospitality. Nevertheless, scholars widely concur that monitoring water and waste management and energy consumption is fundamental to a comprehensive sustainability strategy (Jones & Wynn, 2019). Effective data capture, processing, and reporting systems are essential if businesses aim to make informed decisions, track improvements, and communicate progress to stakeholders.

Restaurants serve as a particularly fertile ground for exploring circular practices (Bux et al., 2025). A considerable portion of research focuses on farm-to-fork initiatives, emphasizing short supply chains, local sourcing, and the responsible use of natural resources. For instance, nutrient recycling, composting, and biodiesel production derived from cooking oil to energy recovery from organic waste (Carmona-Cabello et al., 2018, 2019; Paciarotti & Torregiani, 2018; Scozzafava et al., 2017; Velazquez Abad et al., 2015). By engaging in these practices, restaurants can reduce operational costs, enhance environmental performance, and even generate new revenue streams.

The evolution of food waste management toward circular strategies further testifies to the sector's growing environmental consciousness. Research indicates that integrating CE principles, such as reusing and recycling surplus food, can lead to cost savings, the creation of value-added products, and broader environmental benefits (Haque et al., 2023; Kumar et al., 2022; Lopes de Sousa Jabbour et al., 2021). In addition, restaurant operators are increasingly turning to consumer-oriented approaches like sustainable menu design, local procurement, and sharing economy platforms to divert edible surplus from landfills. Equally important are shifts in consumer choice architecture, wherein diners receive clear information about their selections' environmental and social implications. Such as labeling menus with carbon footprint data or using descriptive language that highlights ethical sourcing can nudge customers toward climate-friendly dining habits (Bacon & Krpan, 2018).

These studies underscore a gradual yet undeniable momentum in the hospitality and tourism sector toward integrating CE strategies. From government policies that incentivize resource-efficient practices to innovations in waste management and educational campaigns targeting consumer awareness, a multifaceted approach is essential for driving meaningful change. As CE research develops, future inquiries may offer deeper insights into holistic methods for reshaping the industry, transforming its impacts on local communities, and ensuring its alignment with broader global sustainability targets. Due to low environmental awareness and infrastructure constraints, it can be difficult for customers to recognize circular practices in less-developed tourism economies, especially in the Global South. Despite efforts such as reusing WCO, aligning with CE goals, tourists often overlook or undervalue these efforts, significantly when economic affordability trumps environmental concerns. A lack of resources may also prevent local businesses from communicating these initiatives, putting them at risk of misinterpretations or failures. Therefore, to increase value recognition in such contexts, communication strategies that are culturally grounded, capacity-building for sustainable innovations, and policy support are needed.

WCO REUTILIZATION STRATEGIES

In the European Union, WCO management is governed by several regulations, notably Directive 2008/98/EC, which defines WCO as non-hazardous but environmentally problematic waste (Commission Decision 2014/955/EU) (Van Caneghem et al., 2019). Each member state has considerable autonomy in designing its collection and recycling systems, creating diverse logistical landscapes. For instance, in Italy, Legislative Decree 152/2006 mandates the participation of operators in specific consortia (e.g., CONOE), which organize the collection, transportation, and recycling of WCO (Lopresto et al., 2024). This structured approach is critical to preventing environmental contamination and promoting resource efficiency.

WCO is generated primarily through repeated frying processes in food services. Its disposal poses significant environmental risks, particularly aquatic contamination and ecosystem damage. Therefore, effective reutilization is economically and environmentally strategic. With the introduction of increasingly hard regulations governing the use of toxic substances in industrial processes, research efforts are turning toward bio-based components as safer and more sustainable alternatives. Such components have gained particular importance in the plastics industry, where they function as additives, most notably in the role of plasticizers (Jia et al., 2018). By incorporating these additives, manufacturers can adjust polymer properties such as flexibility, toughness, and processability, ultimately broadening the range of applications for various plastic products (Bocqué et al., 2015). Plasticizers are essentially low-molecular-weight organic molecules added to polymer formulations to serve as lubricants among polymer chains. Plasticizers lower the polymer's glass transition temperature by reducing intermolecular forces, enhancing its flexibility and ductility. One common industrial example is polyvinyl chloride (PVC), a resin widely employed in food packaging, medical devices, and building materials, which is, by nature, hard and brittle at room temperature. By incorporating suitable plasticizers, PVC can be transformed into a more flexible, user-friendly material (Rahman & Brazel, 2004).

However, conventional plasticizers, particularly phthalates such as dioctyl phthalate (DOP), have attracted considerable scrutiny due to their toxicity and potential to migrate out of polymer matrices. In Europe, for instance, DOP faces REACH restrictions (Annex XVII) that limit its use in toys, food packaging, and medical instruments (Cheng et al., 2020). A significant concern is that these phthalates can leach into their surroundings, especially in contact with fatty foods, solvents, or biological fluids, posing health and environmental risks (Zygoura et al., 2007).

Against this backdrop, the search for safer, bio-based plasticizers has led researchers to explore WCO as a non-toxic, biodegradable, and readily available feedstock for additive manufacturing. By chemically modifying WCO, scientists can create renewable plasticizers that provide comparable or even superior performance to traditional fossil-derived additives, aligning with the global imperative to reduce hazardous chemicals' use and tackle plastic waste more sustainably.

A compelling example is the work of Liu et al. (2020), who developed an acetylated-fatty-acid methyl ester-trimellitic acid ester (AC-FAME-TAE) from WCO. When used as a plasticizer in PVC formulations, this renewable additive endows the plastic with mechanical and thermal properties that closely match those obtained using phthalate-based plasticizers, while exhibiting significantly reduced toxicity and lower environmental impact. This breakthrough underscores WCO's potential as an adequate substitute for hazardous petrochemical additives, offering a safer, cleaner pathway to plastic production.

By harnessing WCO in plastic formulations, manufacturers may meet tightening regulations, enhance product safety, minimize toxic waste, and promote CE principles. Future research is expected to focus on scaling up these technologies, refining cost-efficiency, and optimizing formulations so that WCO-derived additives can seamlessly integrate into existing industrial processes, reinforcing their broad commercial viability and environmental benefits.

SUSTAINABLE BUSINESS MODELS AND APPLICATIONS

Therefore, WCO presents itself as a promising waste source on the creation of "second-life products." Leaving aside its primary use as a renewable source for biodiesel production, WCO can be chemically modified and used as bio-based plasticizers (Landi et al., 2022; Zheng et al., 2018), polymeric materials (Kim & Hall, 2019), bio-lubricants (Mannu et al., 2019, 2020), detergents and soaps (Mannu et al., 2020; Panadare & Rathod, 2016), cosmetics (Escobar Lanzuela et al., 2015), bio-solvents for pollutants (Mannu et al., 2019), and binder additive for aged bitumen (Asli et al., 2012).

The growing emphasis on CE principles and sustainable development spurred by societal, regulatory, and environmental concerns presents a timely opportunity for collaborative partnerships between agri-food operations, local communities, and artisan businesses (Borrero & Yousafzai, 2024). In particular, WCO has emerged as a promising feedstock that bridges environmental responsibility and economic benefit. When collected and processed correctly, WCO can be transformed into a diverse range of bio-based products such as biodiesel, plastic additives, and polyurethane precursors, offering a pathway to resource efficiency and value creation (Bardella et al., 2024).

These opportunities arise most notably through the synergy of agri-food material recovery and the participation of local communities and craft enterprises. Agri-food material recovery can strengthen local supply chains, where producers, restaurants, and households cooperatively gather WCO. Craft enterprises such as small-scale biodiesel producers, artisanal cosmetics makers, and construction material innovators benefit from a consistent, cost-effective supply of renewable raw materials. Meanwhile, local communities gain from reduced environmental pollution and increased green jobs, thereby cultivating pride in eco-friendly initiatives.

CE FRAMEWORK FOR WCO IN THE TOURISM SECTOR

The tourism sector generates significant volumes of WCO, mainly through food preparation activities in hotels, restaurants, and resorts. Often regarded as a pollutant, WCO poses environmental hazards if improperly managed, such as water contamination and increased greenhouse gas emissions. However, applying CE principles can transform this waste into valuable resources, contributing to sustainability, resource efficiency, and local economic development. For this, we developed a framework through a conceptual blend of available literature on CE applications in the tourism sector and WCO management. We adopted the narrative review methodology of peer-reviewed (Sukhera, 2022) studies that allows us to identify key actors, stages, and challenges involved in the WCO management lifecycle within the tourism sector. After carefully reading the relevant studies, we integrated the conceptual connections around the CE and WCO. This framework (Fig. 2.1) outlines a circular approach for managing WCO within tourism settings, consisting of seven interconnected components: generation, collection, logistics, re-utilization, business models, policy, and outcomes.

- The first stage begins with WCO generation during routine cooking in hospitality establishments. Tourism businesses, particularly those with in-house food services, are primary producers of WCO. At this stage, the goal is to recognize WCO not as waste but as a potentially valuable input for other industrial processes.

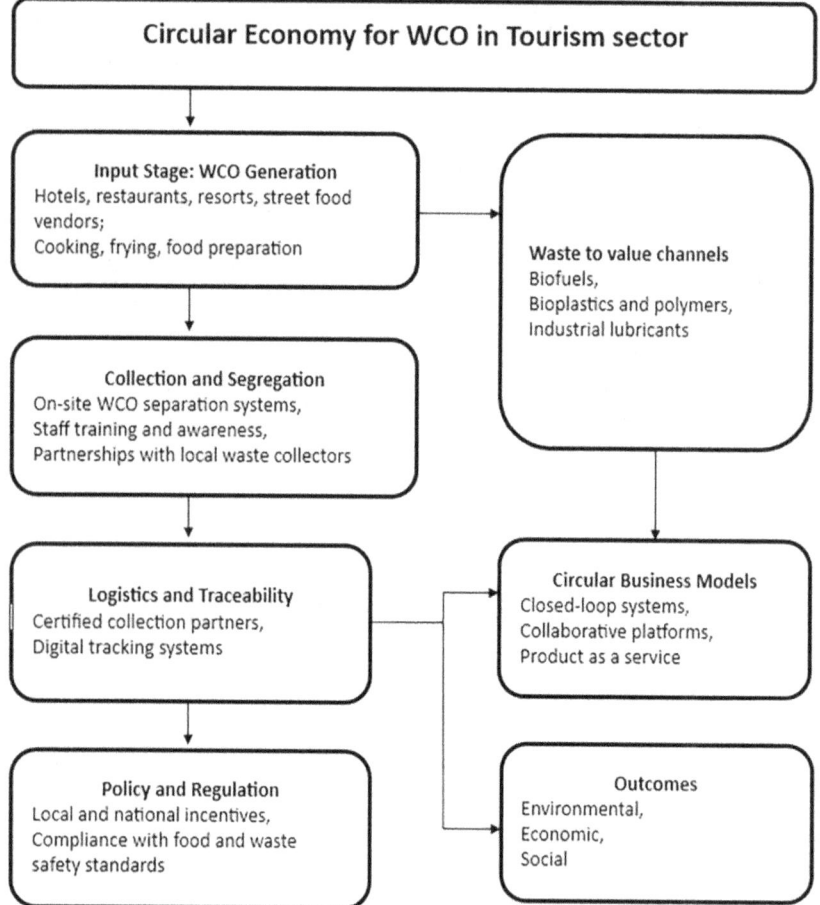

Fig. 2.1. Circular Economy Framework for Waste Cooking Oil (WCO) in the Tourism Sector.
Source: Authors' elaboration.

- Next, collection and segregation are critical. To prevent contamination, WCO must be separated from other waste streams and stored appropriately. Hospitality staff should be trained to handle WCO responsibly, and partnerships should be established with certified collectors. On-site storage systems and periodic pickups by registered handlers ensure safety and efficiency.

- Following collection, the logistics and traceability component emphasizes the importance of transparent and secure transportation. Implementing digital tracking systems can enhance trust and ensure compliance with local regulations. For example, blockchain-based solutions could trace the flow of WCO from source to final product, supporting both sustainability claims and regulatory requirements.

- The center of the framework suggests different value channels for the reutilization of WCO. WCO can be processed into multiple high-value products, such as biofuels, especially biodiesel, for hotel transportation fleets or local energy needs. Bioplastics and polymers are suitable for packaging, utensils, or hotel supplies. Industrial lubricants are used in building maintenance and equipment. The viability of these applications depends on local infrastructure, technology availability, and demand for sustainable alternatives. Innovative circular business models must be adopted to support these practices. For example, closed-loop systems allow hotels to reuse biodiesel from their WCO. Collaborative platforms enable regional tourism clusters to pool shared collection and processing resources. Alternatively, service-based models offer integrated solutions where external providers handle waste and supply bio-based products in return. Policy and regulatory frameworks play a vital enabling role. Government incentives, such as tax reductions or sustainability certifications, can motivate businesses to participate. Clear WCO handling and recycling regulations are essential to ensure health, safety, and environmental protection.

- Finally, this framework's outcomes span multiple domains. Environmentally, it reduces landfill waste and emissions. Economically, it creates new revenue streams, supports green entrepreneurship, and may reduce operational costs. Socially, it fosters job creation in waste management and promotes community participation in sustainable tourism.

This CE framework for the WCO reuse aspect presents a practical and scalable model for integrating sustainability into tourism operations, aligning with global goals for climate action and responsible consumption.

CONCLUSION

Integrating WCO re-consumption into regional economies requires strategic business models involving multiple stakeholders. The Interconnected Nord-Est Innovation Ecosystem (iNEST) project exemplifies integration, linking local communities, craft enterprises, and hospitality businesses. This collaboration encourages innovation in WCO collection and processing, transforming it into marketable products that support regional tourism economies. Living labs established within this project demonstrate practical implementation, where regenerated oils are reintroduced into local economies as sustainable consumer products (e.g., artisanal goods, bio-based plastics). These initiatives illustrate how CE principles can strengthen regional identities, enhance environmental stewardship, and promote inclusive economic development.

By establishing a CE network, municipalities can coordinate logistical support, organize educational campaigns, and provide incentives for participation, while small businesses innovate ways to commercialize WCO-based products. This approach decreases waste disposal costs and stimulates local economies by fostering business innovation. The context of Venice, Verona, and Trento exemplifies how WCO-based partnerships might operate in practice. In Venice, the tourism and hospitality industries generate substantial WCO volumes, making it feasible for local associations to create effective collection points and potentially for small-scale cosmetics producers to market "Venetian-made" products derived from recycled oil. There is also a clear possibility of testing WCO-based biodiesel as a cleaner energy source for the city's water buses or delivery boats, thus reducing emissions in a fragile lagoon environment (Choi et al., 2024).

In the Verona and Vicenza areas, famed for their gastronomic traditions and vineyards, local agritourism, restaurants, and wine producers could collaborate in collecting and processing WCO. These efforts might support the experimentation of WCO-based polyols in eco-friendly foams, insulating panels, or adhesives by local craft enterprises and building-material innovators. The city's emphasis on cultural and culinary heritage and a well-established tourism sector could showcase how heritage can be harmonized with sustainability and innovation (Morea et al., 2022).

With its notable focus on mountain tourism and environmentally conscious visitors, Trento offers yet another compelling case of a region primed for bio-based research and circular initiatives. The local cooperative structure, including mountain huts, hotels, and breweries, could systematically collect WCO and direct it to urban processing facilities managed by a dedicated consortium.

Small-scale chemical laboratories or start-ups backed by Trento's academic network could transform this feedstock into specialized applications such as super-hydrophobic coatings or eco-friendly polyurethane insulation suited to alpine climates. These processes could be integrated into public demonstrations or outreach programs, reinforcing ecological awareness among visitors and residents.

Implementing efficient WCO recovery systems in these regions can yield a double dividend by reducing the environmental impact of used oil disposal and creating economic opportunities across waste management, transportation, and bio-based manufacturing. Local businesses benefit by lowering disposal fees and opening revenue streams from newly developed green products. Policy support is crucial in this regard, since tax incentives, grants, and subsidies are valuable tools for helping small- and medium-sized enterprises adopt WCO-based processes. Equally important is community engagement, which ensures a steady supply of WCO and maintains public enthusiasm through transparent communication about environmental gains. WCO-based initiatives can unify public, private, and communal interests in pursuing ecological and economic resilience. Research in this area is rapidly evolving, and further progress will likely hinge on continued policy support and the widespread recognition that sustainable manufacturing and circular practices are as integral to local economies as they are to the more significant global push for more responsible resource usage.

REFERENCES

Amicarelli, V., Bux, C., & Fiore, M. (2023). Guest editorial: Circular economy in the agri-food, tourism, and hospitality industries in the post-pandemic era. *British Food Journal, 126*(1), 1–12.

Asli, H., Ahmadinia, E., Zargar, M., & Karim, M. R. (2012). Investigation on physical properties of waste cooking oil-rejuvenated bitumen binder. *Construction and Building Materials, 37,* 398–405.

Bacon, L., & Krpan, D. (2018). (Not) eating for the environment: The impact of restaurant menu design on vegetarian food choice. *Appetite, 125,* 190–200.

Bardella, N., Facchin, M., Fabris, E., Baldan, M., & Beghetto, V. (2024). Waste cooking oil as eco-friendly rejuvenator for reclaimed asphalt pavement. *Materials, 17*(7), 1477.

Bocqué, M., Voirin, C., Lapinte, V., Caillol, S., & Robin, J.-J. (2015). Petro-based and bio-based plasticizers: Chemical structures to plasticizing properties. *Journal of Polymer Science Part A: Polymer Chemistry*, *54*(1), 11–33.

Boley, B. B. (2011). Sustainability in hospitality and tourism education: Towards an integrated curriculum. *Journal of Hospitality & Tourism Education*, *23*(4), 22–31.

Borrero, J. D., & Yousafzai, S. (2024). Circular entrepreneurial ecosystems: A Quintuple Helix Model approach. *Management Decision*, *62*(13), 188–224.

Bux, C., Zizzo, G., Roe, B. E., & Amicarelli, V. (2025). A comparative assessment of food waste and carbon footprint toward a more sustainable healthcare foodservice. *Journal of Cleaner Production*, *49*, 145102.

Carmona-Cabello, M., Leiva-Candia, D., Castro-Cantarero, J. L., Pinzi, S., & Dorado, M. P. (2018). Valorization of food waste from restaurants by transesterification of the lipid fraction. *Fuel*, *215*, 492–498.

Carmona-Cabello, M., Sáez-Bastante, J., Pinzi, S., & Dorado, M. P. (2019). Optimization of solid food waste oil biodiesel by ultrasound-assisted transesterification. *Fuel*, *255*, 115817.

Cheng, Z., Yao, Y., & Sun, H. (2020). Comparative uptake, translocation and subcellular distribution of phthalate esters and their primary monoester metabolites in Chinese cabbage (*Brassica rapa* var. *chinensis*). *Science of the Total Environment*, *742*, 140550.

Choi, J., Jeon, H., & Asperin, A. (2024). Popularity paradox in Venice, Italy: A battle of priorities. *Journal of Hospitality & Tourism Cases: An International Case Journal*, *13*(3), 159–168.

de Grosbois, D., & Fennell, D. A. (2021). Sustainability and ecotourism principles adoption by leading ecolodges: Learning from best practices. *Tourism Recreation Research*, *47*(5–6), 483–498.

Dolnicar, S., Juvan, E., & Grün, B. (2020). Reducing the plate waste of families at hotel buffets: A quasi-experimental field study. *Tourism Management*, *80*, 104103.

de Albuquerque Landi, F. F., Fabiani, C., Castellani, B., Cotana, F., & Pisello, A. L. (2022). Environmental assessment of four waste cooking oil valorization pathways. *Waste Management*, *138*, 219–233.

Escobar Lanzuela, N., Ribal Sanchís, F. J., Rodrigo Señer, A., Clemente Polo, G., Pascual Vidal, A., & Sanjuán Pellicer, N. (2015). Uncertainty analysis in the environmental assessment of an integrated management system for restaurant and catering waste in Spain. *The International Journal of Life Cycle Assessment, 20*(2), 244–262.

Geels, F. W., McMeekin, A., Mylan, J., & Southerton, D. (2015). A critical appraisal of sustainable consumption and production research: The reformist, revolutionary and reconfiguration positions. *Global Environmental Change, 34*, 1–12.

Haque, F., Fan, C., & Lee, Y.-Y. (2023). From waste to value: Addressing the relevance of waste recovery to the agricultural sector in line with the circular economy. *Journal of Cleaner Production, 415*, 137873.

Jia, P., Xia, H., Tang, K., & Zhou, Y. (2018). Plasticizers derived from biomass resources: A short review. *Polymers, 10*(12), 1303.

Jones, P., & Wynn, M. G. (2019). The circular economy, natural capital and resilience in tourism and hospitality. *International Journal of Contemporary Hospitality Management, 31*(6), 2544–2563.

Kim, M. J., & Hall, C. M. (2019). A hedonic motivation model in virtual reality tourism: Comparing visitors and non-visitors. *International Journal of Information Management, 46*, 236–249.

Kumar, M., Raut, R. D., Jagtap, S., & Choubey, V. K. (2022). Circular economy adoption challenges in the food supply chain for sustainable development. *Business Strategy and the Environment, 32*(4), Article e3191.

Liu, Y., Yu, Z., Lv, C., Meng, F., & Yang, Y. (2020). Preparation of waste cooking oil emulsion as shrinkage reducing admixture and its potential use in high performance concrete: Effect on shrinkage and mechanical properties. *Journal of Building Engineering, 32*, 101488.

Lopes de Sousa Jabbour, A. B., Frascareli, F. C. de O., Santibanez Gonzalez, E. D. R., & Chiappetta Jabbour, C. J. (2021). Are food supply chains taking advantage of the circular economy? A research agenda on tackling food waste based on Industry 4.0 technologies. *Production Planning & Control, 34*(10), 1–17.

Lopresto, C. G., Gabriela, M., & Calabrò, V. (2024). Importance of the properties, collection, and storage of waste cooking oils to produce high-quality biodiesel: An overview. *Biomass and Bioenergy, 189*, 107363.

Mannu, A., Ferro, M., Pietro, M. E. D., & Mele, A. (2019). Innovative applications of waste cooking oil as raw material. *Science Progress, 102*(2), 153–160.

Mannu, A., Garroni, S., Ibanez Porras, J., & Mele, A. (2020). Available technologies and materials for waste cooking oil recycling. *Processes*, *8*(3), 366.

Morea, D., Fortunati, S., Cappa, F., & Oriani, R. (2022). Corporate social responsibility as a catalyst of circular economy? A case study perspective in agri-food. *Journal of Knowledge Management*, *27*(7).

Paciarotti, C., & Torregiani, F. (2018). Short food supply chain between micro/small farms and restaurants. *British Food Journal*, *120*(8), 1722–1734.

Panadare, D. C., & Rathod, V. K. (2016). Microwave assisted enzymatic synthesis of biodiesel with waste cooking oil and dimethyl carbonate. *Journal of Molecular Catalysis B: Enzymatic*, *133*, S518–S524.

Pattanaro, G., & Gente, V. (2017). Circular economy and new ways of doing business in the tourism sector. *European Journal of Service Management*, *21*, 45–50.

Rahman, M., & Brazel, C. (2004). The plasticizer market: An assessment of traditional plasticizers and research trends to meet new challenges. *Progress in Polymer Science*, *29*(12), 1223–1248.

Scheepens, A. E., Vogtländer, J. G., & Brezet, J. C. (2016). Two life cycle assessment (LCA) based methods to analyse and design complex (regional) circular economy systems: Case: Making water tourism more sustainable. *Journal of Cleaner Production*, *114*, 257–268.

Scozzafava, G., Contini, C., Romano, C., & Casini, L. (2017). Eating out: Which restaurant to choose? *British Food Journal*, *119*(8), 1870–1883.

Sukhera, J. (2022). Narrative reviews: Flexible, rigorous, and practical. *Journal of Graduate Medical Education*, *14*(4), 414–417.

Van Caneghem, J., Van Acker, K., De Greef, J., Wauters, G., & Vandecasteele, C. (2019). Waste-to-energy is compatible and complementary with recycling in the circular economy. *Clean Technologies and Environmental Policy*, *21*(5), 925–939.

Velazquez Abad, A., Cherrett, T., & Holdsworth, P. (2015). Waste-to-fuel opportunities for British quick service restaurants: A case study. *Resources, Conservation and Recycling*, *104*, 239–253.

Zaki, K., & Farrag, M. (2024). The impact of circular economy on environmental performance in the tourism and hospitality industry: The role of low-carbon behavior and eco-friendly behavior. *International Journal of Tourism and Hospitality Studies*, 7(2), 285–304.

Zhang, F., Zhan, J., Li, Z., Jia, S., & Chen, S. (2018). Impacts of urban transformation on water footprint and sustainable energy in Shanghai, China. *Journal of Cleaner Production*, *190*, 847–853.

Zheng, Z., Xie, S., Dai, H. N., Chen, X., & Wang, H. (2018). Blockchain challenges and opportunities: A survey. *International Journal of Web and Grid Services*, *14*(4), 352–375.

Zygoura, P. D., Paleologos, E. K., & Kontominas, M. G. (2011). Changes in the specific migration characteristics of packaging–food simulant combinations caused by ionizing radiation: Effect of food simulant. *Radiation Physics and Chemistry*, *80*(8), 902–910.

3

INCLUSIVE TOURISM DESIGN: BRIDGING THE INFORMATION GAP FACED BY PEOPLE WITH DISABILITIES

ROSSANA DEMURTAS[a], MARIA MENENDEZ-BLANCO[a]
AND ERICA SANTINI[b]

[a]Free University of Bozen-Bolzano, Italy
[b]University of Trento, Italy

ABSTRACT

This chapter explores challenges and opportunities in designing inclusive tourism experiences for people with disabilities (PwD), with a specific focus on the early stages of the tourism journey. Drawing on both qualitative and evaluative methodologies, the study investigates key dimensions of accessibility through web accessibility assessments of major online travel agencies (OTAs) and a thematic analysis of user-generated content from the TripAdvisor forum "Travel with Disabilities." The research maps the primary barriers faced by PwD, ranging from insufficient digital accessibility and fragmented information to a lack of tailored services and support. The findings reveal that current OTAs do not properly address the specific information and planning needs of PwD, often reinforcing exclusion rather than enabling autonomy. This paper opens the discussion on the information gap faced by PwD and the associated costs they incur when participating in the tourism journey and offers design recommendations aimed at fostering greater equity, accessibility, and empowerment within the tourism sector.

Keywords: People with disabilities; tripadvisor; social inclusion; accessibility; digital platforms; online travel agencies

INTRODUCTION

The tourism industry plays a crucial role in fostering cultural exchange and economic growth. It serves as an essential conduit for promoting global cultural understanding, enhancing social cohesion, and facilitating interactions between diverse groups of people. According to the United Nations (2019), accessible tourism expands these benefits by ensuring that tourism opportunities are inclusive, allowing people of all abilities to actively engage and benefit from cultural exchanges. Furthermore, tourism significantly contributes to economic development by creating employment opportunities, stimulating local economies, and encouraging investments in infrastructure and services (Li et al., 2018). By fostering inclusive and accessible tourism practices, the industry not only fulfills social responsibility but also ensures sustainable growth (Aquino et al., 2018; Darcy et al., 2010).

However, despite its numerous benefits, the tourism sector continues to face substantial challenges, particularly in ensuring inclusivity and accessibility for PwD (Agovino et al., 2017; Domínguez Vila et al., 2024; Michopoulou et al., 2015). Bélanger and Jolin (2011) emphasize the significance of a more inclusive and accessible tourism, advocating for the universal right to holidays and tourism as fundamental aspects of human well-being and social integration. Initiatives in this direction not only enable equitable access to leisure and travel but also contribute to the reduction of social inequalities, thus fostering a more inclusive and cohesive society (Wu et al., 2024).

Despite the growing attention and efforts toward creating inclusive tourism, PwD still face numerous barriers and constraints (Portales, 2015). These barriers, ranging from inadequate physical infrastructures and digital accessibility to informational gaps, align closely with the hierarchical model of leisure constraints described by Crawford et al. (1991). Their framework identifies intrapersonal, interpersonal, and structural barriers that sequentially affect individuals' participation in leisure activities, which is particularly relevant for understanding the complexities faced by PwD in tourism contexts. Tourism for PwD extends beyond the need for physical accessibility and delves into a more complex understanding of how digital infrastructures and service design can ensure an inclusive experience. In this regard, McKercher and Darcy (2018) advocate for reconceptualizing disability-related travel barriers by emphasizing a more comprehensive view that incorporates environmental, societal, and personal factors, highlighting the multifaceted nature of these obstacles.

For PwD, traveling remains a significant challenge due to persistent accessibility barriers. The necessity for inclusive tourism has been widely acknowledged, yet many structural barriers remain unaddressed (Bramwell & Lane, 2008; Coleman, 2018). Physical obstacles, inadequate digital information, and a lack of standardized accessibility details create difficulties for PwD in planning and enjoying tourism experiences.

These barriers are present not only during the experience itself but also manifest during the initial planning phase of the tourism journey (Darcy, 2010). While digital technologies have created new opportunities for enhancing accessibility and personalizing travel experiences, they have also introduced additional barriers, particularly when platforms are not designed with inclusivity in mind (Singh & Sibi, 2021). In this regard, investigating the accessibility of OTAs is crucial, as they have become central actors in shaping how tourism services are marketed, booked, and experienced globally throughout the tourism journey (Park et al., 2024; Singh et al., 2021). As intermediaries between service providers and travelers, OTAs significantly shape the planning and decision-making processes of tourists, including PwD (Domínguez Vila et al., 2024).

Despite global efforts to improve accessibility, such as the Web Content Accessibility Guidelines (WCAG) 2.0, many OTA and general travel service providers fail to provide adequate information and solutions to PwD (Domínguez Vila et al., 2024; Vila & Darcy, 2025). This limitation is not attributable to a lack of technological advancement. On the contrary, despite significant progress in digital innovation, many OTAs still exhibit substantial accessibility barriers. These include non-intuitive navigation structures, inadequate alt-text for images, lack of keyboard navigation support, and incompatibility with screen readers and other assistive technologies (Lazar & Jaeger, 2011; Singh & Sibi, 2021). Such design shortcomings can severely hinder the ability of PwD to independently search for information, compare options, and complete bookings. As a result, what should be an empowering digital tool often becomes a source of exclusion, reinforcing systemic inequalities in access to tourism opportunities.

This study enters this debate and seeks to analyze the accessibility of OTAs and examine the concerns expressed by PwD through online travel forums.

Investigating OTAs' accessibility helps identify specific shortcomings and highlights the unique concerns and experiences of PwD, which are frequently discussed within online travel forums. By examining both technical accessibility through evaluation tools and qualitative insights from user-generated content, researchers can pinpoint precise areas for improvement. Ultimately, addressing OTAs' accessibility enhances inclusivity and equality in tourism, empowering PwD to independently embark on their travel journeys with confidence and ease.

Addressing these complex and layered constraints directly supports the achievement of the Sustainable Development Goals (SDGs), specifically SDG 10, which aims to reduce inequalities within and among countries, and SDG 11, which is dedicated to creating inclusive, safe, resilient, and sustainable cities and human settlements. Efforts in overcoming these challenges can significantly enhance the inclusivity, equity, and sustainability of the tourism industry, ultimately promoting a more accessible and empowering tourism experience for PwD.

CONCEPTUAL BACKGROUND

The tourism industry plays a pivotal role in fostering cultural exchange, promoting mutual understanding, and stimulating economic growth globally (Milne & Ateljevic, 2001). By enabling individuals to immerse themselves in diverse cultural settings, tourism actively enhances global interconnectedness, fosters cross-cultural empathy, and promotes tolerance and respect among different communities (Reisinger & Turner, 2012; UNWTO, 2020).

Beyond cultural enrichment, tourism significantly contributes to local and national economies by generating employment opportunities, spurring infrastructure improvements, and increasing consumer spending (Dwyer et al., 2009; Škare et al., 2021). The influx of tourists helps sustain local businesses; encourages investment in facilities such as transportation networks, hotels, and attractions; and can stimulate regional development (Binns & Nel, 2002; Page & Connell, 2020). Furthermore, tourism often acts as a catalyst for preserving cultural heritage, traditions, and natural resources, promoting sustainable practices that benefit both the environment and local communities (UNESCO, 2021; Weaver & Lawton, 2007). Therefore, cultivating an inclusive and accessible tourism industry not only drives economic prosperity but also reinforces social cohesion and cultural appreciation worldwide (Darcy & Dickson, 2009; Michopoulou et al., 2015; Rao & Lai, 2025).

Despite these benefits, PwD often encounter a range of constraints and barriers that limit their full participation in tourism experiences. These obstacles emerge at various stages of the travel journey, from the initial planning phase to the actual destination experience, and can vary in nature, encompassing intrapersonal (e.g., self-perception or lack of confidence), interpersonal (e.g., lack of support or social isolation), and structural (e.g., inaccessible infrastructure or discriminatory practices) barriers and constraints (Crawford et al., 1991; McKercher & Darcy, 2018).

Among the most persistent and overlooked barriers is the information gap, which significantly undermines the autonomy and decision-making capacity of PwD throughout the tourism journey. This gap is not merely a matter of limited content availability, but also of how information is presented, often in inaccessible formats, lacking essential details on accessibility features, or buried within complex digital interfaces (Eichhorn et al., 2008). As a result, PwD are frequently left without the critical knowledge needed to assess the suitability of destinations, accommodations, and services, forcing them to rely on third parties or to take on disproportionate levels of uncertainty and risk when traveling. Addressing this informational asymmetry is essential for creating inclusive tourism ecosystems that support equitable access and participation (Domínguez Vila et al., 2024; Phillips et al., 2013).

In this debate, tourism providers and OTAs might play a central role. Park et al. (2024) underscore that for travelers with disabilities, uncertainty surrounding service accessibility is a central concern throughout the entire travel journey, from the planning stage to the experience itself. Their study reveals that PwD often rely on online platforms to seek and share information that reduces this uncertainty, particularly concerning mobility, safety, and comfort-related services. These issues include accessible transportation options, lift availability, and ADA-compliant facilities, all of which are indispensable for travel but are frequently underrepresented in available travel information. Bridging this information gap is not only a matter of improving digital accessibility but also a critical step toward empowering PwD to make informed travel decisions, thereby fostering a more equitable and inclusive tourism environment. Information barriers pose another critical issue in inclusive tourism: digital accessibility.

In what follows, we investigate the accessibility of selected OTAs using standardized web accessibility tools and analyze thematic content from the "Travel with Disabilities" forum on TripAdvisor. This dual-method approach provides a comprehensive understanding of both the technical and experiential barriers faced by PwD in the early stages of their tourism journey.

METHODOLOGY

The research methodology comprises two primary components: an evaluation of web accessibility and an analysis of information accessibility through user-generated content. The web accessibility evaluation was conducted in February 2024 and focused on assessing the digital usability of seven popular OTAs to determine how well they adhere to WCAG 2.0 guidelines. This involves the application of tools such as AChecker[1] and WAVE[2] to measure elements such as readability, navigation ease, the presence of alternative text for images, and compatibility with screen readers. Compliance is assessed to Level A (minimum level), AA (mid-range), and AAA (highest level), which provide a benchmark for understanding how well digital platforms meet the needs of users with visual, auditory, and cognitive impairments. The target OTAs websites were defined by selecting the five most frequently used OTAs,[3] and supplementing them with two OTAs dedicated to ensuring accessible structures for PwD, namely Bookingbility[4] and Fairbnb.[5] The home pages of the selected OTAs website were chosen for the web accessibility assessment, due to their pivotal role in user navigation experience.

Simultaneously, a qualitative analysis explores the lived experiences of PwD by examining contributions to the "Travel with Disabilities" forum on TripAdvisor. This platform serves as a valuable repository of firsthand travel experiences, concerns, and advice shared by PwD. Forum data from January 2019 to December 2023 were systematically collected and cleaned to eliminate irrelevant, duplicate, or promotional entries. The cleaned dataset ($N = 332$) was imported into NVivo software, where thematic analysis was conducted to identify recurring challenges and concerns. Themes were coded to map the most prominent needs, constraints, and desires in information access and service usability, allowing us to explore barriers to inclusive touristic experiences.

---

[1] AChecker is used to evaluate HTML content for accessibility problems by entering the location of a web page, uploading an html file, or pasting the complete HTML source code from a Web page. AChecker produces a report of all accessibility problems for your selected guidelines.

[2] WAVE is a suite of evaluation tools that helps authors make their web content more accessible to individuals with disabilities. WAVE can not only identify many accessibility and Web Content Accessibility Guideline (WCAG) errors but also facilitate human evaluation of web content.

[3] https://www.statista.com/statistics/1215457/most-visited-travel-and-tourism-websites-worldwide/.

[4] https://it.bookingbility.com/.

[5] https://fairbnb.coop/it/.

Together, these methods enable a multifaceted analysis of both the technical shortcomings and user-experienced limitations in OTA platforms. This integrated approach not only validates the existence of accessibility issues but also provides user-informed insights to guide the design of more inclusive tourism platforms.

RESULTS

The findings from the web accessibility evaluation reveal significant shortcomings in OTA compliance with WCAG 2.0 standards. Across the selected platforms, as we can see from Tables 3.1 and 3.2, common accessibility violations include the absence of alternative text for images and interactive elements (i.e., non-text content), low contrast ratios that hinder readability for users with visual impairments, and non-descriptive link text, which obstructs effective navigation for screen reader users. Additionally, multiple pages lacked proper heading structures and label instructions, creating a disjointed browsing experience for users dependent on assistive technologies. Platforms like Booking and Airbnb were notably deficient in key Level A and AA criteria, as presented in Table 3.2, including keyboard navigability and content clarity. However, these platforms perform similarly to, or even better than, those specifically designed to target PwD and promote inclusion, such as Bookingbility and Fairbnb (see Tables 3.1 and 3.2). These findings highlight the systemic digital barriers preventing PwD from independently accessing essential travel information.

The thematic analysis of user-generated content from the "Travel with Disabilities" forum further underscores these technical deficiencies by illuminating the everyday challenges experienced by PwD. First of all, users frequently report difficulties in obtaining detailed accessibility descriptions for accommodations, transportation options, and tourist sites. Many also express frustrations with contradictory or misleading information provided by service providers.

By exploring the word cloud generated from the forum data (Fig. 3.1), finding highlights recurring themes such as "accessible," "need," "wheelchair," "hotel," "help," and "looking," suggesting that core concerns revolve around physical accessibility and the reliability of service information. Frequent complaints centered on inaccurate descriptions of accommodations, lack of staff training, and discrepancies between advertised and actual accessibility features. Users expressed a strong reliance on peer reviews and personal stories to fill these information gaps, underlining the importance of trust and

Table 3.1. AChecker Standards Evaluation.

	Success Criteria	Booking	Agoda	Bookingbility	Fairbnb	TripAdvisor	Airbnb	Expedia
Level A	1.1.1 Non-text Content	5					N/A	0
	1.3.1 Info and Relationship			9		0	N/A	
	2.4.2 Page Titled		1				N/A	
	2.4.4 Link Purpose (In Context)			4	1		N/A	
	3.1.1 Language of Page						N/A	
	3.3.2 Labels or Instructions			8			N/A	
Level AA	1.4.4 Resize Text	1		35			N/A	
	2.4.6 Headings and Labels			1	1		N/A	

Source: Authors' elaboration.

Table 3.2. Wave Standards Evaluation.

	Success Criteria	Booking	Agoda	Bookingbility	Fairbnb	TripAdvisor	Airbnb	Expedia
Level A	1.1.1 Non-text Content	13	4	12	98	3	25	2
	1.3.1 Info and Relationship	2	4	12	24		22	3
	2.4.1 Bypass Blocks		4	2	2			
	2.4.2 Page Titled		2					
	2.4.4 Link Purpose (In Context)		4	4	27	3	24	
	3.3.2 Labels or Instructions	2		12	22		1	
	4.1.2 Name, Role Value						1	1
Level AA	1.4.3 Contrast (Minimum)	9	24		11			
	2.4.6 Headings and Labels	2	4	12	24		1	2

Source: Authors' elaboration.

Fig. 3.1. Word Cloud of Barriers, Constraints, and Targeted Needs.
Source: Authors' elaboration based on "Travel with Disabilities" forum.

transparency in accessibility reporting. Persons with disabilities, or, in many cases, their caregivers, as indicated by references such as "husband," frequently rely on firsthand reviews from other travelers to assess the credibility of accessibility-related claims. This indicates a fundamental gap in how accessibility information is communicated by OTAs and other service providers. The need for more transparent, detailed, and standardized accessibility information is evident from these findings. These results affirm that digital inaccessibility is not merely a technical flaw but a substantial barrier to equitable tourism participation.

The keywords visualized in the word cloud can be qualitatively grouped into two meaningful clusters. The first cluster relates to different stages of the tourism journey, including terms such as "hotel," "booking," "airport," "transport," "room," and "trip." These terms reflect the temporal and logistical flow of travel, highlighting where accessibility barriers commonly arise. The word cloud vividly illustrates how the lack of clear, accessible, and reliable information can act as a fundamental barrier, beginning as early as the planning phase of the tourism journey. For PwD, this phase is critical, as it involves assessing key elements such as accommodation suitability, transport availability, and mobility-related services. Without accurate and accessible digital information, PwD face heightened uncertainty, which can deter them from initiating travel altogether. This uncertainty not only undermines their ability to make informed decisions but also perpetuates exclusion by reinforcing dependence on informal sources or trial-and-error approaches. The clustering of terms in the word cloud reveals that the planning phase is not just a logistical step – it is a gateway that either enables or obstructs inclusive tourism experiences. As such, bridging the information gap is not merely a technical necessity but a pivotal factor in empowering PwD to travel with confidence and autonomy.

The second cluster centers around disability-specific considerations, with terms such as "wheelchair," "step," "mobility," and "walk" appearing prominently. This vocabulary underscores the dominant visibility of physical and mobility-related concerns within the discourse, highlighting the central role of adaptive infrastructure, such as ramps, lifts, and accessible restrooms, in shaping the tourism experiences of wheelchair users and individuals with mobility impairments. However, the absence or underrepresentation of terms related to other types of disabilities, such as sensory, cognitive, or invisible disabilities, raises important questions. The dominance of mobility-related terms in user-generated content may reflect not only the urgent needs of this user group but also the structural invisibility of other disability types in digital planning tools. Are these travelers less likely to use or benefit from online planning tools due to barriers that are not immediately apparent in the data? Or is their presence underreported because the tools themselves are not designed with their needs in mind? This observation prompts a deeper reflection on the inclusiveness of current digital tourism platforms. It also calls for broader participatory approaches that actively engage individuals with diverse disabilities in the design and evaluation of digital tools, ensuring that tourism accessibility is truly comprehensive and equitable across all needs and abilities.

DISCUSSIONS

The findings of this study underscore the persistent and multifaceted barriers that PwD face in accessing tourism experiences, particularly in the early stages of the travel journey (Loi & Kong, 2017; Rubio-Escuderos et al., 2024). Both the technical assessment of OTAs and the thematic analysis of user-generated content reveal that significant gaps remain in the digital infrastructure that supports inclusive tourism planning, particularly regarding information access.

The web accessibility evaluation reveals substantial non-compliance with WCAG 2.0 standards across major OTAs, suggesting that many platforms are not fully compatible with assistive technologies and inadequately serve users with visual, auditory, or cognitive impairments. These technical deficiencies hinder PwD from independently searching, planning, and booking their travel, thereby reinforcing dependence on others and limiting their autonomy. These findings echo existing research that critiques the tourism industry's slow and uneven adoption of inclusive digital design practices (Darcy et al., 2010; Domínguez Vila et al., 2024; Michopoulou et al., 2015).

The thematic analysis of user-generated content from the "Travel with Disabilities" forum complements the technical assessment by shedding light on the lived experiences of PwD navigating these digital environments. Prominent themes related to physical accessibility (e.g., "wheelchair," "elevator," "step-free") and service-related information (e.g., "staff," "booking," "transport") point to ongoing deficiencies in both infrastructural provision and information clarity.

Notably, the clustering of keywords into stages of the tourism journey – planning, booking, transport, and accommodation – reinforces the importance of addressing accessibility as a continuum rather than a one-time consideration. The findings support the arguments of Park et al. (2024) related to the fact that uncertainty surrounding service accessibility is a critical factor in tourism decision-making for PwD and that reducing this uncertainty through accurate and accessible information is fundamental to enabling participation.

Importantly, the qualitative data also reflect limitations in the digital user experience for individuals with non-mobility-related disabilities. Although less frequently represented in the discourse, the challenges faced by people with sensory, cognitive, or invisible impairments are equally pressing and highlight a broader systemic oversight in current accessibility strategies. The fact that these challenges are less frequently addressed can be the result of limited web accessibility presented by the analyzed OTAs. The results highlight indeed a potential bias in the visibility of certain types of disabilities. The predominance of mobility-related terms in both the word cloud and forum discussions suggests that digital platforms and tourism services may be inadvertently prioritizing the needs of wheelchair users, while the needs of individuals with sensory, cognitive, or invisible disabilities remain underrepresented. This raises important questions about the inclusiveness of existing platforms and suggests a need for further research into how different disability groups engage with digital tourism tools.

Overall, the study affirms that digital inaccessibility is not merely a technical flaw but a structural barrier that limits equal participation in tourism. Addressing this issue requires a systemic approach that combines technological upgrades, inclusive design practices, and participatory engagement with PwD in both the development and evaluation of tourism services.

What if the digital revolution we so proudly celebrate is silently exclud-
ing millions? Despite the global push for inclusivity, the tourism industry
still fails to meet the most basic accessibility needs of PwD, not because the
technology is lacking, but because the will to design inclusively is absent. If
people with sensory, cognitive, or invisible disabilities are not reflected in the
data, is it because they are not traveling, or because they have given up try-
ing? The absence of their voices in forums may be the clearest sign of digital
exclusion.

Finally, the reliance on peer reviews rather than official sources to access
critical accessibility information reveals a failure of institutional communication. Why must PwD rely on anecdotal evidence to plan a trip in 2025? Why
haven't OTAs implemented standardized and certified accessibility filters,
despite years of advocacy and available guidelines? This highlights a broader
systemic issue: accessibility in tourism remains a fragmented promise rather
than an industry-wide standard.

CONCLUSION

The study underscores the pressing need to improve accessibility in the tourism industry by addressing digital, informational, and attitudinal barriers.
The dual-method findings indicate a clear disconnect between the accessibility
needs of PwD and the current design and communication strategies of major
OTAs. Addressing these gaps through standardized accessibility features and
authentic, user-driven content is essential to fostering an inclusive digital tourism ecosystem.

In response to the identified gaps, this study proposes to prioritize enhanced
digital accessibility, standardized accessibility information, and participatory
research methods. Ensuring compliance with WCAG 2.0 guidelines is fundamental to creating an inclusive digital environment that allows PwD to access
necessary travel information seamlessly. Standardized accessibility reporting
mechanisms should be introduced across OTAs, hotels, and tourism service
providers to ensure consistency and reliability in accessibility details. Engaging PwD in participatory research and feedback mechanisms can further
enhance inclusivity in the sector. By encouraging direct contributions from
PwD, service providers can gain valuable insights into the real-world challenges they face and develop more responsive solutions.

Moreover, training programs for tourism professionals should also be
implemented to improve awareness and ensure that accessibility considerations are integrated into service design.

This study makes clear that accessibility in digital tourism is not only a technical issue, but also a matter of equity, autonomy, and social justice. If we are to build an inclusive tourism ecosystem aligned with the Sustainable Development Goals (SDG 10 and 11), then structural and systemic reforms must follow.

For policymakers, the priority should be to legislate mandatory accessibility standards for digital tourism platforms, similar to physical access laws. Public authorities should fund audits, certifications, and co-design programs that include people with different disabilities from the earliest stages of service development. Accessibility should not be aspirational; it should be enforced.

For OTAs, there is a critical opportunity and responsibility to lead innovation in inclusive design. OTAs must go beyond minimal compliance with WCAG standards and invest in universal design principles that embed accessibility into every user interface. Introducing certified filters for accessibility features (e.g., step-free entry, visual alarms, sensory-friendly environments) and ensuring machine-readable accessibility metadata will empower all users, not just those with disabilities.

For tourism practitioners, including hotels, attractions, and transport operators, the call is to recognize that accessibility is not a niche market; it is a growing global demand. Transparent, standardized communication of accessibility features should become part of every booking description. Staff training and digital communication protocols must be updated to reflect diverse needs, especially for non-visible disabilities.

Most importantly, all stakeholders must embrace a participatory approach, actively involving PwD in testing, reviewing, and co-designing both services and digital platforms. Inclusion cannot be retrofitted; it must be embedded from the start.

REFERENCES

Agovino, M., Casaccia, M., Garofalo, A., & Marchesano, K. (2017). Tourism and disability in Italy: Limits and opportunities. *Tourism Management Perspectives, 23*, 58–67.

Aquino, R. S., Lück, M., & Schänzel, H. A. (2018). A conceptual framework of tourism social entrepreneurship for sustainable community development. *Journal of Hospitality and Tourism Management, 37*, 23–32.

Bélanger, C. É., & Jolin, L. (2011). The International Organisation of Social Tourism (ISTO) working towards a right to holidays and tourism for all. *Current Issues in Tourism, 14*(5), 475–482.

Binns, T., & Nel, E. (2002). Tourism as a local development strategy in South Africa. *Geographical Journal, 168*(3), 235–247.

Bramwell, B., & Lane, B. (2008). Priorities in sustainable tourism research. *Journal of Sustainable Tourism, 16*(1), 1–4.

Coleman, L. E. (2018). *Understanding and implementing inclusion in museums.* Rowman & Littlefield.

Crawford, D. W., Jackson, E. L., & Godbey, G. (1991). A hierarchical model of leisure constraints. *Leisure Sciences, 13*(4), 309–320.

Darcy, S. (2010). Inherent complexity: Disability, accessible tourism and accommodation information preferences. *Tourism Management, 31*(6), 816–826.

Darcy, S., Cameron, B., & Pegg, S. (2010). Accessible tourism and sustainability: A discussion and case study. *Journal of Sustainable Tourism, 18*(4), 515–537.

Darcy, S., & Dickson, T. J. (2009). A whole-of-life approach to tourism: The case for accessible tourism experiences. *Journal of Hospitality and Tourism Management, 16*(1), 32–44.

Domínguez Vila, T., Rubio-Escuderos, L., & Alén González, E. (2024). Accessible tourism: Using technology to increase social equality for people with disabilities. *Tourism Review.*

Dwyer, L., Edwards, D., Mistilis, N., Roman, C., & Scott, N. (2009). Destination and enterprise management for a tourism future. *Tourism Management, 30*(1), 63–74.

Eichhorn, V., Miller, G., Michopoulou, E., & Buhalis, D. (2008). Enabling access to tourism through information schemes? *Annals of Tourism Research, 35*(1), 189–210.

Lazar, J., & Jaeger, P. (2011). Reducing barriers to online access for people with disabilities. *Issues in Science & Technology, 27*(2).

Li, K. X., Jin, M., & Shi, W. (2018). Tourism as an important impetus to promoting economic growth: A critical review. *Tourism Management Perspectives, 26,* 135–142.

Loi, K. I., & Kong, W. H. (2017). Tourism for all: Challenges and issues faced by people with vision impairment. *Tourism Planning & Development, 14*(2), 181–197.

McKercher, B., & Darcy, S. (2018). Re-conceptualizing barriers to travel by people with disabilities. *Tourism Management Perspectives, 26*, 59–66.

Michopoulou, E., Darcy, S., Ambrose, I., & Buhalis, D. (2015). Accessible tourism futures: The world we dream to live in and the opportunities we hope to have. *Journal of Tourism Futures, 1*(3), 179–188.

Milne, S., & Ateljevic, I. (2001). Tourism, economic development and the global-local nexus: Theory embracing complexity. *Tourism Geographies, 3*(4), 369–393.

Page, S. J., & Connell, J. (2020). Tourism and entrepreneurship. In *Tourism* (pp. 262–279). Routledge.

Park, H., Park, E., Costa, R., & Lee, M. (2024). Travelers with disabilities: How online information search reduces uncertainty about service accessibility in hospitality and tourism. *Journal of Hospitality & Tourism Research*.

Phillips, J., Walford, N., Hockey, A., Foreman, N., & Lewis, M. (2013). Older people and outdoor environments: Pedestrian anxieties and barriers in the use of familiar and unfamiliar spaces. *Geoforum, 47*, 113–124.

Portales, R. C. (2015). Removing "invisible" barriers: Opening paths towards the future of accessible tourism. *Journal of Tourism Futures, 1*(3), 269–284.

Rao, Y., & Lai, I. K. W. (2025). Understanding how tourists with disabilities' perceptions of residents' emotional solidarity influence their behavioural intention: The mediating role of perceived fairness. *Journal of Sustainable Tourism, 33*(3), 500–519.

Reisinger, Y., & Turner, L. (2012). *Cross-cultural behaviour in tourism.* Routledge.

Rubio-Escuderos, L., García-Andreu, H., Michopoulou, E., & Buhalis, D. (2024). Perspectives on experiences of tourists with disabilities: Implications for their daily lives and for the tourist industry. *Tourism Recreation Research, 49*(1), 48–62.

Singh, R., Ismail, A., PS, S., & Singh, D. (2021). Compliance of accessibility in tourism websites: A pledge towards disability. *Journal of Hospitality and Tourism Insights, 4*(3), 263–281.

Singh, R., & Sibi, P. S. (2021). Accessibility and readability of websites: An analysis of online travel aggregators (OTAs) of India. *E-Review of Tourism Research, 18*(5), 692–716.

Škare, M., Soriano, D. R., & Porada-Rochoń, M. (2021). Impact of COVID-19 on the travel and tourism industry. *Technological Forecasting and Social Change*, *163*, 120469.

UNESCO. (2021). *Reimagining our futures together: A new social contract for education*. Educational and Cultural Organization of the United Nations.

United Nations. (2019). *Promoting accessible tourism for all*. Department of Economic and Social Affairs: Disability.

UNWTO. (2020). *Responsible tourism: The key to building back a better industry*. https://www.unwto.org/covid-19-oneplanet-responsible-recovery-initiatives/responsible-tourism-the-key-to-building-back-a-better-industry

Vila, T. D., & Darcy, S. (2025). Beyond technical website compliance: Identifying and assessing accessible tourism value chain information content on national tourism organisation websites. *Tourism Management Perspectives*, *55*, 101332.

W3C. (2023). *Web Content Accessibility Guidelines (WCAG) 2.0*. https://www.w3.org/TR/WCAG20/

Weaver, D. B., & Lawton, L. J. (2007). Twenty years on: The state of contemporary ecotourism research. *Tourism Management*, *28*(5), 1168–1179.

Wu, L., Fan, A., Hou, Y., & Wei, W. (2024). Unlocking the transformative power of hospitality and tourism experiences: Towards theoretical syntheses and research agenda. *Journal of Hospitality & Tourism Research*.

Part II

ART-BASED BUSINESS MODELS INCORPORATING THE AUTHENTICITY OF PLACES

4

AUTHENTICITY AS WEAVING COHERENCE ACROSS TIME AND PLACE: INSIGHTS FROM CRAFT

CAMILLA FERRIᵃ AND MARIA LUSIANIᵇ

ᵃCopenhagen Business School, Denmark
ᵇUniversity of Bologna, Italy

ABSTRACT

This chapter explores the topic of authenticity work in the development of sustainable business models, referring to craft practices. The debate on authenticity in management and organization studies focuses on authenticity mainly in relation to an audience for competitive advantage, but this reflects a static and functionalist view of authenticity, failing to consider authenticity as exerted by organizations and individuals in the continuous becoming of their work. Using the metaphor of "weaving coherence," the chapter identifies six modes of authenticity work in craft, showing how craftmakers integrate past, present, future, and place into their practices and how this contributes to the development of sustainable business models. This shift in perspective moves the discussion from audience-based narratives to a producer-focused, practice-oriented view, positioning authenticity as an ongoing process. By highlighting the time- and place-based nature of craft, the chapter contributes to the understanding of authenticity as a living practice contributing to business models' sustainability.

The chapter invites further research into the intersection of authenticity, craft, and sustainability, extending its relevance to organizational studies and to practice.

Keywords: Authenticity; authenticity work; craft; coherence; time; place; sustainable business models

INTRODUCTION

In recent years, the concept of authenticity has gained increasing attention across multiple disciplines, from management and organization studies to tourism, cultural and creative industries (Beverland, 2005; Ganzin et al., 2024; Gerosa, 2024; Rickly, 2022). In a world marked by skepticism toward traditional ideologies of progress, rationality, and capitalism, the search for authenticity – whether in personal identities, organizational practices, or consumer experiences – has become an essential concern. As individuals and organizations strive to express genuine, original, and sincere selves, the quest for authenticity is no longer a peripheral interest but a central pursuit in contemporary society. Moreover, recent scholarship in management, geography, and tourism has highlighted how authenticity can serve as a strategic asset for sustainability (Erhardt et al., 2022; Ferreira et al., 2023; Gatrell et al., 2018; Palmi & Lezzi, 2020). Despite its widespread use, the concept of "authenticity" remains ambiguous and elusive across different streams of literature, making its potential impact on business, particularly as a driver of sustainability, difficult to fully grasp. To overcome this, we propose shifting the focus toward a largely overlooked dimension of authenticity: how it is practiced by organizational actors in their everyday work, rather than how it is externally claimed or perceived by audiences. This practice-based perspective allows for a deeper understanding of how authenticity work can contribute to achieving sustainability goals and building sustainable business models, a connection acknowledged in the literature, yet still underexplored. Accordingly, we ask: *How does authenticity work unfold in day-to-day practice, and in what ways does it support the development of sustainable business models?*

This chapter thus explores the notion of "authenticity work" within the context of craft. We propose that craft, as a peculiar form of production, offers a unique lens through which to examine authenticity in its making and in its impact on sustainability, focusing on the practical, producer-related side rather than the audience-related narratives of authenticity. Through an exploration of the time- and place-based nature of craft, and an examination of the intersection of time, place, and the act of making, we note how craft work involves a continuous process of construction of coherence across time and place. We call this *weaving coherence* and conceive it as the very essence of authentic work.

Through proposing authenticity as weaving coherence, this chapter aims to make a contribution to both the study of authenticity, shifting the focus toward its embodied, lived dimensions, and the understanding of craft as a meaningful and evolving form of production, offering valuable new perspectives for research on sustainable business models.

AUTHENTICITY IN MANAGEMENT AND ORGANIZATION STUDIES

In today's postmodern world, marked by declining trust in progress, rationality, and capitalism, the search for authenticity has become a central concern for individuals, organizations, and society. People seek authentic places, organizations value employees who appear true to themselves, and audiences desire authentic experiences, including in tourism. While commonly associated with traits like truthfulness, sincerity, and tradition (Lehman et al., 2019), the meaning of authenticity remains ambiguous.

Lehman and colleagues' (2019) literature review represents a significant effort to organize the complexity surrounding this construct. It shows that authenticity always involves the relationship between an entity and a specific referent: (1) the alignment between an entity's internal values and its external expressions; (2) the conformity of an entity to the norms of its social category; and (3) the connection between an entity and a person, place, or time, as claimed.

In particular, some scholars have specifically focused on "authenticity work," identifying the various strategies through which organizations craft authenticity claims (Beverland, 2005; Dobrev & Verhaal, 2024; Ganzin et al., 2024; Jones et al., 2005; Jones & Smith, 2005; Voronov et al., 2023). Authenticity work is defined as organizations' deliberate efforts to project authenticity to their audiences (Peterson, 2005) or to develop and sustain credible authenticity claims (Voronov et al., 2023). This body of literature suggests that authenticity relates to how well an entity responds to a referent. It is something explicitly claimed, actively pursued, managed, and primarily audience-dependent (Dobrev & Verhaal, 2024), especially when serving strategic purposes such as competitive differentiation (Cattani et al., 2017; Voronov et al., 2023), commercial success, or brand recognition (Beverland, 2005; Koontz, 2010). However, how authenticity is played out in everyday practice, and not only claimed, remains somewhat unaddressed.

AUTHENTICITY AND SUSTAINABLE BUSINESS MODELS

A growing body of research highlights how authenticity can act as a strategic driver in the development of sustainable business models, particularly in sectors where cultural, social, and territorial values are central to value creation (Erhardt et al., 2022; Ferreira et al., 2023; Gatrell et al., 2018; Palmi & Lezzi, 2020).

Erhardt et al. (2022) demonstrate how authenticity-driven enterprises leverage social values such as community collaboration and local embeddedness to create both economic value and social sustainability. They suggest that authenticity plays a central role in building business models that prioritize ethical growth and inclusion. Similarly, Palmi and Lezzi (2020) explore how traditions can be recombined to innovate business models in Italian agritourism, fostering authenticity and aligning inherited values with contemporary sustainability goals, such as ecological responsibility and the preservation of cultural identity.

However, despite the interest in authenticity as a strategic asset for sustainability, there is still limited understanding of how authenticity work can concretely support the design and implementation of sustainable business models (Schaltegger et al., 2016). We argue that adopting a situated perspective on authenticity work can offer valuable insights into this relationship.

In this chapter, we examine the concept of authenticity work in relation to the development of sustainable business models in the context of craft. We suggest that craft represents a unique form of production in which authenticity can be explored through the act of making, focusing on the practical rather than the narrative dimension of authenticity, and on the producer's perspective rather than the audience's. This approach offers a distinctive opportunity to reflect on the ways in which craft makers foster the sustainability of their business models. In the following section, we introduce the concept of craft, highlighting its uniqueness as a form of production and its deep connection to authenticity, time, and place.

CRAFT AS A PECULIAR FORM OF PRODUCTION

Recently, organization and management studies began to dedicate growing attention to crafts (Kroezen et al., 2021), especially for their potential of addressing contemporary grand challenges, such as promoting more sustainable ways of living and producing (e.g., Weber et al., 2008). At the center of all forms of craft is the "craftsmanship" of doing – human know-how, tacit knowledge passed down through generations, and the physical dexterity involved. Unlike other forms of production, crafts typically involve a degree of manual labor – "a skill of making things well" (Sennett, 2008) – and require cultural capital to facilitate esthetic appreciation and practical creativity in blending art with function (Romain, 2016; Takuya & Takayama, 2010). These practices often involve a mix of traditional and modern skills, rooted in local communities (Blundel & Smith, 2013) and are viewed as particularly sustainable forms of production, as opposed to mass industrial ones.

We argue that authenticity, both in the making process and from the perspective of the producer, is deeply embedded in this form of production. Craft provides a vital setting in which to explore and advance the conversation around authenticity work and its connections with sustainability. To further conceptualize this, we examine craft's twofold time-based and place-based nature.

CRAFT AND TIME

Although Kroezen and colleagues (2021) define craft as a *timeless* alternative approach to work, we argue that craft is an inherently temporal concept. We define temporality as the relationships between past, present, and future (Ravasi et al., 2019; Schultz & Hernes, 2013). First of all, craft is a creative act performed in the present, but connecting with the past. In its traditional forms, craft directly reminds the past, for example, thanks to antique materials or techniques used. Also in its neo-craft tendencies (Gandini & Gerosa, 2023), it still evokes some past remnants, even if less directly, because it is related to pre-industrial ways of production, for example, making things slowly, with the use of hands. To this purpose, Bell et al. (2021) speak about "imaginaries of craft" that determine how societies, communities, organizations, and individuals embody temporal relations to the past that extend into the present and future. They argue that most craft imaginaries are past-oriented, since they embed a nostalgic idea of the past, which can be understood as a response to the desire for authenticity and human meaning in modern life (Beverland, 2005), which is often found in relation to the past and to a place. The act of making – whether it is pottery, textiles, or any other craft – becomes a means to engage with the past while contributing to the cultural and social vibrancy of the present.

But also, Bell and colleagues (2021) advocate the concept of "future-oriented craft imaginaries" defined as collective visions that reimagine and adapt traditional craft practices to address contemporary and forthcoming societal challenges. These imaginaries serve as transformative tools for the future, and the authors, therefore, show how craft can be connected to the future too, given that historical craft skills can be innovatively translated to remain relevant in the future, potentially addressing future grand challenges.

CRAFT AND PLACE

Craft, in its various forms such as pottery, glassmaking, textile production, and jewelry, has historically been rooted in specific geographic regions that provide access to necessary materials and energy sources. This place-based nature of craft has given rise to unique dynamics within craft clusters, where regional characteristics – such as availability of raw materials, local skills, and cultural heritage – have shaped both the production and identity of these crafts (Comunian & England, 2019; Gibson, 2016; Tanghetti et al., 2025; Yang et al., 2021).

The place-based nature of craft becomes evident within public debates that have especially regarded the crafts' instrumental role in rural (Jones et al., 2021) or urban (Brandellero & Naclerio, 2025) development. While traditional craft production may not always scale in the same way as other industries, it has nonetheless attracted attention due to its potential to drive educational, cultural, and economic agendas (McHattie et al., 2019). Policymakers have increasingly recognized craft as a means to stimulate local and regional economies, enhance skill development, and promote sustainable practices through the use of local materials and knowledge.

Another significant aspect of craft's role in local development is its ability to foster a sense of place to residents. Craft-making practices, particularly those tied to regional heritage, offer a medium through which communities can celebrate and preserve their local identity. In historic towns, for instance, craft production can serve as a vehicle for reflecting on and revitalizing the role of heritage in everyday life (Kouhia & Rönkkö, 2020).

Additionally, craft practice has the potential to build a sense of community, particularly in urban environments. Groups such as knitting circles or women's collectives demonstrate how craft can facilitate the creation of identity and attachment to place (Platt, 2019). These social spaces, where individuals gather not to produce a marketable product but to engage in affective labor, highlight the emotional and relational aspects of craft.

Moreover, the revival of craft practices plays a crucial role in tourism, especially in the context of the growing demand for authentic experiences.

Tourists seeking genuine, place-based encounters are increasingly drawn to destinations where local crafts offer a tangible connection to the history, culture, and values of the community (Fletchall, 2016). By engaging with local craft traditions, visitors are not only purchasing souvenirs but also participating in the preservation and celebration of regional identities. This trend aligns with the broader global interest in sustainable, culturally rich, and community-oriented tourism, further cementing the value of craft in place-based development strategies (Revilla & Dodd, 2003).

In conclusion, the literature acknowledges that craft's place-based nature offers significant opportunities for local development, not just in economic terms, but also in fostering a deeper sense of community and heritage. Whether through the lens of regional economic revitalization, community cohesion, or tourism, the role of craft in shaping and celebrating a sense of place remains vital in the contemporary world. As such, craft emerges as a fertile ground for the development of sustainable business models, those that not only ensure economic viability but also create and deliver value to a broader range of stakeholders, including local communities and the environment (Schaltegger et al., 2016).

AUTHENTICITY WORK IN CRAFT: WEAVING COHERENCE ACROSS TIME AND PLACE

We argue that weaving coherence in time and place throughout the production process is what makes craft "authentic" and a resource for the development of sustainable business models. But there are different modes of doing so. From a situated perspective on authenticity work – one that focuses on the ongoing practices through which authenticity is practiced in craft work – we propose a framework of six modes of weaving coherence (Table 4.1). We developed this framework conceptually, intersecting the two main streams of literature reviewed above: (a) on one dimension, we identified the *maker* (individual), the *making* (the performance) and the *made object* (the object), as the main targets of authenticity discussed by Lehman et al. (2019); (b) on the other dimension, we identified *time* and *place*, as two relevant dimensions of craft, as discussed in the craft literature (Bell et al., 2021; Comunian & England, 2019). As the framework was built up, we made sense of the six resulting modes, also based on insights from the empirical evidence of an ongoing fieldwork project exploring craft work. We thus followed a rather abductive process in our theorizing process.

Table 4.1.   Craft Authenticity Work as Weaving Coherence in Time and Place.

	Modes of Weaving Coherence in Time	Modes of Weaving Coherence in Place
Maker	*Threading* Connecting craft makers' past experiences and familiar legacy together with identity of the present and the image of the future	*Embroidering* Creating relationships with people on a territory grounded on shared values and common cultural heritage
Making	*Patchworking* Mixing the old and the new as for materials, techniques, final objects	*Knitting* Networking on the territory with local craftmakers in the production process and to solve problems
Made object	*Layering* Adding present meanings and functions to old ones, and embedding makers' past and present identity in the object	*Blockprinting* Relating object's features to the place

Source: Authors' elaboration.

WEAVING COHERENCE IN TIME

Threading. For some artisans, craftmaking was not the first choice in terms of career, but came as a result of multiple, different experiences, in various contexts, for example, education or travels. Nevertheless, these experiences have been fundamental for them to become who they are as craftmakers in the present. As in a thread, they tend to weave together – consciously or unconsciously – elements of their past into their current practice, allowing them to be projected toward the future of their business, imagining it accordingly. This does not mean that their paths are necessarily coherent, but that they could find their own personal way to connect the dots and feel coherent as makers in the present. This also happens when craftmaking is inherited from other family members, posing an issue between the development of the craftmakers' own identity and the still present cultural legacy deriving from the past. From their families, craftmakers take lessons on discipline and attitudes at work, but develop independently, not without difficulties, their own technical style to take distance from the past and move toward the future of their business and their work. This dynamic process of connecting past experiences with present identity and future aspirations enables craftmakers to shape business models that are not only economically viable but also grounded in cultural continuity and personal meaning. In this sense, *threading* becomes a generative resource for sustainable business models, as it informs the maker's value proposition, reinforces long-term commitment, and strengthens the embeddedness of the enterprise in social and territorial contexts.

Patchworking. As in patchwork, the inherent process of making craft is made coherent through time by combining materials, techniques, and objects in a way in which the past is preserved but also projected toward the future through innovations. Craftmakers carry out and balance this mix between the old and the new in different ways. Or also, new and more advanced materials are inserted in traditional manufacturing. New and old materials and techniques can finally be blended for the creation of a new final product. This patchwork-like logic of combining traditional and innovative elements over time is key to the development of sustainable business models in craft. By blending old and new materials and techniques, craftmakers not only preserve cultural heritage and traditional skills but also adapt it to contemporary contexts and future challenges. *Patchworking* enables therefore the creation of a business model that is both rooted in the past and forward-looking, fostering its continuity, innovation, resilience, and long-term viability.

Layering. The main mode through which an artisanal product is made authentic by its own maker is making it coherent with his/her own identity. The product has therefore different layers of meaning, which reflect makers' attitude, values, and thoughts, in its esthetic or in its spirit/functionality. Coherence is created more internally than externally, that is, craft makers care more about their internal judgment of coherence than the external one (e.g., from customers). Layering is even more evident when the products made by artisans nowadays are derived from traditions of the past, but are re-contextualized in the present with new functions to allow the business to be economically sustainable for the future, while also creating value for the community identity by maintaining a connection to heritage. Coherence here is made by finding, not always with ease, a meaningful balance between the new and the old function, so that they can coexist and not exclude one another, allowing craft-based enterprises to remain economically viable and culturally meaningful over time.

WEAVING COHERENCE IN PLACE

Embroidering. As an embroider makes on a surface, coherence is created through place and with place by cultivating relationships with people who are gravitating around the craftmakers and their ateliers, with whom they share the same values. They are not necessarily colleagues (see "making"), but local residents of the street and the neighborhood, or even tourists, with whom craft makers create an interaction that results in being fruitful in one way or another. This can happen even with tourists, "curious travelers" who move away from the beaten tracks and find craft shops where is possible to have a chat with the maker and cultivate a relationship which, even if short, enriches both sides. Many craftmakers decide to stay or to move to a territory, often because that place embodies a specific cultural heritage itself, which acts as an attractor and favorable point of installation of an activity. The place is because it is inherently and coherently connected to the maker's identity and production. Place provides not only materials and work connections (see "making"), but coherent background for one's own job, in terms of culture (e.g., familiar culture), inspiration (e.g., the one given by nature), and presence of a community of peers to which find a more spiritual connection, beyond the practical one. Through embroidering place becomes a generator of social, cultural, and even spiritual capital that supports long-term value creation beyond mere profitability. The situated and relational nature of craft practices enables craftmakers to build resilient models of business grounded in meaningful connections and place-based identity, key elements for sustainability.

Knitting. The construction of coherence in the craft making process is often given by a detailed knitting of collaboration between artisans of the same territory which allows the delivery of an inherently "authentic" final product. Craft makers give value to the collaboration with local suppliers due to a better ability to understand each other, given the similar small dimension, the tailor-made production, and the high quality of the materials. Coherence is also created by a supporting environment that allows the final product to be the result of a shared making process in which craftmakers receive support from other artisans for solving problems of a different nature. Building coherence through *knitting* among local artisans contributes directly to the development of sustainable business models by fostering shared value creation, mutual support, and high-quality production rooted in territorial coherence. This mode of collaboration also promotes the use of local resources and skills, reducing environmental impact and reinforcing the local economy, thus contributing to both social and environmental sustainability.

Blockprinting. In the made object, coherence is created by "blockprinting" a feature of the place on the object. This is often the case when products reproduce architecture or images of territories in their esthetics or shapes. By embedding visual and symbolic references to the local territory into the esthetics or form of the final product, craftmakers transform place into a tangible asset – one that generates cultural, emotional, and commercial value. Therefore, *blockprinting* supports the development of sustainable business models by aligning production with place-based identity, fostering cultural continuity, and enhancing the attractiveness and uniqueness of the offering, key drivers for long-term economic and cultural sustainability.

CONCLUSION

This chapter explores authenticity through the lens of craft, showing how it is not merely claimed but actively constructed in practice. Focusing on the "authenticity work" involved in craft production, we highlight how craftmakers coherently weave their selves, making processes, and objects across time and place. Using the metaphor of weaving, we conceptualize six modes of authenticity work that integrate the past, present, and future of both maker, process and object, and the places where craft is created.

By proposing authenticity as the weaving of coherence across time and place, this chapter shifts the discourse from audience-dependent claims to a producer-oriented, practice-based perspective. It emphasizes authenticity as a dynamic, ongoing process rooted in everyday practice rather than a fixed trait or narrative. The temporal and place-based nature of craft offers a valuable, different lens for understanding how authenticity is built within specific cultural and geographical contexts.

We demonstrate how this authenticity work allows craftmakers to embed identity, values, and locality into their creations, generating multiple layers of value – economic, social, cultural, and environmental. As such, weaving coherence becomes a strategic resource for developing sustainable business models. Craft enterprises can thus deliver value beyond profit, fostering continuity, innovation, and cultural rootedness and care for community and place.

This chapter also contributes to research on craft as a living, evolving practice. It offers new insights into the interplay of authenticity, place, and creative labor in today's society. We encourage further inquiry into how authenticity is actively constructed across diverse forms of production and how these processes can inform both theory and practice in organizational and entrepreneurship studies.

Our framework offers artisans and cultural entrepreneurs a practical tool to reflect on and develop sustainable, authenticity-grounded business models. Rather than relying on externally imposed claims, this perspective highlights the ongoing, situated work through which coherence is built across life experience, material choices, territorial and historical ties.

By connecting personal histories with current practices and future aspirations, artisans can craft models that are economically viable, meaningful,
and resilient. The six modes of authenticity work – such as patchworking
tradition and innovation, layering values into products, embroidering local
ties, and knitting collaborative networks – enable the creation of value-rich
ecosystems. These approaches foster local embeddedness; reduce environmental impact; and build emotional, social, and symbolic capital. Ultimately, this
empowers craft-based and cultural enterprises to move beyond profitability
toward socially inclusive, culturally grounded, and environmentally sustainable forms of entrepreneurship.

REFERENCES

Bell, E., Dacin, M. T., & Toraldo, M. L. (2021). Craft imaginaries – Past,
present and future. *Organization Theory*, 2(1), 263178772199114.

Beverland, M. B. (2005). Crafting brand authenticity: The case of luxury
wines. *Journal of Management Studies*, 42(5), 1003–1029.

Blundel, R. K., & Smith, D. J. (2013). Reinventing artisanal knowledge
and practice: A critical review of innovation in a craft-based industry.
Prometheus, 31(1).

Brandellero, A., & Naclerio, E. (2025). Regenerating urban cultural policy:
Insights on the role of crafts and small-scale production in three European
cities' visions. *International Journal of Cultural Policy*, 31(4), 467–481.

Cattani, G., Dunbar, R. L. M., & Shapira, Z. (2017). How commitment
to craftsmanship leads to unique value: Steinway & Sons' differentiation
strategy. *Strategy Science*, 2(1), 13–38.

Comunian, R., & England, L. (2019). Creative clusters and the evolution of
knowledge and skills: From industrial to creative glassmaking. *Geoforum*,
99, 238–247.

Dobrev, S. D., & Verhaal, J. C. (2024). Organizational authenticity: How
craft-based ventures manage authentic identities and audience appeal.
Strategic Entrepreneurship Journal, 18(4), 740–769.

Erhardt, N., Martin-Rios, C., Bolton, J., & Luth, M. (2022). Doing well by
creating economic value through social values among craft beer breweries:
A case study in responsible innovation and growth. *Sustainability*,
14(5), 2826.

Ferreira, C., Oliveira, J., & Sousa Aroso, M. (2023). Authenticity business model canvas: A new tool applied to the Portuguese Way of St. James. *Journal of Innovation Management, 10*(4), 47–64.

Fletchall, A. M. (2016). Place-making through beer-drinking: A case study of Montana's craft breweries. *Geographical Review, 106*(4), 539–566.

Gandini, A., & Gerosa, A. (2023). What is 'neo-craft' work, and why it matters. *Organization Studies,* 01708406231213963.

Ganzin, M., Chirico, F., Kroezen, J. J., Dacin, M. T., Sirmon, D. G., & Suddaby, R. (2024). Craft and strategic entrepreneurship: Exploring and exploiting materiality, authenticity, and tradition in craft-based ventures. *Strategic Entrepreneurship Journal, 18*(4), 671–685.

Gatrell, J., Reid, N., & Steiger, T. L. (2018). Branding spaces: Place, region, sustainability and the American craft beer industry. *Applied Geography, 90,* 360–370.

Gerosa, A. (2024). *The hipster economy: Taste and authenticity in late modern capitalism.* UCL Press.

Gibson, C. (2016). Material inheritances: How place, materiality, and labor process underpin the path-dependent evolution of contemporary craft production. *Economic Geography, 92*(1), 61–86.

Jones, C., Anand, N., & Alvarez, J. L. (2005). Manufactured authenticity and creative voice in cultural industries. *Journal of Management Studies, 42*(5), 893–899.

Jones, D., & Smith, K. (2005). Middle-earth meets New Zealand: Authenticity and location in the making of The Lord of the Rings. *Journal of Management Studies, 42*(5), 923–945.

Jones, K. E., Van Assche, K., & Parkins, J. R. (2021). Reimagining craft for community development. *Local Environment, 26*(7), 908–920.

Koontz, A. (2010). Constructing authenticity: A review of trends and influences in the process of authentication in consumption. *Sociology Compass, 4*(11), 977–988.

Kouhia, A., & Rönkkö, M.-L. (2020). *Crafting the city: Promoting heritage awareness through craft making in a historical town.*

Kroezen, J., Ravasi, D., Sasaki, I., Żebrowska, M., & Suddaby, R. (2021). Configurations of craft: Alternative models for organizing work. *Academy of Management Annals, 15*(2), 502–536.

Lehman, D. W., O'Connor, K., Kovács, B., & Newman, G. E. (2019). Authenticity. *Academy of Management Annals*, 13(1), 1–42.

McHattie, L.-S., Champion, K., & Johnson, M. (2019). Crafting the local: The lived experience of craft production in the Northern Isles of Scotland. *Cultural Trends*, 28(4), 305–316.

Palmi, P., & Lezzi, G. E. (2020). How authenticity and tradition shift into sustainability and innovation: Evidence from Italian agritourism. *International Journal of Environmental Research and Public Health*, 17(15), 5389.

Peterson, R. A. (2005). In search of authenticity. *Journal of Management Studies*, 42(5), 1083–1098.

Platt, L. C. (2019). Crafting place: Women's everyday creativity in placemaking processes. *European Journal of Cultural Studies*, 22(3), 362–377.

Ravasi, D., Rindova, V., & Stigliani, I. (2019). The stuff of legend: History, memory, and the temporality of organizational identity construction. *Academy of Management Journal*, 62(5), 1523–1555.

Revilla, G., & Dodd, T. H. (2003). Authenticity perceptions of Talavera pottery. *Journal of Travel Research*, 42(1), 94–99.

Rickly, J. M. (2022). A review of authenticity research in tourism: Launching the Annals of Tourism Research curated collection on authenticity. *Annals of Tourism Research*, 92, 103349.

Romain, J. (2016). All art is part of the same constellation: A conversation on craft and artistic practice with Heri Dono. *The Journal of Modern Craft*, 9(2), 183–191.

Schaltegger, S., Hansen, E. G., & Lüdeke-Freund, F. (2016). Business models for sustainability: Origins, present research, and future avenues. *Organization & Environment*, 29(1), 3–10.

Schultz, M., & Hernes, T. (2013). A temporal perspective on organizational identity. *Organization Science*, 24(1), 1–21.

Sennett, R. (2008). *The craftsman*. Yale University Press.

Takuya, K., & Takayama, C. (2010). Traditional art crafts (Dentō Kōgei) in Japan: From reproductions to original works. *The Journal of Modern Craft*, 3(1), 19–35.

Tanghetti, J., Lusiani, M., Panozzo, F., England, L., Comunian, R., & Stevenson, F. (2025). Where has all the knowledge gone? Migrations from industrial to knowledge economy in textile firms. *Knowledge Management Research & Practice*, 23(2), 149–159.

Voronov, M., Foster, W. M., Patriotta, G., & Weber, K. (2023). Distilling authenticity: Materiality and narratives in Canadian distilleries' authenticity work. *Academy of Management Journal*, 66(5), 1438–1468.

Weber, K., Heinze, K. L., & DeSoucey, M. (2008). Forage for thought: Mobilizing codes in the movement for grass-fed meat and dairy products. *Administrative Science Quarterly*, 53(3), 529–567.

Yang, X., Xu, H., & Ni, S. (2021). The creative renewal of a craft cluster: The role of materiality and mobility in cluster evolution. *Regional Studies*, 55(3), 546–555.

5

RETHINKING CULTURAL BUSINESS MODELS THROUGH ARTISTIC INTERVENTIONS IN TOURISM-RELATED CONTEXTS

MARGHERITA DE LUCA, CHIARA CAROLINA DONELLI AND FABRIZIO PANOZZO

Ca' Foscari University of Venice, Italy

ABSTRACT

This chapter explores how artistic interventions in tourism-saturated contexts provide insight into alternative cultural business models (BMs) that could enhance their economic viability. Drawing on critical perspectives from cultural entrepreneurship, the creative industries, and BM theory, the chapter examines how notions such as bricolage, informality, and situated practice help make sense of artistic work that does not conform to standard entrepreneurial frameworks. Through three cases of artistic interventions situated in tourism-driven environments, the chapter identifies four recurring patterns: ultra-light and non-bureaucratic organizational forms, pragmatic yet ethically filtered engagement with markets, a critical stance toward dominant tourism imaginaries, and a shift in artistic labor from authorship to mediation and facilitation. Together, these patterns reveal cultural producers practicing BMs through assemblages, relational networks, and everyday experimentation. By foregrounding bricolage as an organizing logic, the chapter advances a plural, place-based conception of cultural BMs that acknowledges informality, context-specific value creation, and artistic autonomy as pillars of sustainable cultural production.

Keywords: Cultural entrepreneurship; artistic interventions; sustainable tourism; business models; bricolage; creative industries

INTRODUCTION

Although artistic and cultural work has long been associated with the public good, autonomy, and public support, the past few decades have radically transformed how cultural production is conceived and organized. With the rise of the cultural and creative industries (CCI) paradigm in the late 20th century, cultural producers have been increasingly encouraged to operate as market actors, positioning themselves as businesses, thinking entrepreneurially, and devising their own "business models" (O'Connor, 2009). This policy discourse has had a significant impact on cultural organizations' financing, evaluation, and representation. However, this transformation of discourse raises crucial questions: To what extent do cultural producers embrace entrepreneurial logic? Do they internalize marketplace expectations and the BMs? Most importantly, how are these changes being implemented in practice, particularly in tourism-related contexts where artistic activity is intertwined with tourism economies? Conventional tools such as the BM Canvas often fall short in capturing the fluid, adaptive nature of creative and cultural enterprises, especially in the context of heritage tourism (Edensor et al., 2009; Flew & Cunningham, 2010).

This chapter examines the limitations of applying traditional BMs to CCIs operating within tourism-driven contexts and explores alternative practices that promote (economic) sustainability in these settings.

While acknowledging that sustainability is an inherently multidimensional concept encompassing social, environmental, and cultural domains, and that a holistic approach addressing all three is necessary, this study focuses specifically on the economic dimension in relation to the BMs of cultural producers. By examining a variety of practices in photography, video, performance, and participatory arts, this study sheds light on how artists and cultural producers navigate the complexities of tourism economies while balancing creative autonomy with economic sustainability.

To address this question, we first survey the literature on BMs in arts and cultural organizations, before tracing the emergence of new BMs that seek to translate the discourse of strategy and entrepreneurship into the artistic field. We then analyze a qualitative approach comparing three episodes of artistic intervention designed to stimulate a reflection on sustainability issues within tourism-related urban and rural contexts. Shadowing artists during their interventions enabled us to access forms of knowledge and practice typically excluded from mainstream organizational research, while also reflecting on the broader objective of sustainable tourism.

Each case study provided a unique perspective on how cultural producers respond to the pressures, expectations, and opportunities associated with tourism. Rather than viewing these cases as static examples, we interpret them as situated experiments that demonstrate how BMs are constructed, improvised, and reconfigured.

This analysis yields three key insights: the normalization of market orientation among cultural producers; the fragmented, unstructured nature of their operational models; and the emergence of bricolage as a strategic organizing logic.

We conclude by discussing how these findings support a more nuanced understanding of cultural entrepreneurship, one that resists business templates and instead centers on the adaptive, collaborative, and context-specific nature of artistic production in tourism-related contexts. We also propose future research directions aimed at advancing sustainable tourism and culturally sensitive urban development through inclusive, artist-led innovation.

LITERATURE REVIEW: BMS IN THE CULTURAL SECTOR

BMs have become a central focus of management studies, providing a conceptual lens to understand how organizations create, deliver, and capture value (Teece, 2010). However, mainstream BM literature has traditionally prioritized large, profit-driven industrial companies in Western economies, with a strong emphasis on technological innovation and financial outcomes (Chesbrough & Rosenbloom, 2002; Foss & Saebi, 2017). This leaves important gaps when analyzing small- and medium-sized enterprises, particularly in the cultural sector, where organizations often pursue ecological, social, and artistic goals alongside economic viability (Gasparin et al., 2022).

Challenges of BMs in the Cultural Sector

The cultural sector poses unique challenges for BM research. Cultural organizations often pursue dual objectives: maintaining financial viability while preserving creative autonomy and delivering social impact (Spieth et al., 2019). Unlike traditional industries, which follow standardized frameworks (Osterwalder & Pigneur, 2010), CCIs operate through fluid, hybrid structures that resist rigid categorization (Fillis, 2023). Emerging from this industrial legacy, the diffusion of BM thinking in the cultural sector has been shaped by the rise of the CCI paradigm. Within this framework, culture is reframed as an economically productive activity, increasingly detached from traditional expectations of public subsidy and evaluated by its potential to drive innovation, growth, and urban regeneration (Hesmondhalgh & Pratt, 2005). As a result, cultural producers are routinely exposed to external pressures, operating in environments where accessibility, clarity, and responsiveness to audiences often take precedence over artistic autonomy.

Consequently, many resist adopting business-related terminology for fear that it may compromise their artistic integrity. As Rex (2018, p. 6) observes: "The majority of practitioners would not describe the way they manage resources using this terminology [business model]."

Expanding the BM Framework

To address these tensions, Schiuma (2017) proposes the Business Model Prism (BMP), a multidimensional framework that integrates economic sustainability with non-financial values, such as social and cultural capital. Although the BMP provides a more comprehensive perspective, it still tends to overlook the lived experiences of individual cultural producers, many of whom operate through temporary collaborations or informal networks rather than stable organizations (Banks & O'Connor, 2017). This challenges conventional BM models, which assume linear hierarchies and fixed organizational structures.

Similarly, Moureau and Sagot-Duvauroux (2012) identify four distinct BMs employed by contemporary artists, highlighting the diversity of economic practices in this field. Some rely on traditional gallery systems, while others leverage digital platforms and participatory methods to diversify their revenue streams. Yet, as Fillis (2023) notes, BMs in the cultural sector tend to be reactive rather than strategic, developed out of necessity rather than opportunity. Beckman (2022) takes this further by describing this dynamic as a "tyranny" (p. 14), in stark contrast to mainstream entrepreneurship literature, which is premised on deliberate planning and scalability (Banks & O'Connor, 2017).

The Artist as Entrepreneur

The literature on entrepreneurship offers alternative insights, particularly through the figure of the "artist-entrepreneur" (Beckman, 2022; Oakley, 2014). This perspective highlights artists' ability to create cultural value through visionary entrepreneurial actions (Klamer, 2011). Cultural policy is increasingly promoting self-reliance, innovation, and adaptability as core competencies for creative workers, reflecting broader neoliberal transformations in cultural labor (McRobbie, 2016).

From a critical standpoint, entrepreneurialism in the cultural field can also be understood as a discourse that reframes structural challenges as personal opportunities. Rather than identifying systemic constraints that limit agency, the entrepreneurial discourse encourages individuals to innovate and "disrupt" structures. It emphasizes personal creativity and treats external barriers as individual challenges, rather than issues to be addressed through collective social or political action.

Überbacher et al. (2015) examine how artists acquire entrepreneurial competencies and become "skilled cultural operators," highlighting the dynamic, context-specific nature of these transformations.

Two key approaches emerge from this literature:

- *Survival approach*: Many artists engage in entrepreneurial activities, such as self-promotion, grant writing, and side jobs, primarily out of necessity, driven by unstable income streams and shrinking public support (Fillis, 2023; Hesmondhalgh & Baker, 2013).

- *The passion economy paradox*: Digital platforms offer enhanced visibility and market access but often require constant self-branding and emotional labor. As Duffy (2017) and Poell et al. (2021) argue, this form of platform-driven entrepreneurship can intensify rather than alleviate precarity.

Cultural entrepreneurship thus unfolds through informal networks and temporary collaborations, rather than formal institutions (Bilton, 2017). It combines hybrid revenue streams, including public funding, commissions, commercial ventures, and joint projects (Bilton & Cummings, 2010), and often occurs in project-based economies marked by discontinuity (Sydow & Staber, 2002).

Despite theoretical advancements, existing models still struggle to capture the improvisational, fragmented nature of artistic careers, characterized by unstable and interdependent income streams (Fillis, 2023). The precariousness of cultural work (Hesmondhalgh, 2013; McRobbie, 2016) underscores the need for hybrid economic structures and strategic skillsets, such as teaching, grant-seeking, and merchandizing (Comunian et al., 2015).

RESEARCH GAP AND CONTRIBUTION

This review reveals a persistent gap in the literature: the absence of an artist-centered, dynamic BM theory that reflects the precarity and non-linear trajectories typical of cultural work. The present study contributes to the existing literature by exploring how cultural producers in tourism-related contexts develop sustainable BMs.

METHODOLOGY

This study uses a multiple case study approach to examine how cultural producers operate within tourism-driven contexts and to identify the alternative practices they employ, beyond conventional BMs, to achieve economic sustainability.

The three cases are artistic interventions conducted through art-based research (Barone & Eisner, 2011; Leavy, 2015) and developed in tourist-related contexts: urban or rural settings where tourism is pervasive or emerging, often raising complex questions about sustainability, identity, and cultural representation. These interventions followed a dialogical and interventionist approach, in which researchers and artists collaboratively shaped the research agenda and co-developed the research questions (Cacciatore & Panozzo, 2025).

Methodologically, our approach included:

1. Ethnographic observation of the artistic interventions before, during, and after their development;

2. Semi-structured interviews conducted at the conclusion of each intervention (approximately 90 minutes in length), during which artists reflected on their process, the context, and their working models.

Interviews were conducted with the following artists involved in the three case studies:

• Filippo Tognazzo, actor and director at Zelda Teatro (*Souvenir*).

• Andrea Signori, photographer (*Souvenir*).

- Giovanni Pellegrini, video maker and director at Ginko Film (*Venezia è Africa*).

- Fabio Bonelli, sound artist and musician (*TOTEM*).

These interviews offered valuable insights into the artists' BMs and the nature of their interventions. The dialog between practice and analysis revealed several key findings concerning the role of artistic work in relation to heritage, tourism, and contemporary cultural production.

ARTISTIC INTERVENTIONS

To provide a practical context for these theoretical discussions, we analyze three artistic interventions: two in Venice, a city that embodies the tensions between heritage and mass tourism, and one in Roana, a small mountain town in the Veneto region that has a strong local identity and is environmentally fragile. These cases, developed in collaboration with Ca' Foscari University, show how artists can translate their creative practice into adaptive BMs, engaging new stakeholders and rethinking the relationship between culture, community, and tourism.

Souvenir: An Exploration of Artisan Memory

Souvenir: An Exploration of Artisan Memory was a project conducted by Ca' Foscari University of Venice in collaboration with the theater company Zelda Teatro and photographer Andrea Signori in the summer and autumn of 2024. The project addressed a shared research question: how can artistic languages contribute to creating new imaginaries associated with Venice and its artisan traditions? It explored the relationship between material culture and the transmission of artisanal knowledge, prompting reflection on the survival of craft skills in a changing urban context.

The project combined photography, storytelling, and academic inquiry to document the lives and practices of retired artisans. Theatre director Filippo Tognazzo (Zelda Teatro) wrote monologs based on interviews, while photographer Andrea Signori produced a series of dual portraits. Each artisan was represented by two images: one with a glitched face that foregrounded the crafted object, and another focusing solely on the individual, creating a visual contrast between identity and labor.

The project was previewed on October 5, 2024, at the *Salone dell'Alto Artigianato Italiano*, which was held at the Arsenale in Venice. The *Souvenir* exhibition featured six panels combining photographic portraits, excerpts from the monologues, statistical data on Italian craftsmanship, and QR codes linking to the recorded stories performed by actors.

In a city shaped by mass tourism and commercial pressures, *Souvenir* revisited the stories of retired artisans to explore the interplay of skill, identity, and cultural resilience. Using photography and performative storytelling, the project challenged romanticized narratives of artisanal heritage, positioning artists as cultural mediators. Beyond its artistic dimension, *Souvenir* also informed policy discussions on knowledge transmission and was submitted to international exhibitions to increase public engagement.

Venezia è Africa

Venezia è Africa was developed in summer 2024 through a collaboration between Wetlands Books, a publisher focusing on social and environmental sustainability and the challenges of the Anthropocene, and Ginko Film, a film and audiovisual production company specializing in auteur cinema and creative documentaries. The project once again addressed the shared research question of how artistic languages can contribute to generating new imaginaries associated with Venice and its productive heritage. It responded by reinterpreting the city through an Afro-diasporic lens, aiming to decolonize cultural narratives and situate Venice within a broader transnational dialog.

Combining literature, cinema, and academic inquiry, the project focused on a series of video interviews with African and Afro-descendant authors in artistic residency. Conducted by Ginko Film, these conversations used Venice as a reflective space to explore the historical entanglements between Africa and Europe. The authors' observations challenged Eurocentric heritage frameworks, revealing traces of African presence often erased from mainstream narratives. They reflected on how the city's enclosed form shapes perception, particularly through sound, silence, and spatial memory.

The project culminated on September 1, 2024, during the Venice Film Festival, one of the world's most prominent cultural stages. The videos were also showcased at the launch of Afterwords, Wetlands' latest literary series, curated by the author Maaza Mengiste. This dual cinematic and editorial platform extended the work's public resonance across artistic and cultural circuits. In a city where global tourism often reduces complexity to spectacle, *Venezia è Africa* offered an alternative vision grounded in absence, dialog, and cultural entanglement. By foregrounding marginalized voices and repositioning Venice within a decolonial framework, the project broadened the city's imaginary beyond dominant tropes, fostering a connection between artistic creation and critical discourse.

TOTEM – The Sound of Memory

TOTEM – The Sound of Memory was developed in early 2025 by sound artist and musician Fabio Bonelli, in collaboration with Ca' Foscari University as part of the iNEST Spoke 6 Lab Village initiative. Based in Roana, a small mountain town in the Veneto region, the project addressed a shared research question: how can artistic languages be used to re-narrate the identity of a mountain landscape that is experiencing ecological and cultural erosion, including the disappearance of snow and other emblematic features?

Despite being geographically distant from Venice, Roana provided a significant contrast, offering an alpine setting where cultural identity is closely intertwined with memory, landscape, and local storytelling traditions.

The project explored the relationship between sound, memory, and place through a participatory process involving Roana's residents. Bonelli invited locals to share personal objects linked to their past, using them as prompts for storytelling and sonic interpretation. Instead of documenting these stories in traditional formats, he reworked them into a layered soundscape – blending voices, ambient recordings, and musical composition – to create a multisensory experience.

The project culminated in February 2025 with a video performance at Museo Radici, Lavarone's cultural hub. Here, the collected voices and compositions merged to create an immersive installation, offering audiences a resonant, sound-based experience of the town's heritage.

Set in an area distant from mass tourism yet not untouched by tourism-related pressures, TOTEM questioned the role of contemporary art in sustaining local identity. Developed within the community, the project avoided extractive dynamics and presented artistic practice as a form of cultural inquiry. By amplifying personal memory through sound, it showed how artistic interventions can strengthen the bonds between people, place, and heritage, while exploring new forms of storytelling and cultural preservation.

FINDINGS

We identified four recurring patterns across the artists' narratives about their BMs, which diverge from the configurations proposed by traditional BMs. These dimensions emerged inductively through the coding and interpretation of interviews and field observations. Their identification of four patterns contributes to the debate on BMs in the cultural sectors, particularly by shedding light on how cultural producers operate within tourism-driven contexts and the alternative practices they adopt to achieve economic sustainability.

The first pattern concerns the operational model of artistic work: how artists structure their practice, the types of organizational or legal frameworks they adopt (if any), and whether their work follows a continuous or project-based logic.

The second pattern focuses on the artists' market orientation, examining to what extent their work is financed through public funding and private commissions, as well as how they position themselves in relation to commercial demands.

The third pattern explores the artists' attitude toward tourism, and the effect that working in a highly touristic city like Venice, or in contexts marked by tourism, has on their practice, both materially and symbolically.

Finally, the fourth pattern examines the artists' self-perception in their work: whether they see themselves exclusively as creators or tend to identify with other roles.

Operational Model

Across the four interviews, a shared operational logic emerges: artistic production is predominantly project-based (Davies et al., 2011) and developed within lightweight organizational structures that rely more on informal networks than on hierarchical institutions. While some adopt legal business forms (such as an Srl in Zelda Teatro's case or as a production company in Ginko Film's case), these are used pragmatically to secure fiscal and contractual legitimacy, rather than as markers of market-driven enterprise. The artists' working methods reveal a distinct artisanal, reticular model based on collaboration, temporality, and mobility. Projects are developed around specific contexts and then disbanded, requiring the continual reactivation of professional and personal connections. While flexible and adaptive, this model complicates long-term planning and underscores the need for intermediary structures capable of sustaining dissemination and continuity beyond the ephemeral moment of creation.

Revenue Stream: At the Crossroads of Market Orientation and Public Funds

Market orientation varies, but all four practitioners navigate a mixed economy of cultural production. While some rely more on public funding (e.g., Bonelli and Tognazzo), others, such as Signori and Pellegrini, more regularly integrate corporate commissions into their practice. Interestingly, private commissions do not entail a wholesale shift toward commercial language. Instead, all interviewees describe a delicate negotiation in which their artistic voice is preserved, even when operating within marketing contexts. For Pellegrini, private work subsidizes documentary filmmaking; for Signori, it provides a platform for conceptual experimentation within esthetic boundaries set by the client. While all these artists acknowledge increasing market pressure on cultural production, none adopt a fully market-oriented logic. Instead, they pursue "meaningful" collaborations, often turning down projects that do not align with their ethical or creative standards.

Spatial and Symbolic Context of Intervention

A key dimension in the discussion of cultural BMs is the spatial and symbolic context in which artistic practices unfold, in line with tourism studies that conceptualise tourism products as culturally embedded, co-produced, and shaped by extended networks of actors rather than by firms alone (García-Rosell et al., 2007). In this case, Venice emerges not only as a physical site of work and residence but also as a powerful cultural and economic framework. The artists' engagement with the city reveals a deliberate and critical distance from its dominant tourism-driven economy. While Venice's esthetic and symbolic weight undeniably shapes audience perception, as noted by Signori, the practitioners consistently resist allowing tourist imaginaries to dictate the terms of their work. For example, Tognazzo asserts that the city's touristic identity had no influence on the artistic structure of *Souvenir*, while Pellegrini reflects on the challenge of eluding the "tourist gaze," even in politically engaged projects. Bonelli, who works primarily outside the city, articulates this dynamic most explicitly: "In highly touristic contexts, culture is often swallowed up by tourism." In all these cases, tourism emerges not as a productive opportunity but as a structural constraint that reduces artistic complexity to spectacle unless it is actively challenged. This tension reveals how cultural BMs in tourist-saturated environments must not only navigate economic pressures but also engage in symbolic negotiations, balancing visibility with integrity and resisting commodification through deliberate positioning.

Beyond Authorship

Finally, all four artists assume roles that transcend conventional definitions of authorship. Tognazzo and Pellegrini challenge the label of "artist," leaning instead toward terms such as cultural artisan or visual craftsman. Signori identifies as a cultural mediator, while Bonelli emphasizes the pedagogical and relational aspects of his work. These redefinitions reposition the artist as not only a creator but also a researcher, facilitator, educator, and translator. In doing so, they illustrate how contemporary artistic work, especially in a tourist setting, intersects the symbolic, social, and economic domains to shape relationships and enable new forms of civic engagement.

DISCUSSION: EXPANDING CULTURAL BMs

The four patterns identified in our fieldwork reveal how cultural producers adapt their practices in tourism-driven contexts through pragmatic and flexible forms of entrepreneurship. These practices challenge traditional assumptions about BMs by prioritizing informality, improvisation, and context-specific value creation.

Operational Models: Non-organizational Infrastructures and Informal Architectures

In all four cases, cultural production is structured through temporary, project-based arrangements rather than stable organizations. Artists operate with minimal internal infrastructure, and any legal entities primarily serve to secure fiscal legitimacy. This organizational fluidity is not a sign of immaturity but a strategic adaptation to the constraints of the field. As Bilton (1999) and Moureau and Sagot-Duvauroux (2012) have noted, informal coordination is a defining feature of cultural work, offering agility and reduced overheads. Our findings support this view, showing that artistic production relies on networked collaboration, ephemeral teams, and relational maintenance rather than institutional consolidation. This challenges conventional BM frameworks, which often assume structured firms with managerial continuity (George & Bock, 2011; Ghezzi & Cavallo, 2020).

Market Orientation: Situated Pragmatism over Ideological Resistance

The artists in our study display a clear and context-sensitive engagement with market dynamics. This engagement is not an ideological capitulation but a strategic response to precarious funding landscapes and fragmented audiences. They navigate between public funding and private commissions, tailoring their outputs to multiple stakeholders while preserving creative autonomy. This reflects what Flew and Cunningham (2010) and Schramme (2023) describe as tactical deployment of entrepreneurial rationality. Rather than aspiring to growth or profit maximization, the artists build project portfolios, minimize fixed costs, and cultivate meaningful collaborations, often refusing projects that conflict with their values. Such practices challenge the binary opposition between market-driven and publicly subsidized cultural work.

Spatial and Symbolic Context of Intervention: Anticipatory Calibration and Critical Distance from Tourism

Operating in a tourism-saturated environment such as Venice can put specific pressures on cultural production. Rather than passively responding to tourist demand, our interviewees *anticipate* and negotiate it. This anticipatory calibration reshapes their practice stylistically, logistically, and symbolically without fully aligning with the commodified "cultural delivery" logic often found in heritage cities (Evans, 2009; Richards, 2014). These artists resist allowing tourism imaginaries to frame their work and often express concern about the risk of cultural homogenization. Nevertheless, the tourism economy creates a structural demand for accessibility, which many address by adopting flexible modes of production, rather than by contesting tourism ideologically. This reinforces the need to conceptualize entrepreneurship in place-based and tourism-influenced terms.

Artists' Role: Beyond Authorship, Toward Facilitation, and Translation

The fourth pattern highlights how cultural producers reframe their role beyond traditional notions of authorship. They see themselves as facilitators, educators, mediators, or artisans – roles that emphasize process, participation, and knowledge exchange. This resonates with Gherardi's (2000) concept of *knowing-in-practice*: a form of embedded coordination and learning that emerges from doing, adjusting, and improvising. The BM here is not a pre-defined plan but an ongoing enactment. These artists compose rather than plan; they repurpose resources, reconfigure teams, and build momentum iteratively. This actor-dependent, improvisational mode of action aligns with the idea of bricolage described by Duymedjian and Rüling (2010) and Glasbeek (2024): a form of strategic improvization under constraint.

Bricolage as a BM Logic

Far from being marginal or deficient, bricolage emerges as the dominant BM logic in our cases, in line with the definition of entrepreneurial bricolage proposed by Baker and Nelson (2005). It reflects how artists mobilize symbolic capital, relationships, and infrastructure through informal, responsive, and iterative means. This logic is similar to Actor–Network Theory (Latour, 1987), which defines innovation as the process of assembling and maintaining provisional alliances. While bricolage fosters adaptability and resilience, it also limits the artists' ability to meet institutional expectations for growth, visibility, and formalization (Bhardwaj et al., 2024; Valliere & Gegenhuber, 2014). Our study highlights this tension: the very features that ensure survival – flexibility, improvization, and fluidity – can undermine legitimacy in fields that reward standardization.

Challenging Assumptions in BM Theory

Taken together, these patterns challenge the foundational assumption in BM theory that the organization is the natural unit of analysis. In the cultural field, BMs are not organizational blueprints but situational practices grounded in material constraints, ethical orientations, and place-based dynamics. Recognizing this paves the way for a more pluralistic and situated theory of cultural entrepreneurship, one that measures success not by growth or scale, but by sustainability, relevance, and adaptive coherence in uncertain environments. These dynamics reflect deeper structural transformations, prompting a rethinking of how cultural BMs are theorized and supported. Building on these findings, the concluding section identifies key implications and outlines directions for future research.

CONCLUSIONS

This study has illuminated three interrelated shifts that challenge dominant assumptions about cultural entrepreneurship and BMs in heritage tourism contexts. First, we have shown that market orientation is increasingly normalized among cultural producers, not as an ideological capitulation to neoliberalism, but as a pragmatic and often ethically mediated response to external demand and resource scarcity. Second, we have identified a clear departure from the firm-based, growth-driven assumptions that underpin much of the BM literature. In contrast, cultural work emerges here as fluid, fragmented, and project-based, resisting institutionalization and long-term consolidation. Third, we have proposed bricolage not as a residual or deficient mode, but as a strategic organizing logic: one particularly well-suited to the complex, uncertain, and materially constrained environments in which many artists operate.

These findings call for a rethinking of how cultural BMs are conceptualized and supported, particularly in tourism-related contexts where cultural policy, market logics, and sustainability agendas intersect. Rather than evaluating cultural entrepreneurship in terms of scalability, efficiency, or organizational maturity, we argue for a more situated and pluralistic perspective, one that acknowledges informality, relational coordination, and context-specific improvization as legitimate and strategic features of cultural economic life.

Ultimately, this study contributes to a growing body of work that seeks to decenter standardized templates and firm-based theories of entrepreneurship. We advocate an expanded understanding of BMs in the cultural field – one that recognizes artistic autonomy, organizational fluidity, and adaptive creativity not simply as survival tactics, but as core strategic resources essential for building more resilient and sustainable forms of cultural production in heritage cities.

Future research could build on these insights by:

- Investigating how bricolage strategies evolve in response to shifting policy frameworks, audience expectations, or funding conditions;

- Comparing these dynamics with non-tourism-driven contexts, to better understand how exposure to tourism reconfigures cultural business practices;

- Exploring how cultural producers construct legitimacy and continuity in the absence of stable organizational forms;

- Examining the role of intermediaries, infrastructures, or support mechanisms that can sustain fragmented cultural actors without imposing formalization;

- Expanding the notion of value by exploring how cultural BMs contribute to sustainability in ways that go beyond economics, such as memory-making, community engagement, pedagogical functions, and decolonial perspectives.

REFERENCES

Baker, T., & Nelson, R. E. (2005). Creating something from nothing: Resource construction through entrepreneurial bricolage. *Administrative Science Quarterly, 50*(3), 329–366.

Banks, M., & O'Connor, J. (2017). Inside the whale (and how to get out of there): Moving on from two decades of creative industries research. *European Journal of Cultural Studies, 20*(6), 637–654.

Barone, T., & Eisner, E. W. (2011). *Arts based research*. Sage.

Beckman, G. D. (2022). *The new arts entrepreneur: Navigating the art ecologies*. Routledge.

Bhardwaj, R., Bindra, S., Singh, T., & Sahay, A. (2024). Toward a typology of entrepreneurial bricolage and its capabilities. *Journal of Entrepreneurship in Emerging Economies, 16*(6), 1453–1480.

Bilton, C. (1999). *The new adhocracy: Strategy, risk and the small creative firm*. University of Warwick, Centre for Cultural Policy Studies.

Bilton, C. (2017). *Management and creativity: From creative industries to creative management* (2nd ed.). Wiley-Blackwell.

Bilton, C., & Cummings, S. (2010). *Creative strategy: Reconnecting business and innovation*. Wiley.

Cacciatore, S., & Panozzo, F. (2025). Rethinking research through artistic experimentation. *European Journal of Cultural Management and Policy, 14*, Article 13047.

Chesbrough, H., & Rosenbloom, R. S. (2002). The role of the business model in capturing value from innovation: Evidence from Xerox Corporation's technology spin-off companies. *Industrial and Corporate Change, 11*(3), 529–555.

Comunian, R., Gilmore, A., & Jacobi, S. (2015). Higher education and the creative economy: Creative graduates, knowledge transfer, and regional impact debates. *Geoforum, 59*, 1–6.

Davies, A., Brady, T., & Prencipe, A. (2011). Innovation in complex products and systems: Implications for project-based organising. *Advances in Strategic Management, 28*, 3–26.

Duffy, B. E. (2017). *(Not) getting paid to do what you love: Gender, social media, and aspirational work*. Yale University Press.

Duymedjian, R., & Rüling, C. C. (2010). Towards a foundation of bricolage in organization and management theory. *Organization Studies, 31*(2), 133–151.

Edensor, T., Leslie, D., Millington, S., & Rantisi, N. (Eds.). (2009). *Spaces of vernacular creativity: Rethinking the cultural economy* (Vol. 30). Routledge.

Evans, G. (2009). From cultural quarters to creative clusters creative spaces in the new city economy. In M. Legner (Ed.), *The sustainability and development of cultural quarters: International perspectives* (pp. 32–59). Institute of Urban History.

Fillis, I. (2023). *Business models for the arts and creative industries.* Routledge.

Flew, T., & Cunningham, S. (2010). Creative industries after the first decade of debate. *The Information Society, 26*(2), 113–123.

Foss, N. J., & Saebi, T. (2017). Fifteen years of research on business model innovation: How far have we come, and where should we go? *Journal of Management, 43*(1), 200–227.

García-Rosell, J. C., Haanpää, M., Kylänen, M., & Markuksela, V. (2007). From firms to extended markets: A cultural approach to tourism product development. *Tourism: An International Interdisciplinary Journal, 55*(4), 445–459.

Gasparin, M., Green, W., Lilley, S., Quinn, M., Saren, M., & Schinckus, C. (2022). Business as unusual: A business model for social innovation. *Journal of Business Research, 125,* 698–709.

George, G., & Bock, A. J. (2011). The business model in practice and its implications for entrepreneurship research. *Entrepreneurship Theory and Practice, 35*(1), 83–111.

Gherardi, S. (2000). Practice-based theorizing on learning and knowing in organizations. *Organization Studies, 21*(6), 1051–1075.

Ghezzi, A., & Cavallo, A. (2020). Agile business model innovation in digital entrepreneurship: Lean startup approaches. *Journal of Business Research, 110,* 519–537.

Glasbeek, L. (2024). Bricolage and its strategic connotations: A study of Greek social entrepreneurs in times of crisis. *British Journal of Management, 35*(1), 45–63.

Hesmondhalgh, D. (2013). *The cultural industries* (3rd ed.). Sage.

Hesmondhalgh, D., & Baker, S. (2013). *Creative labour: Media work in three cultural industries*. Routledge.

Hesmondhalgh, D., & Pratt, A. C. (2005). Cultural industries and cultural policy. *International Journal of Cultural Policy, 11*(1), 1–13.

Klamer, A. (2011). Cultural entrepreneurship. *Review of Austrian Economics, 24*(2), 141–156.

Latour, B. (1987). *Science in action: How to follow scientists and engineers through society*. Harvard University Press.

Leavy, P. (2015). *Method meets art: Arts-based research practice*. Guilford Publications.

McRobbie, A. (2016). *Be creative: Making a living in the new culture industries*. Polity.

Moureau, N., & Sagot-Duvauroux, D. (2012). Four business models in contemporary art. *International Journal of Arts Management, 14*(3), 44–56.

O'Connor, J. (2009). Creative industries: A new direction? *International Journal of Cultural Policy, 15*(4), 387–402.

Oakley, K. (2014). Good work? Rethinking cultural entrepreneurship. In C. Bilton & S. Cummings (Eds.), *Handbook of management and creativity* (pp. 145–159). Edward Elgar.

Osterwalder, A., & Pigneur, Y. (2010). *Business model generation: A handbook for visionaries, game changers, and challengers*. Wiley.

Poell, T., Nieborg, D., & van Dijck, J. (2021). Platformisation. *Internet Policy Review, 8*(4).

Rex, B. (2018). *New business models for cultural organisations: A critical literature review*. Creative Lenses Working Paper No. 1.

Richards, G. (2014). Creativity and tourism in the city. *Current Issues in Tourism, 17*(2), 119–144.

Schiuma, G. (2017). The business model prism: Managing and innovating business models of arts and cultural organisations. *Journal of Open Innovation: Technology, Market, and Complexity, 3*(3), 1–13.

Schramme, A. (2023). Cultural entrepreneurship and funding policies in Europe. In S. Comunian, B. E. Mitchell, & S. K. Watson (Eds.), *The handbook of cultural work* (pp. 229–244). Bloomsbury Academic.

Spieth, P., Schneckenberg, D., & Ricart, J. E. (2019). Business model innovation – State of the art and future challenges for the field. *R&D Management, 44*(3), 237–247.

Sydow, J., & Staber, U. (2002). The institutional embeddedness of project networks: The case of content production in German television. *Regional Studies, 36*(2), 215–227.

Teece, D. J. (2010). Business models, business strategy and innovation. *Long Range Planning, 43*(2–3), 172–194.

Valliere, D., & Gegenhuber, T. (2014). Entrepreneurial remixing: Bricolage and postmodern resources. *International Journal of Entrepreneurial Innovation, 15*(1), 29–38.

Part III

PARTICIPATORY BUSINESS MODELS FOR CREATING SHARED VALUE

6

COMMUNITY-BASED ENTERPRISES AS A SUSTAINABLE BUSINESS MODEL FOR TOURISM DESTINATION REGENERATION

STEFANIA DENISE ESCOBAR[a], CHIARA MASSACESI[a], LINDA OSTI[b], PAOLA ROVELLI[a] AND FEDERICA VIGANÒ[a]

[a]Competence Centre for Mountain Innovation Ecosystems,
Free University of Bozen-Bolzano, Italy
[b]Bangor Business School, UK

ABSTRACT

Community-based enterprises (CBEs) represent a sustainable business model where communities act entrepreneurially and cooperatively to establish enterprises that prioritize community goals alongside profit. As such, CBEs can be a viable strategy for regenerating tourism destinations. CBEs can help small local communities retain and attract new residents by building social capital, strengthening social cohesion, and enhancing the community's quality of life. In this chapter, we present the case of the "Cooperativa di Comunità Valle del Vanoi," which approached this business model in March 2023. The aim is to shed light on the development of a CBE, unveiling antecedents, development processes, and actual and expected outcomes for sustainability and community development. This case highlights how a CBE business *model can serve as a pathway to community revitalization and the development of sustainable tourism strategies.*

Keywords: Community-based enterprises; regeneration; tourism destinations; sustainable tourism; sustainable business model

INTRODUCTION

CBEs represent a business approach in which a community acts both entrepreneurially and cooperatively to establish a business enterprise (Valchovska & Watts, 2016). CBEs aim at profits "only insofar as profits are instrumentally effective at achieving other community goals" (Peredo & Chrisman, 2006, p. 28). As such, they engage in commercial activities and operate for the development of the local community by bringing economic, social, and environmental benefits (Buratti et al., 2022).

CBEs emerge as a strategic response to complex challenges such as economic decline, social disintegration, and lack of services, especially in marginal areas (Sharma & Shenoy, 2024; Valchovska & Watts, 2016). Therefore, CBEs have been used as an alternative form of business development compared to traditional companies that are often detached from the territory, especially in small places (Walzer, 2021). Indeed, CBEs can provide advantages to local communities (Morrison et al., 2017) and positively impact societal issues locally (Bacq et al., 2022; Deschamps & Slitine, 2024; Lumpkin et al., 2018; Mitzinneck et al., 2024; Peredo & Chrisman, 2017). An important component of CBEs is entrepreneurship, which is recognized as a tool for economic development and social transformation (Daskalaki et al., 2015; Lumpkin et al., 2018). In particular, CBEs are praised for their strategic potential to use entrepreneurial means not primarily for private gain but for communal benefits (Mitzinneck et al., 2024) and tourism destination regeneration (Dolezan & Novelli, 2022). Unlike traditional businesses, CBEs are deeply rooted in the territory and leverage local participation, often mobilizing residents as investors and volunteers in shared projects. This model has proven effective in building social capital and enhancing the quality of life, particularly in small or declining communities (Morrison et al., 2017; Renkert, 2019).

Recently, the concept of CBE has been used as an alternative model for tourism development that can boost community empowerment through fairer redistribution of tourism value among community members due to its greater involvement of residents in community development (Aquino, 2022; Dolezal & Novelli, 2022; Rocca & Zielinski, 2022; Zielinski et al., 2020).

Indeed, tourism can be a key driver for social value creation and social change (Altinay et al., 2016; Higgins-Desbiolles et al., 2019; Scheyvens, 1999). This study aims to expand this debate by exploring the development of a CBE to unveil antecedents, development processes, actual and expected benefits for the regeneration of the tourism destination in which it is embedded, with a particular focus on long-term sustainability and community development. Therefore, we aim to answer the following research question: *how do CBEs contribute to the regeneration and sustainability of tourism destinations?*

To answer this question, we explore the "Cooperativa di Comunità Valle del Vanoi" in the Trento province of the Trentino Alto Adige Region through a case study approach. The case presents a prospective development of a CBE, considered by the local stakeholders as a suitable business model since the beginning of their internal discussion in March 2023, as an endogenous expression of local governance, independent from the influences or pressures of external actors. This model has been widely used in Italy, with more than 300 CBEs developed in 2023 (EURICSE, 2024). The choice made by the community of Vanoi is also strongly related to the local cooperative culture (Sforzi & Borzaga, 2019). This case is particularly interesting because the CBE is in the process of developing the organizational model, which enabled us to investigate the decision-making process at a community level. The process shows significant changes in terms of the purpose envisioned behind the choice of a CBE and allows the community to deeply debate on the role of tourism and the type of visitor needed to enhance the revitalization of the territory, unveiling the importance of having the resident as a primary recipient of the CBE benefits. From a methodological standpoint, the use of a case study allowed us to pursue an in-depth investigation and analysis of the phenomenon (Baxter & Jack, 2008). Data collection entailed seven semi-structured interviews combined with secondary data from multiple sources. Findings are analyzed through the lens of sustainable business model archetypes to unveil the process of value creation, value capture, and value proposition of a CBE. In addition, the development process analysis is guided by the CBE development phases framework (Valchovska & Watts, 2016).

THEORETICAL FRAMEWORK

To investigate antecedents, development processes, actual and expected benefits of adopting a CBE model as a strategy for regenerating tourism destinations, we first explain the concept of regeneration in the context of tourism.

Afterwards, we employ two theoretical lenses: the sustainable business model archetypes (Bocken et al., 2014) and the CBE development process framework (Valchovska & Watts, 2016).

Regeneration in Tourism Destinations

Renewing a territory or a tourism destination involves restoring and enhancing the ecological integrity and social well-being of anthropocentric and natural systems (Dredge, 2022; Ferretti, 2021). Regeneration goes beyond tackling challenges and entails working together with communities to plan in an inclusive and proactive way (Dredge, 2022). Ferretti (2021) explains that regeneration involves an analysis of the key issues and limitations to be addressed and which actors should be involved. In tourism, regeneration aims to improve the local community's and the environment's well-being. Dredge (2022) and Bellato and Pollock (2025) describe regenerative tourism as a new way of thinking that focuses on caring for places and helping them thrive, not just avoiding harm. Suárez-Rojas et al. (2023) show how this approach can help tourism activities become more respectful of local communities and natural ecosystems. Hussain (2021) adds that regenerative tourism also means traveling more consciously, thinking about how and why we travel and how it affects others. A process of regeneration can lead to social innovation models such as CBEs that boost community stakeholder involvement, promoting social connections and restoring the social capital of a destination (Della Lucia & Trunfio, 2018).

Sustainable Business Models Archetype

Sustainable business models are "business models that incorporate pro-active multi-stakeholder management, the creation of monetary and non-monetary value for a broad range of stakeholders, and hold a long-term perspective" (Geissdoerfer et al., 2018, p. 404). Sustainable business models aim to generate economic, social, and environmental value by addressing the needs of a broad range of stakeholders (Bocken & Geradts, 2020; Bocken et al., 2014).

These models are characterized by three core elements: *value proposition, value creation and delivery*, and *value capture* (see Table 6.1). Moreover, sustainable business models encompass a variety of archetypes according to their focus area and purpose (Bocken et al., 2014). CBEs are considered a concrete form of sustainable business model that pertains to the archetype aiming to "repurpose for society/environment" (Bocken et al., 2014).

Table 6.1. Business Model Framework Applied to the Case of the CBE.

Components of a Sustainable Business Model	General Description	CBE
Value proposition	Developing an offer of products and services that generates economic value along with social and environmental value for a multitude of stakeholders (Baldassarre et al., 2017; Bocken & Geradts, 2020; Bocken et al., 2014; Yang et al., 2017)	Prioritizing social and environmental benefits rather than economic value by integrating firms with community stakeholders
Value creation and delivery	Capturing emerging business opportunities, explore new markets, and generate additional revenue streams (Aagaard, 2018)	Developing benefits for society and its environment, thereby enhancing the community's quality of life and preserving and regenerating the natural ecosystem, through participatory actions that involve multiple stakeholders (Bocken & Geradts, 2020)
Value capture	Generating revenue by delivering goods, services, or data/information to customers and users (Aagard, 2018; Bocken & Geradts, 2020; Bocken et al., 2014)	Delivering products and services with the lowest possible environmental impact and integrating the community and its inhabitants (Bocken et al., 2014)

Source: Authors' elaboration.

The CBEs examined in this study adopt a cooperative structure, which aligns with the archetype "repurposing for society/environment," which prioritizes, as the cooperatives do, to reinvest profits into social and environmental benefits rather than economic profit (i.e., shareholder value) maximization (Bocken et al., 2014).

Table 6.1 reports on the characteristics of a CBE based on the three components of sustainable business models.

This framework allows us to understand how CBEs can operate as viable business models that promote the long-term regeneration of tourism destinations while ensuring community well-being.

CBEs' Development Process

To analyze the dynamics behind the emergence of a CBE, we adopt the framework developed by Valchovska and Watts (2016), which identifies three key stages in the formation process: antecedents, gestation process, and enterprise start-up.

1. *Antecedents* – the set of socio-economic and territorial conditions that motivate local stakeholders to consider a CBE model, such as depopulation, lack of services, or housing constraints.

2. *Gestation phase* – a phase of vision-building, stakeholder engagement, and collective alignment toward shared goals. It involves community meetings, idea co-creation, and negotiation of the cooperative's future identity.

3. *Enterprise set-up* – the operationalization of the CBE through concrete investments, legal set-up, and the actual launch of services.

This process-based lens allows us to explore how communities transition from recognizing challenges to taking concrete collective action through entrepreneurship.

METHODOLOGY

This research adopts an exploratory approach and employs qualitative methods through a single case study methodology. This approach facilitates an in-depth examination of a phenomenon within its authentic, real-world context (Riddler, 2017; Yin, 2003) while being well-suited for emerging topics where existing theories and frameworks may not be able to explain the phenomenon completely (Creswell & Poth, 2016). To enhance the understanding of the phenomenon, we used an abductive approach that allowed us to move between theory and empirical data (Awuzie & McDermott, 2017).

We analyzed the case of the "Cooperativa di comunità Valle del Vanoi" in the Italian region of Trentino-Alto Adige, due to its potential to provide valuable insights into the relationship between sustainable business models and tourism regeneration. This region is characterized by a strong cooperative tradition, especially in rural and mountain areas, which facilitates the emergence of community-led initiatives (EURICSE, 2024; Sforzi & Borzaga, 2019). The valley community started recognizing the challenges related to living conditions in its territory and aimed to identify a sustainable business model that aligns with its community development goals. In this context, the community is considering the creation of a CBE as a way to retain enterprise value locally and ensure a fair redistribution of benefits among stakeholders.

We conducted seven semi-structured interviews (Rubin & Rubin, 2011). The interviewees were selected based on their active involvement in the envisioning and gestation phases of the CBE, including local administrators, representatives of community groups, and stakeholders from the housing and tourism sectors. Before the interviews, which were conducted in Italian and then translated into English, we requested the interviewees' explicit consent to record the interview; each interview lasted approximately 50 minutes and was conducted between April and September 2024. To ensure the validity and reliability of primary sources, we combined these interviews with information from secondary sources, including project reports, newspaper articles, and academic papers (Yin, 2017). We analyzed the data following the three stages of Gioia et al. (2013): the number of codes progressed from 51 first-order concepts to 12 second-order themes to 6 aggregate dimensions.

RESULTS

The CBE examined in this study adopts a cooperative structure, which aligns with the "repurposing" archetype of sustainable business models. The analysis highlighted the key features of the development process that the CBE is following in terms of antecedents, gestation process, and enterprise set-up (Valchovska & Watts, 2016).

Antecedents

Three main interrelated antecedents triggered the development of a CBE in the Vanoi Valley: valley depopulation, decrease of essential services, and increase in second homes.

Driven by an aging population and a decline in younger generations settling in the Vanoi Valley, valley depopulation emerged as a pressing issue. As interviewee 1 highlights, "the valley suffers from demographic fragility," and interviewee 6 emphasizes that "we are 1500 inhabitants in 7 hamlets, we are becoming 'extinct'". This demographic fragility reflects a broader trend of depopulation and aging, threatening both the economy and essential services as reported by respondent 6 "The population has aged, [...] in Caoria the average age is 48, in 1951 was 36 years." Addressing this crisis requires efforts to "regenerate the social fabric – lowering the average age by introducing new families" (interviewee 1). However, achieving this is not straightforward, as interviewee 2 points out the need "[...]to repopulate the mountain" and "the challenge is to make the owners understand this need." Without action, public and private services risk disappearing since, as explained by interviewee 1, "we must be aware that public and private services can continue to exist if there is a mass of not considering the need to [...] improve settlement of new families."

The survival of valley communities depends on maintaining a stable population, as even small changes can make a difference. Interviewee 2 points out that "even just adding 3 families per year allows the services (school, bar, etc.) to remain open." Basic services are essential to sustaining local life, as explained by interviewee 7, stating that "basic services, if lacking, impoverish the community itself." In some areas of the Vanoi Valley, the decline of basic services is even more evident, like in Caoria, where interviewee 6 recalls, "in 1987, it was something else, 350 people, a post office, a nursery, schools, various shops, bars, etc. two hotels, things worked. Now we have almost none of these services anymore, 1 hotel, 1 B&B, there is something, there are few of us." The closure of schools, in particular, accelerates the decline, as interviewee 5 explains: "if we keep a certain number of users, certain services remain; otherwise, services are destined to disappear (e.g. schools). And take away the schools, exponential fall." Without intervention, these valleys risk becoming places for retirees and second homes rather than active communities.

The third interrelated condition triggering the CBE's development is the increase in second homes, which represents a significant challenge in the Vanoi Valley, as it limits housing availability for permanent residents. Second homes dominate the housing market in some areas, making it difficult for new families to settle. As interviewee 1 points out, "some areas of the valley reach 70% of second homes (e.g., Zortea has 68%), all have over 50% of houses being second homes." One of the key issues in this respect is the large number of vacant houses that remain unused for most of the year. Indeed, according to interviewee 2, "there are more than 400 houses that are closed right now. We need to convince owners about the importance of letting families live in those houses." Young families are discouraged from settling in the valley without access to affordable and permanent housing, contributing to depopulation and the disappearance of essential services.

Gestation Process

The gestation process of the development of the CBE has been a challenging journey (see Fig. 6.1), involving various phases and stakeholders. It began in April 2023, with initial meetings held in the valley's hamlets to discuss with

Fig. 6.1. Gestation Process.
Source: Authors' elaboration.

the local community and gather input on local concerns. The first official meetings took place in Autumn 2023, forming three working groups focused on territory, housing, and tourism. Each group held two to three meetings and developed specific action plans, which were later consolidated into a broader presentation. Recognizing the need for institutional support, the project was then presented to the Province of Trento, emphasizing that local efforts alone would not be enough.

However, the project was temporarily put on hold due to the election campaign from October to December 2023, which also put all decision-making on hold. Further delays followed in early 2024 as leadership changes, council renewals, and new responsibilities took priority. By the summer of 2024, efforts resumed with an invitation to the Pro Loco, aiming to involve them in the process despite local political tensions. Finally, by autumn 2024, another formal presentation to the Province of Trento was scheduled, marking a crucial moment in seeking official funding to ensure the project's continuity.

Initial Vision: Tourism-driven Regeneration

The initial vision originated from the recognition that tourism in the Vanoi Valley was underdeveloped due to a lack of available and organized tourism infrastructure. As interviewee 1 explains, "The cooperative was initially born because there is no tourism project in the valley, and it is missing because there is a lack of tourism supply. The idea, therefore, is to give a touristic boost through something more organized." Instead of building new structures, the plan initially focused on revitalizing existing housing infrastructure, as interviewee 4 highlighted: "put in place accommodation facilities of apartments, which need renovation, which is empty [...], we do not create new cubic meters, we take properties and renovate them." To achieve this, the community turned toward the choice of a CBE model. One major advantage is that "the economic value of the cooperative returns to the members. The cooperative does not have to make a profit, the benefits must be invested in the community" (interviewee 1). This aligns with a long-standing local tradition of working together. However, shifting toward a cooperative mindset has not been easy. Interviewee 6 acknowledges, "creating a service cooperative is already a big step, defeating this mentality, we have always been very much on our own, each fraction." Despite these challenges, many see this model as the best solution for sustaining local businesses and services. As interviewee 5 puts it, "the community cooperative can give the possibility to maintain activities that otherwise would not be able to sustain themselves (mountain shop, services, and future for the valley), even in the tourism sector, it could give us good results. I struggle to see an alternative to a project like this." Therefore, the initial vision of the valley entails the development of a CBE that aims to address the challenges of the territory through a tourism development plan that helps revitalize and regenerate the economic and social fabric of the valley.

Shift of Focus: Community Needs and Demographic Sustainability

Initially, the CBE project was centered around tourism as a means of territorial regeneration. However, over time, the focus shifted from tourists to residents as the importance of addressing demographic challenges became clearer. As interviewee 1 explains, "These analyses have shifted the focus of the cooperative project from tourists to residents. At the beginning, the project had tourism in mind – tourism brings income – but along the way, we consolidated the importance of the demographic situation and therefore shifted the focus to the resident." While tourism remains relevant within the gestation process, interviewee 3 reinforces this shift, stating, "tourism may play a role, but it is not the priority." The real goal has been creating the conditions and services that make the area attractive for current and potential residents (interviewee 6).

Together with the new focus, the Vanoi Valley is still rediscovering the form of tourism that aligns with the local identity and supports the community. Rather than large-scale tourism, the valley focuses on slow, sustainable experiences that highlight nature, local culture, and traditions (interviewee 5). Interviewee 1 describes this vision as "a family-sized, slow stroll, food and wine traditions, semi-sporty, valley and mountain huts, lodges. The actions to be promoted must be consistent with the community." In addition, the community aims to attract tourists "who seek contact with the territory [...] and the local culture" (interviewee 1). Another interviewee emphasizes the importance of niche tourism that attracts visitors who truly appreciate the main characteristics of the valley: "nature, silence, walks, [...] having a type of tourist who appreciates the nature where I live as I do." By attracting a tourism segment that aligns with the territory, "one goal, for example, could be to transform some of these tourists into residents" (interviewee 3).

This approach also considers how tourism infrastructure is developed. The goal is not to create tourism accommodations and amenities that could exist anywhere, but rather to create a "tourism that does not become something disconnected from our past and present," and therefore tourism accommodations and amenities that are authentic to the valley (interviewee 4). This means increasing hospitality capacity to benefit the local economy, using existing family-owned properties rather than relying on outside investors (Interviewee 4). This increase remains within the limitations of local settings and refers to a desirable quantity identified by the community. Respondents advocate for sustainable growth, with interviewee 4 explaining that to be financially viable, a CBE should manage "20-30 tourist accommodations, working together with local businesses, farms, and restaurants, hiring local services, and keeping economic benefits within the valley."

Finally, tourism can be developed only based on existing essential local services. As interviewee 6 claimed, "we need to create services, and then we can talk about tourism. We are not interested in mass tourism, even at the hotel level [...]. First, we create the conditions, and then we can talk about the rest." This strategic shift ensures that tourism plays a supportive role in the broader process of destination regeneration and long-term community development.

Challenges in the Gestation Process: Participation Fatigue and Entrepreneurial Gaps

The initial excitement gradually faded during the gestation process, resulting in a significant decrease in local participation. Specifically, the gestation process encountered challenges related to the loss of enthusiasm and the need for a more concrete and entrepreneurial approach. One major issue has been the difficulty in maintaining participation: "Many of us started out, but now we are about ten. Every time new people came, and the mayor repeated everything, it was a bit of a waste of time, and people lost enthusiasm. It is the administration that dictates the process. We need to move on to the operational part" (interviewee 2). The slow progress and repetitive discussions caused frustration among participants, making it harder to keep up momentum. Another interviewee echoes this concern, saying, "at a certain point, after 3–4 meetings, I understood that we were still in a 'very working-class' part – I didn't see any concrete things" (interviewee 4). While enthusiasm was strong in the beginning, maintaining engagement over time has thus been difficult. Interviewee 4 notes that after the initial phase, "those who work there must have a job, people who dive into this thing need economic response. You can volunteer for a cultural association, not for a productive activity – either you work there, or you don't work there. If your head is somewhere else, the thing doesn't work." This highlights the need for a structured working scheme rather than relying purely on volunteer efforts.

Another major challenge was the lack of an entrepreneurial mindset and risk-taking culture. While the municipality can provide initial funding, interviewee 4 warns, "you can also start with the money from the municipality, but then you have to know how to walk on your own, or you will make a big flop." Similarly, interviewee 2 adds, "you can find funding to start, but after that, you have to stay on your feet, so the problem is not starting, but after a year, what happens?." The cooperative needs a long-term funding scheme model to ensure it does not collapse after the initial excitement fades.

Despite these difficulties, the project has laid an important foundation by conducting demographic and housing research and community meetings. Interviewee 1 explains, "we have held meetings of fractions – April 2023, and now we will repeat them in October 2024. We have done some research: demographic analysis, housing and real estate analysis." However, the challenge has been developing this research and discussions into tangible action and successful examples that can inspire confidence in the local community. Interviewee 2 says, "there is distrust; therefore, we need to show two successful experiences." Best practices from other valleys must thus be shown to restore motivation and participation.

Enterprise Set-up Phase

During the start-up phase, the approach to establishing the enterprise shifted from launching a cooperative immediately to first creating an association as a stepping stone. Interviewee 1 explains, "during this time, we also understood that it is more useful to start with an association that then, transforms into a cooperative, rather than starting immediately with the cooperative." This change allows for a more flexible structure in the beginning, focusing on organizing and guiding the project rather than immediately managing production. Interviewee 4 supports this decision, emphasizing that an association can act as a bridge guiding "them towards the cooperative. They understood that the cooperative has a production structure, they start with something that gives direction, it could also be a right choice." This change may help reduce the initial risks, as it allows time for planning, regaining community support, and testing ideas before transitioning into a fully operational cooperative. By starting with an association, the project can build a strong foundation so that it is structured for long-term sustainability when the cooperative is eventually formed.

The future role of the association is to build the foundation for the CBE while addressing key community challenges related to housing, funding, and the lack of professional expertise. One of its primary objectives is to secure provincial funds to renovate buildings, which is crucial for attracting new residents. Interviewee 1 explains, "provincial funds are needed for the renovation of buildings. On October 25th, the province will present what it intends to implement on this issue (interventions with 40% non-repayable funds)." These funds could support restoring unused homes and making them available for families interested in moving to the valley. Beyond housing, the association will also serve as a transitional phase before establishing the cooperative. The association relies on members' voluntary contributions, while the cooperative will require a more professional structure with expertise in finance, taxation, networking, law, and technical skills (interviewee 1).

CBEs as a Sustainable Business Model for Community and Destination Regeneration

The current "Vanoi futura" and future CBE "Cooperativa di comunità Valle del Vanoi" has the potential to represent a sustainable business model that supports the social sustainability of the Vanoi community. Indeed, the value proposition of the CBE prioritizes community development rather than economic profits through revitalizing current housing infrastructure to enhance the quality of life for current and future residents. Indeed, for the Vanoi Valley, the CBE needs to create value that remains in the community, as interviewee 2 said, "the economic value of the cooperative returns to the members. The cooperative does not have to make a profit; the benefits must be invested in the community." Tourism is considered a tool for attracting potential new residents that align with the values and culture of the community rather than the main priority. The value creation component lies in the focus on territorial

and destination regeneration, which requires the active participation of community stakeholders. The aim is to enhance the quality of life for residents by
developing new working opportunities that allow residents to live and work
in the territory and develop services that align with the community's needs.
Finally, the value capture of the CBE relates to generating revenue by renting
properties and tourist services that will be reinvested in the cooperative to
develop new projects and provide additional services for community members. This was confirmed by interviewee 5: "The income will be generated
by renting, hosting, providing tourist services [...] and reinvested in [...] new
innovative projects."

In this way, the priority of the association and future CBE remains the development of a business model that involves the creation of a system that guaran-
tees the economic and social well-being of the local community and promotes
sustainable tourism. Consequently, by means of a CBE, destination regeneration can be accomplished through community and territory regeneration.

DISCUSSION AND CONCLUSION

This chapter analyzes the Vanoi Valley and the process that led to approach a
CBE model, which represents a viable strategy for addressing the local critical challenges of depopulation, the disappearance of basic services, and loss
of social and economic fabric. The study reveals that the CBE can serve as a
sustainable community and territorial regeneration business model. However,
the findings are based on an early-stage initiative still in its gestation and pre-
startup phase. Further longitudinal research is needed to assess the long-term
viability of this model. Without intervention, the valley risks transforming
into a place primarily for seasonal visitors rather than an active, permanent
community. However, this process requires a delicate balance between long-
term vision and practical implementation to ensure sustainable growth and
stakeholder participation.

One of the most significant insights from the findings is prioritizing residents' needs over tourism development. While tourism remains an important
economic driver, it is secondary to the fundamental goal of attracting and
retaining residents. Initially, the gestation process focused on tourism as a
tool for territorial regeneration, yet the vision gradually shifted toward creating conditions conducive to permanent settlement. This transition underscores the realization that sustainable tourism cannot thrive without a stable
resident population (Cheung & Li, 2019; Khater & Faik, 2024). The shift
in focus from tourism-centered regeneration to community-based regeneration highlights the need for local services and stable housing options before

tourism can be effectively developed. In this way, the community is empowered to welcome the kind of tourist that aligns with local culture and traditions, a slow and sustainable tourist. This reorientation ensures that tourism becomes a complementary strategy rather than a primary objective.

This study contributes to the literature regarding the role of tourism in CBEs, showing that tourism can represent an important driver of destination regeneration. So far, the destination has regenerated the community's social fabric first. Our findings align with recent research emphasizing the primacy of community well-being as a prerequisite for regenerative tourism (Dredge, 2022; Suárez-Rojas et al., 2023). Moreover, it contributes to destination management, showing how community regeneration can help make tourism a tool to tackle depopulation. Indeed, promoting the destination to tourists in a way that aligns with local culture and values might turn some tourists into permanent residents who can contribute to enhancing local services.

REFERENCES

Aagaard, A. (2018). Identifying sustainable business models through sustainable value creation. In *Sustainable business models: Innovation, implementation and success* (pp. 1–24). Springer International Publishing.

Altinay, L., Sigala, M., & Waligo, V. (2016). Social value creation through tourism enterprise. *Tourism Management, 54*, 404–417.

Aquino, R. S. (2022). Community change through tourism and social entrepreneurship. *Annals of Tourism Research, 95*, 103442.

Awuzie, B., & McDermott, P. (2017). An abductive approach to qualitative built environment research: A viable system methodological exposé. *Qualitative Research Journal, 17*(4), 356–372.

Bacq, S., Hertel, C., & Lumpkin, G. T. (2022). Communities at the nexus of entrepreneurship and societal impact: A cross-disciplinary literature review. *Journal of Business Venturing, 37*(5), 106231.

Baldassarre, B., Calabretta, G., Bocken, N., & Jaskiewicz, T. (2017). Bridging sustainable business model innovation and user-driven innovation: A process for sustainable value proposition design. *Journal of Cleaner Production, 147*, 175–186.

Baxter, P., & Jack, S. (2008). Qualitative case study methodology: Study design and implementation for novice researchers. *The Qualitative Report, 13*(4), 544–559.

Bellato, L., & Pollock, A. (2025). Regenerative tourism: A state-of-the-art review. *Tourism Geographies, 27*(3–4), 558–567.

Bocken, N. M., & Geradts, T. H. (2020). Barriers and drivers to sustainable business model innovation: Organization design and dynamic capabilities. *Long Range Planning, 53*(4), 101950.

Bocken, N. M., Short, S. W., Rana, P., & Evans, S. (2014). A literature and practice review to develop sustainable business model archetypes. *Journal of Cleaner Production, 65*, 42–56.

Buratti, N., Sillig, C., & Albanese, M. (2022). Community enterprise, community entrepreneurship and local development: A literature review on three decades of empirical studies and theorizations. *Entrepreneurship & Regional Development, 34*(5–6), 376–401.

Cheung, K. S., & Li, L. H. (2019). Understanding visitor–resident relations in overtourism: Developing resilience for sustainable tourism. *Journal of Sustainable Tourism, 27*(8), 1197–1216.

Creswell, J. W., & Poth, C. N. (2016). *Qualitative inquiry and research design: Choosing among five approaches*. Sage.

Daskalaki, M., Hjorth, D., & Mair, J. (2015). Are entrepreneurship, communities, and social transformation related? *Journal of Management Inquiry, 24*(4), 419–423.

Della Lucia, M., & Trunfio, M. (2018). The role of the private actor in cultural regeneration: Hybridizing cultural heritage with creativity in the city. *Cities, 82*, 35–44.

Deschamps, B., & Slitine, R. (2024). The creation of collective enterprises for social impact: An agency perspective. *International Small Business Journal, 42*(1), 14–38.

Dolezal, C., & Novelli, M. (2022). Power in community-based tourism: Empowerment and partnership in Bali. *Journal of Sustainable Tourism, 30*(10), 2352–2370.

Dredge, D. (2022). Regenerative tourism: Transforming mindsets, systems and practices. *Journal of Tourism Futures, 8*(3), 269–281.

EURICSE. (2024). *Le imprese di comunità in Italia. Tratti distintivi e traiettorie di sviluppo* (Euricse Research Reports No. 36/2024).

Ferretti, V. (2021). Framing territorial regeneration decisions: Purpose, perspective and scope. *Land Use Policy, 102*, 105279.

Geissdoerfer, M., Vladimirova, D., & Evans, S. (2018). Sustainable business model innovation: A review. *Journal of Cleaner Production, 198*, 401–416.

Gioia, D. A., Corley, K. G., & Hamilton, A. L. (2013). Seeking qualitative rigor in inductive research: Notes on the Gioia methodology. *Organizational Research Methods, 16*(1), 15–31.

Higgins-Desbiolles, F., Carnicelli, S., Krolikowski, C., Wijesinghe, G., & Boluk, K. (2019). Degrowing tourism: Rethinking tourism. *Journal of Sustainable Tourism.*

Hussain, A. (2021). A future of tourism industry: Conscious travel, destination recovery and regenerative tourism. *Journal of Sustainability and Resilience, 1*(1), 5.

Khater, M., Ibrahim, O., Sayed, M. N. E., & Faik, M. (2024). Legal frameworks for sustainable tourism: Balancing environmental conservation and economic development. *Current Issues in Tourism*, 1–22.

Lumpkin, G. T., Bacq, S., & Pidduck, R. J. (2018). Where change happens: Community-level phenomena in social entrepreneurship research. *Journal of Small Business Management, 56*(1), 24–50.

Mitzinneck, B. C., Coenen, J., Noseleit, F., & Rupietta, C. (2024). Impact creation approaches of community-based enterprises: A configurational analysis of enabling conditions. *Journal of Business Venturing, 39*(6), 106420.

Morrison, C., Ramsey, E., & Bond, D. (2017). The role of social entrepreneurs in developing community resilience in remote areas. *Journal of Enterprising Communities: People and Places in the Global Economy, 11*(1), 95–112.

Peredo, A. M., & Chrisman, J. J. (2006). Toward a theory of community-based enterprise. *Academy of Management Review, 31*(2), 309–328.

Peredo, A. M., & Chrisman, J. J. (2017). Conceptual foundations: Community-based enterprise and community development. In *Entrepreneurial neighbourhoods* (pp. 151–178). Edward Elgar Publishing.

Renkert, T. (2019). 05| An approach to understand the subura: The "Argiletum" and its function between public and private spaces in Rome. *Public| Private*, 102.

Rocca, L. H. D., & Zielinski, S. (2022). Community-based tourism, social capital, and governance of post-conflict rural tourism destinations: The case of Minca, Sierra Nevada de Santa Marta, Colombia. *Tourism Management Perspectives, 43*, 100985.

Rubin, H. J., & Rubin, I. S. (2011). *Qualitative interviewing: The art of hearing data*. Sage.

Scheyvens, R. (1999). Ecotourism and the empowerment of local communities. *Tourism Management, 20*(2), 245–249.

Sforzi, J., & Borzaga, C. (2019). *Imprese di comunità e riconoscimento giuridico: È davvero necessaria una nuova legge?* Impresa Sociale.

Sharma, A., & Shenoy, S. S. (2024). Bibliometric portrait of the theory of community-based enterprise: evolution and future directions. *Cogent Business & Management, 11*(1), 2315685.

Suárez-Rojas, C., Hernández, M. M. G., & León, C. J. (2023). Sustainability in whale-watching: A literature review and future research directions based on regenerative tourism. *Tourism Management Perspectives, 47*, 101120.

Valchovska, S., & Watts, G. (2016). Interpreting community-based enterprise: A case study from rural Wales. *Journal of Social Entrepreneurship*.

Walzer, N. (Ed.). (2021). *Community owned businesses: International entrepreneurship, finance, and economic development*. Routledge.

Yang, M., Evans, S., Vladimirova, D., & Rana, P. (2017). Value uncaptured perspective for sustainable business model innovation. *Journal of Cleaner Production, 140*, 1794–1804.

Yin, R. K. (2003). *Designing case studies*. Sage.

Yin, R. K. (2017). *Case study research and applications* (Vol. 6). Sage Publications.

Zielinski, S., Kim, S. I., Botero, C., & Yanes, A. (2020). Factors that facilitate and inhibit community-based tourism initiatives in developing countries. *Current Issues in Tourism, 23*(6), 723–739.

7

SOCIAL INNOVATION AND NETWORKING IN TOURISM: INSIGHTS FROM CASE STUDIES IN NORTHEAST ITALY

MAURIZIO BUSACCA[a], SILVIA SACCHETTI[b] AND OLGA TZATZADAKI[a]

[a]University Ca' Foscari of Venice, Italy
[b]University of Trento, Italy

ABSTRACT

This chapter explores the role of networks in social innovation in tourism (SIT), focusing on their capacity to foster inclusive and sustainable practices. Drawing on the concept of structural embeddedness, it highlights how networks mediate between individual actions and institutional frameworks. Using a mixed-methods approach, including literature review, desk research, and 39 qualitative interviews, the study analyzes two case studies: Bassano del Grappa and the Trentino province. Findings show that networks, particularly those linked to festivals and local heritage, enhance collaboration, trust, and innovation across urban and rural contexts. Brokers and stakeholder engagement emerge as key elements in shaping effective and resilient networks. The research underscores the importance of balancing inclusive and specialized initiatives and calls for policies that support community-driven collaboration. Understanding how networks evolve and generate

both tangible and intangible outcomes contributes to advancing
SIT as a tool for local regeneration and long-term community
development. The chapter concludes by highlighting the theoretical
and practical implications.

Keywords: Social innovation; sustainable tourism; networks;
festivals; community participation

INTRODUCTION

The chapter explores the intersection of SIT, focusing on the role that networks play in fostering innovation within local contexts. SIT is an evolving
field, with significant implications for both social inclusion and sustainable
tourism practices. Theoretical perspectives on SIT highlight the importance of
networks as critical drivers for innovation, bridging the gap between individual actors and broader institutional frameworks. Drawing from the concept of
structural embeddedness, the paper argues that networks not only shape individual actions but also influence the outcomes of social innovation by mediating between micro-level behavior and macro-level institutional structures.

The research examines two distinct geographical areas – Bassano del
Grappa and the broader Trentino province – as case studies for understanding
how networks operate in regions varying degrees of social and institutional support. Bassano del Grappa, with its rich cultural heritage and growing
tourism sector, offers a compelling case for studying how local actors, ranging from businesses to community organizations, create networks that support evolving sustainable tourism practices based on the valorization of local
cultural heritage and social inclusion. The Trentino province, renowned for
its natural beauty and established tourism infrastructure, provides a different perspective. Here, the focus is specifically on festivals, which serve as an
important focal point for the research. Interviews with festival organizers and
related stakeholders in the Trentino area offer valuable insights into how networks are formed, maintained, and leveraged to create innovative cultural
and tourism experiences. Festivals in this region play a central role in connecting local actors and facilitating collaboration, making them an ideal case for
studying the operational dynamics of networks in tourism.

Through these case studies, the paper explores how networks influence
the adoption of SIT, highlighting the importance of both formal and informal
networks, the role of brokers in connecting disconnected actors, and how the
density of networks impacts cooperation, trust, and innovation. The findings

offer a deeper understanding of how local networks in tourism can be har-nessed to foster social innovation, creating a more sustainable and inclusive tourism industry in both Bassano del Grappa and the Trentino province.

FRAMING STAKEHOLDER INVOLVEMENT WITHIN SOCIAL INNOVATION

Social innovation and stakeholder involvement are essential for regenerating local contexts, revitalizing communities, and promoting sustainable develop-ment. Social innovation starts by identifying community-specific challenges, such as economic decline or social inequality, and developing tailored solu-tions to address them (Moulaert et al., 2013; Nicholls & Murdock, 2012). By involving community members in creating new services or initiatives, social innovation fosters empowerment, resilience, and long-term sustainability (Franz et al., 2012). It also contributes to economic revitalization by support-ing community-based enterprises and social entrepreneurship, which create jobs and attract investment (Defourny & Nyssens, 2010). Furthermore, social innovation enhances cultural and social revitalization by preserving local tra-ditions, boosting community pride, and fostering cohesion (Manzini, 2015).

Stakeholder involvement complements social innovation by ensuring that diverse local actors – residents, businesses, and local authorities – are included in decision-making (Freeman, 2010; Greenwood, 2007). Involving stake-holders from the start ensures that regeneration initiatives are supported by the community and are more likely to be sustained over time (Reed et al., 2009). The collaborative approach between social innovation and stakehold-er involvement ensures that solutions are deeply rooted in the community's needs, making them more relevant and impactful (Cajaiba-Santana, 2014). Shared ownership and responsibility enhance the success and sustainability of these initiatives (Sørensen & Torfing, 2011).

Key variables drive the success of social innovation, including identify-ing community needs, engaging stakeholders, and mobilizing resources such as finance, human capital, and material assets (Mulgan, 2006). Engag-ing diverse stakeholders ensures that solutions align with the community's desires, increasing acceptance and the likelihood of successful implementa-tion (Sacchetti & Borzaga, 2021). Collaborations across public institutions, private enterprises, and community groups are crucial for pooling resources and expertise (Sørensen & Torfing, 2011).

Social innovation, when combined with stakeholder involvement, creates a framework that fosters holistic regeneration. The integration of grassroots initiatives, organizational competencies, and a deep understanding of community needs promotes economic sustainability and new ways of living and thinking. Analyzing this process from a social innovation perspective reveals how stakeholder involvement fosters heterarchical organizations (Stark, 2009), where decision-making and resources are distributed across networks of actors and the local community (Da Roit & Busacca, 2024). Studying these networks and their interactions with the community helps understand the operational mechanisms underlying successful social innovation.

METHODOLOGY

The research methodology adopted in this study is a mixed methods approach that triangulates literature review, secondary data, and qualitative data, all centered around the concept of networks, particularly within the context of SIT in the Bassano del Grappa territory and the Trentino province. The study began with a theoretical exploration of the topic of SIT, focusing on the main trends and emerging micro-focus areas within the sector. This initial phase involved the collection of key theoretical frameworks and concepts, which provided a foundation for understanding how networks play a role in driving innovation and collaboration. The exploration also included identifying critical challenges and opportunities, shedding light on the evolving dynamics and the impact of networked collaborations in the tourism industry.

In addition to the theoretical exploration, a desk analysis was conducted, examining institutional reports on tourism in these specific geographical areas (DMP Terre Vicentine, 2016; Veneto Tourism Strategic Plan 2022–2024, 2022; DMO Veneto regional orientations, 2024). This helped to identify regional policies, strategies, and challenges that influence network dynamics and the broader context of tourism development. The desk research also provided a concrete backdrop for the empirical findings, grounding them in the real-world context of Bassano del Grappa and Trentino.

The third component of the methodology involved in-depth interviews with local stakeholders engaged in SIT initiatives and the valorization of local cultural heritage. For the Bassano del Grappa area and its surroundings, 12 interviews were analyzed through their representatives. For the Trentino region, 3 festival organizations located in both rural and urban areas were involved in an in-depth interview process with internal and external stakeholders (27 interviews). These interviews were designed to gather first-hand insights into how networks operate on the ground, with a particular focus on how actors collaborate, share resources, and co-create initiatives around social innovation and local heritage. The representatives and key witnesses of these initiatives provided valuable perspectives on the challenges they face and the strategies they employ to build and sustain effective networks, emphasizing the importance of trust, shared goals, and long-term cooperation.

CASE STUDIES

We have chosen the two case studies we are going to introduce in this section for their capacity to explore the relationship between social innovation, networks, and local communities. The first case, Bassano del Grappa, focuses on the functioning of the network per se; the Trentino case delves into the relationship between network and local community.

BASSANO DEL GRAPPA

In the Bassano del Grappa town and surroundings, social networks play a crucial role in shaping community initiatives, fostering collaboration, and driving local development. The following section illustrates how both formal and informal networks have contributed to the area's growth and vibrancy. Through interviews, we uncover the importance of creating and nurturing relationships between local actors, businesses, and cultural organizations. The section highlights how the strength of these networks, built on trust and shared goals, enables innovation, enhances community engagement, and creates a lasting impact. The insights shared offer a deeper understanding of how Bassano's network-driven culture contributes to the greater area's dynamic and interconnected ecosystem.

THE POLICY CONTEXT

Over the years, Bassano del Grappa has developed a distinct and original network DNA, which has been significantly fostered by projects such as the OperaEstate Festival and various community-driven initiatives. This unique characteristic of the city, built on collaboration and shared values, has evolved through various activities and programs, with the Festival playing a central role in supporting these efforts.

The OperaEstate Festival, founded in 1981, has been instrumental in fostering a cultural network that spans the entire region. By working in close collaboration with local institutions, the Festival has helped to strengthen the city's cultural policies and promote local initiatives. It is not just an artistic event but also a catalyst for creating connections between the public, private, and cultural sectors. The Festival has also demonstrated the city's long-standing commitment to cultural innovation, as evidenced by its collaboration with several local administrations over its 34 years. These partnerships have created a lasting impact on the community and continue to enhance Bassano's reputation as a cultural hub.

Furthermore, the Musei Civici di Bassano, with their rich history and collections, have also played a role in solidifying the city's cultural policies and its connection with the broader community. The museum's continuous expansion and community donations reflect a commitment to preserving and sharing Bassano's heritage, supporting both local pride and cultural tourism.

In addition to these institutions, other initiatives have contributed to the city's collaborative spirit. For instance, in 1999, the Cittadinanza e Volontariato initiative was launched, engaging local youth in projects that would later empower them to take on leadership roles in various sectors of Bassano, such as welfare, public services, businesses, and local communities. Similarly, in 2003, the Festival supported the creation of the Casa sull'Albero association, a collaboration that brought together volunteers, local leaders, and citizens to build a space for children and families in need. This was followed by La Terra di Mezzo, a network of 45 local associations aimed at connecting young people to hands – on volunteer work, further enhancing the sense of community in the area.

These initiatives, alongside the Festival's activities, exemplify how Bassano's cultural and social networks have flourished thanks to continuous collaboration. From school programs fostering inter-school communication to fundraising campaigns supporting local projects, the presence of OperaEstate Festival has helped reinforce these local alliances. It has contributed to creating a cultural environment where community-driven solutions are nurtured and supported by strong partnerships across different sectors, including education, business, and social services.

NETWORKING IN BASSANO

As stated by Interviewee 1: "You should imagine this place a bit like a forest, where what is visible are the trees. [...] we like to represent ourselves this way, saying that, in reality, the vitality of this place lies in the roots, which are the daily exchanges between the different realities. And it's precisely there that the true creativity and generativity of the projects are found." The interviewee highlights that the network is a living ecosystem, where collaboration and exchange generate creativity. The complexity and richness of the network emerge only when viewed through a collective perspective.

According to Interviewee 2: "This metaphor, suggested to me by a craftswoman and artist, deeply struck me, so much so that I am adopting it as a description of our work. We are 'weavers of relationships', a material just as valuable, if you will, as high craftsmanship, which is delicate and precious." Networks, like relationships, require care and attention to weave meaningful and valuable connections. This view underscores that networks are not just about visible connections but about deeper, more meaningful bonds that create real value.

Interviewee 3 provides another example: "Do you know those grants that, starting from hotels, end up with twenty electric bikes? So, I call the nearest bike shop and propose renting the bikes to tourists. At what price? 25 euros an hour, I say to them, I agree at 25 euros. You don't buy the bikes, you don't think about maintenance, but you create a network." This example demonstrates how collaboration between local businesses, like bike shops, restaurants, and tourist attractions, creates a synergistic ecosystem. The network allows for resource-sharing and interaction without the need for ownership or direct management, resulting in a more dynamic, sustainable approach to tourism and business.

Shared goals and mutual interests are vital to a network's success. Interviewee 4 notes: "If there is adherence to the goals and a strong interest in the actions that realize them, these generate positive impacts on the work and organization of each member. Otherwise, participating in the network would become truly burdensome. More than internal difficulties, challenges are often found outside the network." When members align with common objectives, the network becomes more sustainable and effective, but external challenges like a lack of support from institutions can hinder success.

Interviewee 5 reflects on the collaborative culture in Bassano: "In my opinion, the most general answer is that Bassano, and the Bassano area in general, has a rather unique and original network DNA compared to many other areas. [...] I believe our presence in the territory over the years has nonetheless facilitated and strengthened this characteristic." Bassano's strong network culture has been built over time through continuous collaboration, involving local actors such as businesses, cultural institutions, and community-driven initiatives. This collaboration has created a fertile environment for relationships, trust, and cooperation, making the network resilient and adaptable.

Interviewee 5 continues: "Being, so to speak, genetically oriented towards the concept of networks, for us it is something natural, almost spontaneous. [...] one of our most appreciated 'creations' is the project 'Ci sto Affare Fatica.' In just a few years, we created it, we really committed ourselves, and little by little we faded from the spotlight, but today 'Ci sto' has become a public asset of the territory." This example illustrates how the network transcends individual efforts, creating a collective, shared value. The project evolved into a public asset, demonstrating how collaboration and community involvement can lead to long-lasting impact. The approach emphasizes that networks must continually grow, innovate, and expand rather than remain static.

Interviewee 6 discusses the network as a system that includes both formal structures (like schools and families) and informal elements (like markets and entertainment spaces): "The fundamental idea is that connecting these diverse elements creates a support system that can help address issues faced by young people. Despite challenges, this network has been essential in fostering volunteerism and supporting individuals dedicated to the cause." This network is critical for building community-driven initiatives and addressing collective needs effectively.

The insights from the interviewees highlight the crucial role of networks in driving innovation, collaboration, and community development. Tight-knit networks, based on trust and shared norms, foster smooth collaboration, while looser networks encourage new ideas. Brokers – individuals who connect different parts of the network – are essential for facilitating collaboration and creating positive change, guiding resources and opportunities through the system.

The deeply embedded collaborative culture in Bassano, as pointed out by Interviewee 5, shows how networks are an instinctive part of the social fabric, with projects like "Ci sto Affare Fatica" thriving due to mutual support and shared responsibility. Interviewee 1 emphasizes that "the vitality of this place lies in the roots, which are the daily exchanges between the different realities. And it's precisely there that the true creativity and generativity of the projects are found." Dense networks create a foundation of trust that allows projects to come to life, while looser networks, as seen in local tourism initiatives, foster innovation, as demonstrated by Interviewee 3.

Effective networks rely on ongoing engagement, collaboration, and external support from institutions and the broader community. The role of brokers is crucial in maintaining cohesion and the success of networks. In conclusion, networks are dynamic systems that enable collaboration, resource sharing, and the achievement of collective goals, based on the commitment of participants and institutional support.

TRENTINO PROVINCE – THE CULTURAL POLICY CONTEXT

In the Trentino case, the meritorious value of culture is recognized by the 1987 law on cultural promotion and subsequently by the provincial law on cultural activities 15/2007. Civil society is given a special proactive role. It is, in fact, by empowering civil society organizations that the norm aims to implement a principle of participation in the development of culture. A key practical implication of this principle is the development of actions toward the participatory planning, coordination, and evaluation of cultural activities, together with an emphasis on the economic sustainability of cultural organizations, stressing public support as well as the autonomous role of cultural organizations in developing cultural entrepreneurial capacity. There is, in other words, the promotion of both community engagement and of a cultural industry attitude. This law has provided the normative context for the development of cultural organizations, which fall within the realm of the social and solidarity economy, including both voluntary organizations, foundations, cooperatives of artists, as well as (more rarely) social enterprises. Moreover, it has supported community competences that in large part already existed within voluntary associations such as brass bands, choirs, cultural heritage associations, and amateur theatre companies. From the point of view of distributional effects, it has supported cultural services in multiple and remote locations, rather than focusing on a few (urban) centers. Cultural activities of local relevance are given special attention. Article 8 addresses this point, emphasizing the need to identify, within the community, the local cultural and creative venues and networks "that can integrate the different forms of cultural and artistic expression of the residents and for the participation of cultural operators in the enhancement of local creativity."

FESTIVAL ORGANIZATIONS

The festivals analyzed focus on performing arts, music, and audiovisual media. Three festivals were considered: Contavalle, located in the rural Cembra Valley, and two urban festivals in Rovereto: Oriente Occidente (an international dance festival) and RAM (an archaeological film festival). Contavalle aims to regenerate community identity amidst challenges like depopulation and the decline of the local porphyry industry. The urban festivals focus on specific cultural interests and also engage in cultural and creative management activities, fostering local community connections and contributing to a cohesive social fabric. These festivals enhance synergies with institutions, increasing opportunities for local and external partnerships through the search for funding.

The key competencies identified for successful festival management include community engagement (especially in rural areas), economic and organizational skills, and proficiency in communication, marketing, and competitive selection for funding. Festival organizers express confidence in their ability to secure and manage both public and private funding for project implementation and sustainability. Over time, these cultural organizations have increased their fundraising efforts through local and national funding, which has been crucial for sustaining activities and events beyond the festival's peak period.

CONNECTIVITY WITH LOCAL BUSINESSES AND CIVIL SOCIETY ORGANIZATIONS

The network perspective suggested by the local cultural policy reinforces mutually supportive strategies, which are again incentivized by the public resources available for joint projects and by community organizations' capabilities to design and implement joint projects. The interplay between the pillar organizations of this cultural policy has emerged through the events and activities that have been developed over time. Festival events, for example, are often produced not by one single organization but through the partnership of multiple associations and with the cooperation between two or more local authorities. The president of one of the Festivals commented on the collaborative linkages with private citizens and volunteers, as well as with local associations, who represent the social capital of the place. Another festival manager observed the relevance of cooperation with local associations and cultural institutions. The production of events is also beneficial for young professionals and artisans who can contribute their work to the staging of events, and it also creates opportunities for small hospitality businesses. However, the involvement of small entrepreneurs also has another meaning related to a sense of belonging to the community. One local entrepreneur observes: "The need for community made me gladly accept the opportunity to participate, and in fact, I have always done so willingly. Participating in initiatives like those of RAM or Oriente Occidente is not a commercial endeavor – it's not done for promotional or economic reasons. There might be some return, but it is relatively minor."

COMMUNITY INVOLVEMENT AND MULTIPLE RELATIONSHIPS

The Contavalle Festival, located in the Cembra Valley and coordinated by the Puntodoc association, operates in a rural, isolated area. It combines high and popular culture and engages the community through participatory theater and decision-making activities throughout the year. Artists conduct listening sessions with locals to incorporate their stories into performances, fostering inclusivity. Collaborations with art companies, volunteers, community associations, and local businesses are central to the festival's success. Support from municipalities, regional institutions, and national partners helps sustain the festival's community-driven approach. The artistic director plays a pivotal role in engaging locals and ensuring the festival's relevance. Puntodoc has been nurturing these values since 2011.

In contrast, the urban festivals RAM and Oriente Occidente cater to niche communities with educational goals. Oriente Occidente, established in 1981, was created by a group of professionals in Rovereto passionate about dance. It has since grown internationally, addressing themes like migration, rights, and sustainable development. In 2003, it expanded to include production, training, and dance culture promotion, and it is now part of the European Dancehouse Network. The festival also engages local communities through dance projects and supports young choreographers from Trentino.

The RAM Film Festival, focused on archeology and cultural heritage, is more community-oriented, engaging a diverse audience with a range of activities, including workshops and masterclasses. It has a strong international presence, with past editions attracting figures from 20 countries. Both urban festivals are more globally focused compared to Contavalle's locally rooted approach.

DIVERSITY OF APPROACHES TO COMMUNITY INVOLVEMENT AND VALUE CREATION FOR COMMUNITIES

Despite the diversities of approach toward the community of the three in – depth cases, overall, if we consider all the 16 festivals, we could observe that festivals generally tend to use culture as a tool for education and skills development, on one hand, and for participation, relationships, and the promotion of community identity, on the other hand. They aim to create both personal and collective benefits, primarily of an intangible nature.

Their cultural activities activate a community's vitality in various ways, depending on the territorial and social context, as well as on organizational aims and choices. In rural settings, the adaptive and emergent nature of cultural initiatives, following engagement with the community members on the definition of activities and interests, proves to be essential. In urban contexts, festivals are more exclusively shaped by expert groups and cater to more specific communities of interest. However, through the diversification of activities, they still aim to create broader cultural exchanges, at least in terms of audience engagement.

On one hand, there are predominantly inclusive festivals where communities actively contribute or are consulted in defining the content. This does not usually lead to localism but rather leverages high culture as a tool to enhance popular culture and address local needs. On the other hand, some festivals have adopted an international approach from the outset, with the goal of establishing themselves as cultural enterprises recognized as key players in their field. These festivals cater to niche groups by promoting high culture, focusing on capacity-building for specific audiences, and indirectly generating positive external effects for the broader community. The skills developed within this framework enable the creation of cutting-edge expertise and innovative projects for targeted social groups.

CONCLUSION

The cases presented above allow us to highlight two key findings. First, local networks take forms that depend on their institutional and social context. In this sense, the presence of public policies that continually act to foster the creation of networks is an important resource because it contributes to creating a system of relations that is more prone to building partnerships and trust.

In Bassano, networks function as dynamic ecosystems grounded in trust, reciprocity, and shared purpose. Local actors – such as artisans, educators, and cultural operators – foster micro-regeneration by activating both dense and flexible ties. Their actions are sustained by a culture of collaboration and the presence of brokers who connect diverse initiatives and translate local knowledge into shared opportunities. These networks are not passive contexts but active infrastructures of care and innovation, essential for inclusive and sustainable development (Da Roit & Busacca, 2024).

Second, involving local communities in networks enables people and organizations to build cultural and social inclusion pathways that reinforce local resources and make territories more dynamic and innovative. The Trentino case study, based on 16 cultural festivals, shows how events can enhance education, identity, and civic participation. Rural festivals often emerge from community involvement, while urban ones are more curated and audience-specific. Both, however, contribute to social vitality and cultural exchange. A balance between inclusive, grassroots events and specialized festivals is key to fostering both local engagement and broader cultural dialogue (Sacchetti, 2015).

In both cases, regarding networks, they are essential for fostering community development, innovation, and collaboration. Their success depends on continuous exchanges of ideas, resources, and support. Networks thrive when participants align around common goals, creating benefits such as trust, community vitality, and social capital. However, a lack of commitment can hinder their success (Sacchetti & Borzaga, 2021).

Future research should delve deeper into understanding the temporal evolution of networks, particularly within community and cultural contexts. This includes examining how networks respond to shifting community needs, emerging challenges, and changing socio-economic environments. A dynamic approach is necessary to trace how relationships within networks strengthen or weaken over time, how new actors are integrated, and how roles such as brokers adapt to facilitate evolving forms of collaboration. Additionally, research should address the conditions that enable networks to remain inclusive and resilient, especially in contexts where resources and trust are limited (Kazepov, 2008). Evaluating the sustainability of these networks involves not only tracking their immediate outputs but also their long-term outcomes in terms of community empowerment, shared governance, and social innovation (Heidenreich & Aurich-Beerheide, 2014; Sacchetti & Sugden, 2009). This line of inquiry will provide valuable insights into the effectiveness of networks in promoting equitable development and offer practical frameworks for designing and supporting durable, community-oriented organizational ecosystems (Da Roit & Busacca, 2024; Kazepov & Cefalo, 2022).

On a practical level, the findings highlight the need for policies that foster not only inclusive networks but also those that support specialized functions within communities (Sacchetti & Borzaga, 2021). Particular attention should be paid to brokers and to mechanisms of external institutional support, which are vital for maintaining healthy and adaptive networks (Sacchetti, 2015). At the same time, it is essential to encourage forms of enterprise and cultural organization that are generative for both communities and territories – models of governance and access that are inclusive, responsive to local needs, and oriented toward shared benefits rather than the appropriation of value by a few (Sacchetti, 2015). This can be facilitated through co-programming processes between public and private actors and by promoting initiatives that intensify meaningful interactions among local stakeholders (Sacchetti & Sugden,

2009). These interactions build mutual understanding, trust, and cooperation, forming the social foundations necessary for effective network work. Without these conditions, networks may become inefficient or even counterproductive (Sacchetti & Borzaga, 2021), risking extractive uses of local resources rather than fostering shared, community-based development.

REFERENCES

Cajaiba-Santana, G. (2014). Social innovation: Moving the field forward. A conceptual framework. *Technological Forecasting and Social Change*, 82, 42–51.

Da Roit, B., & Busacca, M. (2024). Street-level netocracy: Rules, discretion and professionalism in a network-based intervention. *International Journal of Sociology and Social Policy*, 44(3–4), 296–310.

Defourny, J., & Nyssens, M. (2010). Conceptions of social enterprise and social entrepreneurship in Europe and the United States: Convergences and divergences. *Journal of Social Entrepreneurship*, 1(1), 32–53.

Franz, H.-W., Hochgerner, J., & Howaldt, J. (Eds.). (2012). *Challenge social innovation: Potentials for business, social entrepreneurship, welfare, and civil society*. Springer.

Freeman, R. E. (2010). *Strategic management: A stakeholder approach*. Cambridge University Press.

Greenwood, M. (2007). Stakeholder engagement: Beyond the myth of corporate responsibility. *Journal of Business Ethics*, 74(4), 315–327.

Heidenreich, M., & Aurich-Beerheide, P. (2014). European worlds of inclusive activation: The organisational challenges of coordinated service provision. *International Journal of Social Welfare*, 23, S6–S22.

Kazepov, Y. (2008). The subsidiarization of social policies: Actors, processes and impacts. Some reflections on the Italian case from a European perspective. *European Societies*, 10(2), 247–273.

Kazepov, Y. A. K., & Cefalo, R. (2022). The territorial dimension of social investment in Europe. In *The handbook of urban social policies: International perspectives on multilevel governance and local welfare*.

Manzini, E. (2015). *Design, when everybody designs: An introduction to design for social innovation*. MIT Press.

Moulaert, F., MacCallum, D., Mehmood, A., & Hamdouch, A. (Eds.). (2013). *The international handbook on social innovation: Collective action, social learning and transdisciplinary research*. Edward Elgar Publishing.

Mulgan, G. (2006). The process of social innovation. *Innovations: Technology, Governance, Globalization, 1*(2), 145–162.

Nicholls, A., & Murdock, A. (Eds.). (2012). *Social innovation: Blurring boundaries to reconfigure markets*. Springer.

Reed, M. S., Evely, A. C., Cundill, G., Fazey, I., Glass, J., Laing, A., Newig, J., Parrish, B., Prell, C., Raymond, C., & Stringer, L. C. (2009). What is social learning? *Ecology and Society, 15*(4), Article 4. http://www.jstor.org/stable/26268235

Sacchetti, S. (2015). Inclusive and exclusive social preferences: A Deweyan framework to explain governance heterogeneity. *Journal of Business Ethics, 126*, 473–485.

Sacchetti, S., & Borzaga, C. (2021). The foundations of the public organisation: Governance failure and the problem of external effects. *Journal of Management and Governance, 25*(3), 731–758.

Sacchetti, S., & Sugden, R. (2009). The organization of production and its publics: Mental proximity, market and hierarchies. *Review of Social Economy, 67*(3), 289–311.

Sørensen, E., & Torfing, J. (2011). Enhancing collaborative innovation in the public sector. *Administration & Society, 43*(8), 842–868.

Stark, D. (2009). *The sense of dissonance: Accounts of worth in economic life*. Princeton University Press.

Part IV

REGENERATIVE BUSINESS MODELS FOR SUSTAINABLE PLACE DEVELOPMENT

8

RETHINKING CULTURAL HERITAGE IN PLACEMAKING: FROM PRESERVATION TO REGENERATIVE DEVELOPMENT IN CASTEL CAMPO

MARIA DELLA LUCIA°, GIULIA DORE°, STEFAN LAZIC° AND
MARINA CLERICI RASINI[b]

°University of Trento, Italy
[b]Castel Campo, Italy

ABSTRACT

Contemporary placemaking increasingly focuses on managing bio-regional and participatory processes that integrate cultural landscapes, human–nature relationships, ecological health, and lived experiences, while remaining open to external influences and creative reinterpretation of place. Cultural heritage plays a key role in contemporary placemaking, moving beyond static preservation toward dynamic, future-oriented place regeneration. This shift is particularly relevant in peripheral areas, where placemaking must navigate challenges but also holds potential for alternative, place-based development models. The chapter explores the role of cultural heritage in placemaking through the Castel Campo case study, a historic, family-run, and women-led estate in Trentino, Italy. The study highlights how a hybrid business model grounded in respect for time, place, and community enabled regenerative development by integrating living heritage, regenerative agriculture, and social *care. It illustrates how cultural heritage management can bridge historical continuity and contemporary experimentation to support innovative and inclusive forms of placemaking.*

Keywords: Placemaking; cultural heritage; regenerative development; family-run enterprise; Castel Campo

INTRODUCTION

In recent decades, *placemaking* has emerged as a prominent, interdisciplinary framework for rethinking the relationship between people and the places they inhabit, even temporarily (Lew, 2017). Emerging from late 20th-century urban design and planning, placemaking has evolved into a holistic, participatory approach rooted in living systems (Lew, 2017; Silberberg et al., 2013). At its core, placemaking seeks to create not only functional or aesthetic spaces but places that are healthy, meaningful, accessible, inclusive, and resilient, where people enjoy living, working, interacting, and having meaningful experiences.

Today, placemaking must navigate a landscape marked by complex societal transitions. Recent global crises have deepened socio-ecological inequalities (Rodríguez-Pose, 2018), contributing to rising social tensions, displacement, and vulnerability. One key expression of this inequality is the growing divide between urban centers and peripheral areas. Metropolitan areas, including newly built areas, concentrate on people, resources, services, and opportunities. Peripheral areas – whether rural, post-industrial, or suburban – instead face depopulation, reduced public services, and a weakened social fabric (Rodríguez-Pose, 2018). This divide also plays out culturally and ecologically. Cities champion diversity, connectivity, and innovation at the expense of ecological pressure and gentrification. Peripheral communities prioritize tradition, social cohesion, ecological stewardship, and local autonomy but are vulnerable to neglect, exploitation, or abandonment. Yet, these peripheral areas are increasingly recognized for their cultural richness, ecological value, and potential to foster alternative, place-based models of development (De Vidovich, 2022).

In response, contemporary placemaking is adopting bio-regional and participatory processes integrating cultural landscapes, human–nature relationships, ecological health, and lived experiences (Courage et al., 2021) while remaining open to external influences and creative reinterpretation of places. This openness encourages diverse perspectives and knowledge systems in placemaking. Within this evolving process, *cultural heritage* is gaining renewed importance, not as a static legacy to preserve, in isolation, to prevent degradation or return sites to a perceived original state, but as a *living*, dynamic force for regeneration (Duxbury et al., 2015). Cultural heritage management harnesses this potential through co-creation, interdisciplinarity, and adaptive reuse. These dynamics promote shared responsibility (Zagato, 2015), democratic participation (Dore & Turan, 2024), and bridge past narratives with future possibilities (Labadi & Logan, 2016), empowering private initiatives, encouraging community engagement, and enabling cross-sector and public–private experimentation and collaboration. Culture-led place regeneration activated by these dynamics (Della Lucia & Trunfio, 2018) may also foster regenerative development (Du Plessis & Brandon, 2015) and creative and regenerative forms of tourism (Bellato et al., 2022; Richards, 2014). However, challenges remain that may limit the scope for participation and innovation (Rizzo, 2020).

This chapter explores the role of cultural heritage management in placemaking, focusing on the intertwining processes of heritage preservation, culture-led regeneration, and regenerative development. Through qualitative analysis, the chapter examines how family-run and women-led enterprises contribute to these dynamics using the case study of Castel Campo, a historic estate in Trentino, northern Italy. Acquired by the Rasini family in 1920, the castle is inhabited and managed by their descendants. The first section outlines the key drivers and models of cultural heritage regeneration (Della Lucia & Pashkevich, 2022; Della Lucia & Trunfio, 2018) and its potential to catalyze regenerative development (Bellato et al., 2022), along with women's leadership in family enterprises (Cameron & Gibson-Graham, 2003). The following sections present the Castel Campo case and the research methodology, and discuss findings. The analysis positions Castel Campo as a dynamic, multidimensional hybrid enterprise that combines living heritage, regenerative agriculture, and social care. Its business model, anchored in respect for time, place, and community, demonstrates how cultural heritage management can connect historical continuity with contemporary innovation to support inclusive, future-oriented placemaking.

FROM HERITAGE PRESERVATION TO CULTURE-LED REGENERATION AND REGENERATIVE DEVELOPMENT

The dynamics of integrating cultural heritage management into contemporary placemaking are complex. One central challenge is reconciling heritage protection with culture-led regeneration processes that drive economic development, social innovation, and individual and collective well-being (Della Lucia & Trunfio, 2018). Balancing heritage's intrinsic value protection through conservation with its enhancement and innovative use (Sacco et al., 2014) encourages engagement with heritage and its hybridization with creativity (Booth et al., 2022; Della Lucia & Trunfio, 2018). At the same time, it rejects heritage misuse and commodification (Macmillan, 2021; Nhambura, 2023). Striking this balance ensures heritage remains a protected yet dynamic resource.

The theoretical and analytical framework (Della Lucia & Pashkevich, 2022) that has addressed the tensions and opportunities generated by these dynamics across multiple levels of placemaking integrates the institutional setting (Palthe, 2014) with the key drivers, change factors, and models of culture-led regeneration (Della Lucia & Trunfio, 2018). At institutional level, the regulative, normative, and cognitive systems (Palthe, 2014) provide legitimacy to discourses on cultural heritage conservation and regeneration, each grounded in different premises. While the regulative system relies on legal obligations and coercive mechanisms, such as cultural and heritage policies (Barnett & Carroll, 1993), the normative system emphasizes moral and ethical obligations (Selznick, 1948), shaping how actors perceive their role in preserving heritage and engaging with communities. The cognitive dimension is particularly relevant for transformational change, underpinning cultural identity and participatory practices. In this space, change is driven by personal values, beliefs, and assumptions, often catalyzed through narratives, symbols, and place-based storytelling (Powell & DiMaggio, 1991).

These institutional systems, explaining *what* drives change, *how*, and *why* different actors engage with it, are reflected in *stakeholder participation and heritage-creativity hybridization*. These drivers of culture-led regeneration correspond to the levels of social inclusion and innovation within the regeneration processes, which shape the models adopted and their evolution over time (Della Lucia & Pashkevich, 2022; Della Lucia & Trunfio, 2018). The *Patronage model* emphasizes the static preservation of cultural heritage, while the *Creative City* model promotes the dynamic transformation of heritage and its surroundings. The transition between these models reflects a shift from top-down governance to participatory and shared governance and from conservation to an integrated development strategy that blends heritage with creativity, fostering innovation and new forms of tourism (Richards, 2014). Transitional models include the *Managerial Innovation* model, which values heritage innovation as a source of enriched experiences and value creation, and the *Social Innovation* model, which promotes community involvement in heritage conservation to strengthen social ties and regenerate social capital.

When approached holistically, culture-led regeneration has the potential to catalyze *regenerative development* (Reed, 2007) and a regenerative approach to tourism. Rooted in an ecological worldview (Du Plessis & Brandon, 2015), regenerative development emphasizes co-evolutionary relationships among different forms of capital (Caniglia et al., 2019) in a bioregional context through development models grounded in mutual care and co-evolution (Benne & Mang, 2016). Their connection is activated through the *sense of place*, which encompasses the meanings, emotions, and memories that individuals associate with a specific place, as well as *place-sourced knowledge* derived from ecological understanding, local practices, and lived experiences over time (Mehmood et al., 2020; Reed, 2007). In this perspective, the place becomes an active stakeholder in regenerative development (Chambers & Buzinde, 2015). Similarly, regenerative tourism (Bellato et al., 2022) encourages communities and visitors to contribute actively to local biocultural vitality and flourishing.

Individuals and communities developing a keen sense of place become primary holders and custodians of this knowledge, guiding place-specific processes that reflect the ways humans can relate to a place, give back to it, and support its holistic flourishing (Bellato et al., 2023; Mehmood et al., 2020). Regenerative efforts unfold through various culture-based and biodiversity-stewarding activities, including agriculture, handicrafts, hospitality, and education, that are catalyzed by family-run enterprises. They often encompass local collaborations, transgenerational succession, and strategic foresight to define economic and non-economic goals toward innovation and long-term impact (Micelotta et al., 2023). Female leadership in family-run enterprises often stands out, shaping conscious business practices to foster a "more equitable, gender-balanced, and ecologically conscious future" (Henderson, 1998, p. 9). *Feminizing* the economy (Cameron & Gibson-Graham, 2003, p. 4) means restructuring the economic systems by recognizing female leaders as agents of change in regional development and fostering interconnections among all living beings within socio-ecological systems. Female agency supports the creation of empowering businesses that integrate social cooperation, innovation, and respect for nature, while improving the role of people within economic activities. Redefining women's role in entrepreneurship not only transforms how women see themselves but also reshapes societal perceptions and expands the ways women experience being and belonging in the world.

CASTEL CAMPO CASE STUDY

Castel Campo (https://www.castelcampo.com) is a historic castle in the small municipality of Fiavè (approximately 1,000 inhabitants) in the Giudicarie Valleys of Trentino, northern Italy. This region maintains a strong, traditional, agricultural-based economy while being part of the broader Garda Dolomiti tourism destination (https://www.gardatrentino.it/en). The historic estate is surrounded by a garden and dense wood covering 38 ha. It includes the castle and the adjoining Chapel of San Nicolò. Nearby, in the village of Curé, are the Church of San Vigilio and Maso Pacomio, a typical Trentino farmstead (Fig. 8.1, View of Castel Campo estate).

Castel Campo has long symbolized power and influence in the Giudicarie Valleys. The Da Campo family reportedly controlled it as early as 1211, establishing it as a political fortress. In the 15th century, it witnessed violent conflict, especially between the Da Campo and Lodron families. From 1468 to 1885, it was granted as a fief to the Von Trapp family, who performed major architectural and decorative renovations. During World War I, the castle was a support hub for nearby villages. In 1920, Milan entrepreneur Cesare Luigi Silvio Rasini purchased the estate and entrusted it to his son Giovanni and daughter-in-law, the sculptress Thea Casalbore. Under their care, Castel Campo became a cultural landmark, even during wartime, occasionally hosting artists and intellectuals such as the poetess Ada Negri. It still remains in the hands of their descendants, who continue to preserve its legacy.

Artist Marina Clerici Rasini and her daughters Sofia, Olivia, and Thea Rasini own and manage the property as a family enterprise. After Marina permanently moved to Castel Campo in 2003, following the passing of her husband, Michele Rasini, the family undertook a significant restoration of

Fig. 8.1. View of the Castel Campo Estate.
Source: Lorenzo Clerici (2024).

the castle. In 2012, they also completed the full renovation of Maso Paco-mio, using traditional materials and building techniques. Today, they operate through four areas integrated into the *Castel Campo hub*: the castle as a his-torical place, the limited company "Il Campo s.r.l.," the organic farm "Castel Campo," and the non-profit organisation "Associazione Campo Base Onlus."

METHODOLOGY

This study examines the processes of heritage preservation, culture-led regen-eration, and regenerative development through the case of Castel Campo, fea-turing a holistic single-case study (Yin, 2018). This private estate integrates diverse cultural, social, economic, and agricultural activities, functioning as a complex yet cohesive system (Benne & Mang, 2016). The case was selected for its national recognition in social and civic engagement and its capacity to gen-erate unique insights into the themes under investigation. This approach aligns with scholarly recommendations for purposeful case selection in qualitative research, emphasizing cases with high analytical value (Eisenhardt, 1989). In 2024, Marina Clerici Rasini was awarded the Order of Merit of the Italian Republic by the President of Italy, an honor conferred upon individuals who have distinguished themselves through ethical entrepreneurship, social inclu-sion, solidarity, and public service. She was recognized for "giving impetus to a family activity aimed at welcoming and providing hospitality to people with illnesses or psychosocial difficulties" (Presidenza della Repubblica, 2024).

Primary and secondary data were collected from multiple sources to ensure methodological rigor through data triangulation (Vivek, 2023). Pri-mary data were collected through freely structured interviews (Foote Whyte, 1982) with the Castel Campo owners. Questions were open-ended and served as a rough template (O'Dwyer, 2004) to explore key topics related to the Castel Campo business model, such as rootedness in place, family-business goals and initiatives, and female leadership, among others. Eight interviews (approximately one hour each) were conducted during four in-field visits and observations from spring to fall 2024. Secondary data encompass print and electronic documents published over the years, including archival materials from state archives and other institutions, national and local press articles, catalogs, and booklets documenting the history and the activities of Castel Campo (about 400 pages). Data were analyzed manually to generate in-depth insights. The involvement of Maria Clerici Rasini, as a crucial knowledge holder (Bellato et al., 2024) and co-author, strengthened the validity of the data interpretation. To address the inherent limitations of the single case study design (Flyvbjerg, 2006), particularly the challenge of generalizing findings to other contexts, the authors ensured detailed documentation of the research processes, including transparent reporting and detailed contextual description (Gibbert, 2008).

CASTEL CAMPO'S HISTORICAL CONTINUITY AND CONTEMPORARY EXPERIMENTATION

Research findings highlight the role of the family-run enterprise at Castel Campo in heritage preservation, regenerative agriculture, and social entrepreneurship. The insights for each area are detailed in the following chapter's sections. They showcase how private, women-led stewardship co-exists and co-evolves with culture-led regeneration in a systemic process (Fig. 8.2, Castel

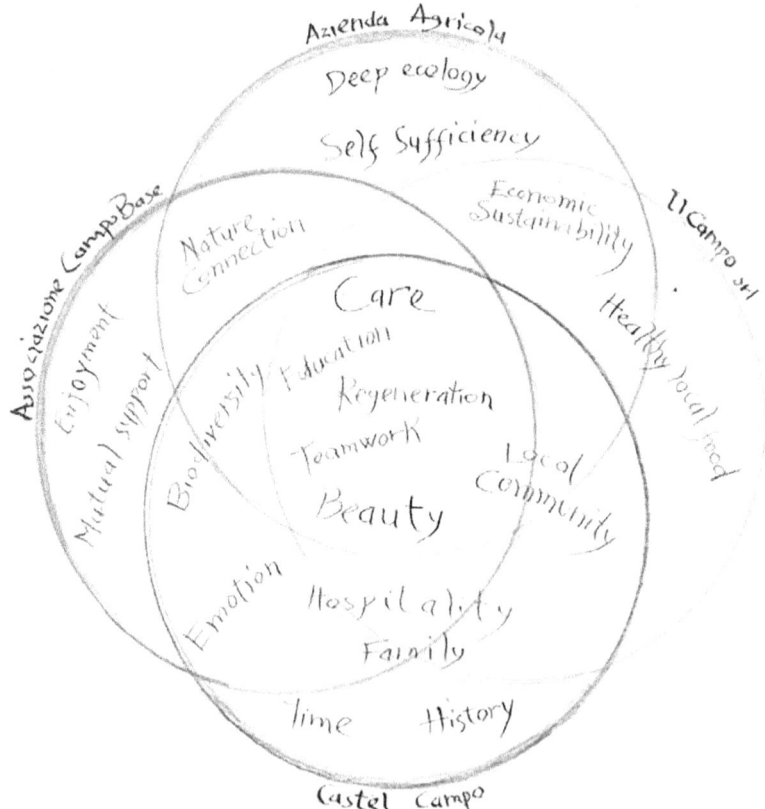

Fig. 8.2.   Castel Campo Hub.
Source: Marina Clerici Rasini (2020).

Campo hub). As the owner notes, this process reflects a deep, ongoing relationship with Castel Campo's living natural and cultural heritage, shaped by female leadership:

> *In managing both the land and the castle, I try to follow the ways of nature [...], and in doing so, I align my intention with the intention of nature. (Marina Clerici, 2020)*

> *A woman has a unique ability to care for both people and places. This allows us to work harmoniously and recognize our strengths and weaknesses. Most importantly, it sparks the courage to dare and fuels the belief that we can make it. (Marina Clerici, 2020)*

HERITAGE PRESERVATION

Castel Campo is a listed building of special historic-artistic interest under Italian law and is subject to cultural heritage protection restrictions justified by the interest in its public fruition (ItCCHL, 2004). The local heritage authority (Soprintendenza) supervises all major restoration and maintenance work. Its preservation has been possible through private family and public funding, most notably from the Autonomous Province of Trento, which partially funded the initial restoration work (2001–2005). These joint efforts required constant dialog between the owners and the stakeholders, leading to collaborative preservation actions. This process also demanded careful management of resources, prioritizing what to preserve.

> *It is essential to gauge one's resources when carrying out castle activities, find ways to spend less while maintaining an acceptable aesthetic, and preserve or select to preserve wherever possible. (Marina Clerici, 2020)*

Preserving has meant safeguarding its historic structure and its intangible heritage – the stories of who lived there and the enduring sense of mystery that enshrouds it. As the owner notes, being custodians of this private estate is a "true privilege": not a luxury, but the honor and responsibility of sharing its beauty and legacy with the community, guests, and future generations, while protecting its value.

> *Privilege is the opportunity to connect with time, to be penetrated by the presence that has built these walls. It's about living in harmony with the rhythms and seasons of a place that is constantly*

evolving. Above all, it's about the possibility offered by this place to meet and work with families, professionals, and individuals who take part in our non-profit activities and are so often a great example of courage and selflessness. (Marina Clerici, 2020)

Preservation at Castel Campo goes beyond the castle and its outbuildings. It includes frescoes and interiors from various periods and styles, a remarkable art collection featuring sculptures and plaster casts by Thea Casalbore Rasini, and a valuable library of rare books on natural history and science by Tito Vignoli, alongside a unique collection of tribal art from Africa and Oceania.

REGENERATIVE AGRICULTURE

The farm is integrated into the Castel Campo wildlife reserve, which includes estate lands and adjacent areas. The project reconnects cultivation with the natural environment, healing and revitalizing the soil, water systems, and the rural landscape through conscious, small-scale practices rooted in regenerative agriculture (Müller, 2020):

We must let the land guide us toward natural, sensible respect for nature and experiment with agriculture without interfering with wildlife. (Marina Clerici, 2020)

The project centers on *soil health*, *biodiversity*, and *ecological resilience*. Natural methods – composting, green manure, crop rotation, and cover cropping – increase organic matter, support microbial life, and improve water retention with minimal disturbance. The farm grows a variety of crops, walnuts, and both wild and cultivated herbs. It also produces organic alfalfa and hay for a nearby livestock farm and makes "Liber-tè" herbal tea. Hedgerows, trees, and mixed habitats support pollinators and beneficial wildlife, creating a self-regulating environment through regenerated natural cycles. Grains are milled on-site just before sale to preserve their freshness. Seeds are saved and replanted each year. Other plans include employing livestock grazing to prepare soil, ideally in collaboration with nearby farms. These efforts contribute to Castel Campo's food self-sufficiency.

Education and community involvement are integral to the project. Merging traditional rural knowledge with contemporary ecological innovation, the farm is active in networks like Donne in Campo and has collaborated with institutions such as Fondazione Mach of San Michele all'Adige. It also hosts local markets, and educational programs. This participatory approach positions farming as a web of relationships – with the land, other local actors, and across generations – showing how historical practices can inspire contemporary farming while enhancing local culture.

SOCIAL ENTREPRENEURSHIP

Social entrepreneurship is a key pillar of the Castel Campo hub, primarily expressed through the non-profit Campo Base Onlus. Its mission is to foster well-being, personal growth, independence, joy, and community spirit, all grounded in a deep connection to nature:

> *Campo Base is a safe place, a starting point for exploring, a destination, a place to rest, and a place to move forward. (personal communication, 2024)*

The projects help children and adults facing serious illness by offering retreats, hospitality, and tailored activities. Marina Clerici's daughters have expanded their mission to include stays for families in need, teenage summer camps, and residential retreats for adults and families, delivered in partnership with local and international organizations through donations and sponsorships.

Setting the base camp for these social initiatives within the estate reinforces Castel Campo's historical bond with local communities while opening to international collaborations. These are aided by the Rasini family's international experience in cultural exchange and volunteering, in Italy and abroad. The social mission operates alongside Il Campo S.r.l., which ensures financial sustainability for the hub's activities. The company deals with the administrative and commercial aspects of managing hospitality-related, educational, and recreational meetings, concerts, and other cultural performances. These activities, which take place throughout the estate, are all connected by a common thread, the land, offering visitors immersive, nature-based experiences. One example is the "Labyrinth," which marks the conclusion of the summer camps, a unicursal maze with only one way to reach the center. This ritual space, inspired by ancestral practices, reflects Castel Campo's philosophy of presence, healing, and connection.

DISCUSSION

Over time, the preservation of Castel Campo, the development of the farm, and the establishment of the social enterprise have embodied different models from the cultural regeneration matrix (Della Lucia & Trunfio, 2018), respectively, patronage, social innovation, and managerial innovation. Each model is driven by different goals and premises, involving varying degrees of stakeholder engagement and heritage-creativity hybridization. In preserving Castel Campo (*Patronage model*), the Rasini family's stewardship is closely tied to a broader commitment to the public good. Their investment in cultural heritage preservation and enhancement reflects both a legal duty and a moral responsibility. On the one hand, joint private–public collaboration was key for preserving the castle. On the other hand, sharing the estate's beauty, meaning, and history exemplifies modern patronage grounded in the family's generosity, responsibility, and community engagement. The farm at Castel Campo (*Social innovation*) serves as a platform that reconnects land, traditional knowledge, and people. It reimagines agriculture as a social act of care that nourishes both ecosystems and the family, while inspiring local communities with contemporary practices rooted in ancient wisdom. Community participation grows through educational and hands-on experiences. Finally, Campo Base Onlus (*Managerial innovation*), in synergy with Il Campo s.r.l., represents a hybrid, impact-driven organization. It gives new social purpose to local natural and cultural heritage, offering tailored, creative activities for vulnerable individuals and families, and people who want to reconnect with themselves and nature. Collaborations with international partners introduce a networked, globally informed approach to social value creation.

Despite their differences, the Castel Campo Hub activities coexist and coevolve into a systemic, place-based approach to regenerative development at Castel Campo (Fig. 8.3). This organic process emerges naturally from experience rather than being strategically deliberated by a shared family-and-women-led vision. Decision-making around the management of Castel Campo – its land, property, and heritage – continues to be rooted in an ongoing, deeply felt sense of place, reflected in respect and care for the site's natural and cultural legacy, while decisive female leadership plays a key role in shaping a hybrid entrepreneurial mindset and conscious business practices. The distinctive female sensitivity to sensing, understanding, and reinterpreting the place is reflected in living heritage experiences, regenerative agriculture, and social care and captured in the family's cherished motto: "If you build it, he will come!" (Clerici, 2017).

The place's legacy and the family's history relate dynamically to its members' interests and international experiences, and contributions from guests and partners. This interplay fosters the capacity and sensitivity for creative reinterpretations of Castel Campo's identity. Transgenerational succession – evident in the involvement of Marina's daughters in the Castel Campo Hub – infuses fresh energy into this evolving development model. The

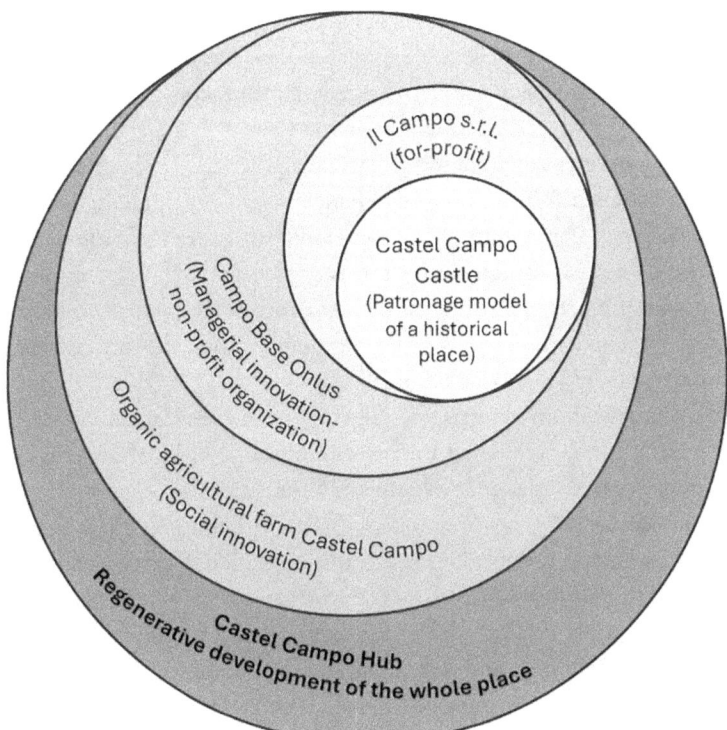

Il Campo s.r.l.
(for-profit)

Castel Campo
Castle
(Patronage model
of a historical
place)

Campo Base Onlus
(Managerial innovation-
non-profit organization)

Organic agricultural farm Castel Campo
(Social innovation)

Regenerative development of the whole place
Castel Campo Hub

Fig. 8.3. Systemic Place-based Development at Castel Campo.
Source: Authors' elaboration.

development of social projects initially attracted more participation from international partners and sponsors than local stakeholders, who are now increasingly involved, however. This openness brings innovation, benefiting the organization and broader efforts toward local regenerative development. However, implementing these initiatives continues to be mediated by the family, as Castel Campo remains a private home, retaining the privilege to shape its path and share it with those who resonate with its worldview. Enduring women's leadership remains a strength marked by their distinct voices and resilience, affecting future development.

CONCLUSION

This chapter contributes to the academic debate on cultural heritage management in placemaking by offering an actionable, real-world business model that can inspire private initiatives for heritage regeneration elsewhere.

Castel Campo is a dynamic, family-run enterprise whose hybrid business model combines living heritage experiences, regenerative agriculture, and social care in a systemic, place-based regenerative process. Within this model, the women-led entrepreneurial approach is key to shaping the enterprise's socio-ecological goals and conscious business practices. Their existential and business projects involve a distinctive female sensitivity, bridging respect for time, place, and community with contemporary experimentation, thereby supporting innovative and inclusive forms of placemaking. The family acts as a custodian of place and a catalyst of regenerative development trajectories, fostering human–nature synergy and harmony, embracing stewardship and care, and enhancing the living heritage.

Several implications emerge for stakeholders involved in cultural heritage management. First, private-led initiatives embedded in bioregional contexts can support viable forms of development in rural areas aimed at a more equitable and ecologically conscious future. Second, supporting and recognizing women's leadership is critical, as it can foster relational, caring, and resilient approaches to development well suited to regenerative models and contemporary placemaking. Third, greater attention should be given to the distinctive goals of family-run and women-led enterprises, which often prioritize long-term social and environmental value creation over short-term economic gain. To maximize impact, stakeholders should actively position regenerative initiatives within broader debates on alternative economies and sustainable and conscious business models. Strengthening these connections will not only validate the relevance of localized, privately-led practices but also contribute to more inclusive and resilient forms of territorial development.

This research is limited by restricted contact with local actors and the exploratory nature of the analysis conducted. Future studies could benefit from a deeper immersion in the context of Castel Campo, through participatory action research, embedded ethnography, focus groups, and interviews with a broader network of stakeholders, which would allow for a more detailed exploration of each dimension of their existential and business vision. Identifying ways to measure the long-term impact of their work, whether in terms of ecological health or human well-being, would also be valuable.

REFERENCES

Barnett, W. P., & Carroll, G. R. (1993). How institutional constraints affected the organization of early U.S. telephony. *The Journal of Law, Economics, and Organization*, 9(1), 98–126.

Bellato, L., Frantzeskaki, N., & Nygaard, C. A. (2022). Regenerative tourism: A conceptual framework leveraging theory and practice. *Tourism Geographies*, 25(4), 1026–1046.

Bellato, L., Frantzeskaki, N., & Nygaard, C. A. (2024). Towards a regenerative shift in tourism: Applying a regenerative conceptual framework toward swimmable urban rivers. *Tourism Geographies*, 26(8), 1361–1380.

Bellato, L., Frantzeskaki, N., tebrakunna country, Lee, E., Cheer, J. M., & Peters, A. (2023). Transformative epistemologies for regenerative tourism: Towards a decolonial paradigm in science and practice? *Journal of Sustainable Tourism*, 32(6), 1161–1181.

Benne, B., & Mang, P. (2016). Working regeneratively across scales – Insights from nature applied to the built environment. *Journal of Cleaner Production*, 109, 42–52.

Booth, P., Navarrete, T., & Ogundipe, A. (2022). Museum open data ecosystems: A comparative study. *Journal of Documentation*, 78(4), 761–779.

Cameron, J., & Gibson-Graham, J. K. (2003). Feminising the economy: Metaphors, strategies, politics. *Gender, Place & Culture*, 10(2), 145–157.

Caniglia, B. S., Frank, B., Knott, J., Sagendorf, K. S., & Wilkerson, E. A. (Eds.). (2019). *Regenerative urban development, climate change and the common good*. Routledge.

Chambers, D., & Buzinde, C. (2015). Tourism and decolonisation: Locating research and self. *Annals of Tourism Research*, 51, 1–16.

Clerici, M. (2017). *Il Pacomio di Castel Campo. Castel Campo*.

Clerici, M. (2020). [unpublished diary].

Courage, C., Borrup, T., Jackson, M. R., Legge, K., McKeown, A., Platt, L., & Schupbach, J. (2021). *The Routledge handbook of placemaking*. Routledge.

De Vidovich, L. (2022). Different forms of welfare provision for diverse suburban fabrics: Three examples from Italy. *Urban Planning*, 7(3), 86–97.

Della Lucia, M., & Pashkevich, A. (2022). A sustainable afterlife for post-industrial sites: Balancing conservation, regeneration, and heritage tourism. *European Planning Studies*, 31(3), 641–661.

Della Lucia, M., & Trunfio, M. (2018). The role of the private actor in cultural regeneration: Hybridizing cultural heritage with creativity in the city. *Cities*, 82, 35–44.

Donders, Y. (2020). Cultural heritage and human rights. In F. Francioni & A. F. Vrdoljak (Eds.), *The Oxford handbook of international cultural heritage law* (pp. 379–406). Oxford University Press.

Dore, G., & Turan, P. (2024). When copyright meets digital cultural heritage: Picturing an EU right to culture in freedom of panorama and reproduction of public domain art. *IIC – International Review of Intellectual Property and Competition Law, 55*, 37–65.

Du Plessis, C., & Brandon, P. (2015). An ecological worldview as basis for a regenerative sustainability paradigm for the built environment. *Journal of Cleaner Production, 109*, 53–61.

Duxbury, N., Garrett-Petts, W. F., & MacLennan, D. (Eds.). (2015). *Cultural mapping as cultural inquiry* (1st ed.). Routledge.

Eisenhardt, K. M. (1989). Building theories from case study research. *Academy of Management Review, 14*(4), 532–550.

Flyvbjerg, B. (2006). Five misunderstandings about case-study research. *Qualitative Inquiry, 12*(2), 219–245.

Foote Whyte, W. (1982). Interviewing in field research. In R. G. Burgess (Ed.), *Field research: A sourcebook and field manual* (pp. 111–122). Routledge.

Gibbert, M., Ruigrok, W., & Wicki, B. (2008). What passes as a rigorous case study? *Strategic Management Journal, 29*(3), 1465–1474.

Henderson, H. (1998, December 4). The breaking point. *The Australian Financial Review*, 1–9.

Italian Code of Cultural Heritage and Landscape (ItCCHL). (2004). DLgs 42/2004, GU 45.

Labadi, S., & Logan, W. S. (Eds.). (2016). Urban heritage, development and sustainability: International frameworks, national and local governance. Routledge.

Lew, A. A. (2017). Tourism planning and place making: Place-making or placemaking? *Tourism Geographies, 19*(3), 448–466.

Macmillan, F. (2021). Western dualism and the regulation of cultural production. *Brill Research Perspectives in Art and Law, 4*(4), 1–116.

Mehmood, A., Marsden, T., Taherzadeh, A., Axinte, L. F., & Rebelo, C. (2020). Transformative roles of people and places: Learning, experiencing, and regenerative action through social innovation. *Sustainability Science*, *15*(2), 455–466.

Micelotta, E., Benedetti, C., & Rovelli, P. (2023). *Family firm: A distinctive form of organization*. Cambridge University Press.

Müller, E. (2020). Regenerative development as natural solution for sustainability. In F. O. Sarmiento & L. M. Frolich (Eds.), *The Elgar companion to geography, transdisciplinarity and sustainability* (pp. 201–217). Edward Elgar.

Nhambura, C. (2023). Indigenous people and the protection of intellectual property rights (IPRs) in Zimbabwe. In S. G. Barnabas (Ed.), *Indigenous and minority populations*. IntechOpen.

O'Dwyer, B. (2004). Qualitative data analysis: Illuminating a process for transforming a 'messy' but 'attractive' 'nuisance.' In C. Humphrey & B. Lee (Eds.), *The real life guide to accounting research* (pp. 391–407). Elsevier.

Palthe, J. (2014). Regulative, normative, and cognitive elements of organizations: Implications for managing change. *Management and Organizational Studies*, *1*(2), 59.

Powell, W. W., & DiMaggio, P. (Eds.). (1991). *The new institutionalism in organizational analysis*. University of Chicago Press.

Presidenza della Repubblica. (2024, March 20). *Il Presidente Mattarella ha consegnato le onorificenze dell'Ordine al Merito della Repubblica italiana conferite motu proprio*. https://www.quirinale.it/elementi/109208

Reed, B. (2007). Shifting from 'sustainability' to regeneration. *Building Research & Information*, *35*(6), 674–680.

Richards, G. (2014). Creativity and tourism in the city. *Current Issues in Tourism*, *17*(2), 119–144.

Rizzo, I. (2020). Regulation of heritage. In R. Towse & T. N. Hernández (Eds.), *Handbook of cultural economics* (pp. 474–484). Edward Elgar.

Rodríguez-Pose, A. (2018). The revenge of the places that don't matter (and what to do about it). *Cambridge Journal of Regions, Economy and Society*, *11*(1), 189–209.

Sacco, P., Ferilli, G., & Blessi, G. T. (2014). Understanding culture-led local development: A critique of alternative theoretical explanations. *Urban Studies*, *51*(13), 2806–2821.

Selznick, P. (1948). Foundations of the theory of organization. *American Sociological Review*, *13*(1), 25.

Silberberg, S., Lorah, K., Disbrow, R., & Muessig, A. (2013). *Places in the making: How placemaking builds places and communities*. Massachusetts Institute of Technology.

Vivek, R. (2023). A comprehensive review of environmental triangulation in qualitative research: Methodologies, applications, and implications. *Journal of European Economy*, 22(4), 517–532.

Yin, R. K. (2018). *Case study research and design methods* (6th ed.). Sage.

Zagato, L. (2015). The notion of "heritage community" in the Council of Europe's Faro Convention: Its impact on the European legal framework. In N. Adell, R. F. Bendix, C. Bortolotto, & M. Tauschek (Eds.), *Between imagined communities of practice* (pp. 141–168). Göttingen University Press.

9

CRAFT-BASED EXPERIENCES TO REVITALIZE TOURISTIC URBAN CENTERS: THE VENETIAN CASE STUDY

STEFANO MICELLI AND SOFIA MIZZAN

Ca' Foscari University of Venice, Italy

ABSTRACT

Craft enterprises can play a crucial role in revitalizing urban centers generating positive externalities for local communities and territorial ecosystems from both economic and social perspectives. Their impact can benefit from the increasing interest among tourists in search of authentic interactions with local SMEs. This paper introduces a literature review framing culture-based regeneration projects as initiatives aimed at promoting territorial heritage, local know-how, working practices, and overall local attractiveness. Craft businesses can indeed play a pivotal role in this context, especially when their offerings combine educational features and tailored services that respond to the curiosity of an increasingly sophisticated tourist demand. The analysis of three case studies involving craft enterprises in Venice's historic center illustrates the links between craftsmanship, territorial economic growth, social benefits, and enhanced city attractiveness. The chapter aims to demonstrate that through strategic management consulting and effective ecosystem integration, it is possible to foster urban and social regeneration, leveraging local and mindful touristic demand.

Keywords: Craft enterprises; new technologies; strategic management; experiential tourism; sustainability; urban regeneration

INTRODUCTION

Craft enterprises have been considered for a long time incapable of growth and technology adoption. A number of studies have highlighted the limits of such a stereotype. Not only are these firms now utilizing digital technologies in different realms (production, administration, and communication), but when guided by strategic management and anchored in a robust territorial ecosystem, they emerge as catalysts of culture-based urban regeneration. Traditionally bounded by distribution constraints, these firms are increasingly discovering new communication and distribution channels related to tourism. By translating traditional know-how into authentic and immersive experiences, these firms are indeed able to meet a sophisticated tourist demand. When properly guided, these firms benefit from these emerging opportunities while safeguarding intangible heritage and strengthening place identity. The success of these online and offline experiences depends not only on appropriate managerial decisions but also on a variety of actors, resources, and relationships provided by the local community.

This chapter takes into consideration critical success factors, analyzing three case studies in the problematic context of Venice. The paper also evaluates the role of public institutions and other enabling territorial actors that shaped and amplified firms' economic, cultural, and social trajectory.

In conclusion, the chapter identifies guidelines to develop local companies, to connect small craft firms to technology providers, and to foster local policies to favor a positive business environment.

CULTURE-BASED URBAN REGENERATION

Culture-based urban regeneration involves comprehensive approaches targeting both infrastructural and intangible urban elements. This regeneration type emphasizes creative and cultural interventions aimed at revitalizing neglected urban spaces, such as abandoned buildings or deteriorated areas. By reactivating these underutilized assets, culture-led regeneration transforms them into vibrant, multifunctional spaces that enhance urban livability and accessibility (Cancellieri & Ostanel, 2014).

Research emphasizes the potential of culture-based regeneration to activate local community resources, thereby fostering new socio-cultural dynamics that extend beyond traditional economic outcomes. Hybrid cultural spaces emerge as pivotal points within these initiatives, offering platforms for innovation, social interaction, and cultural engagement. Such spaces contribute significantly to the urban landscape, functioning as centers for communal activities, cultural promotion, and sustainable economic practices, thus increasing the overall attractiveness and the livability of the urban area (Lusiani & Panozzo, 2016).

Craft enterprises significantly influence urban regeneration, offering crucial economic contributions to communities (Li et al., 2020). These businesses generate employment opportunities, particularly enhancing the economic well-being of the middle-class segment. They strengthen the competitiveness of local economies by integrating specialized skills into global value chains and by providing distinctive products and tailored services that appeal to both residents and tourists (Bettiol & Micelli, 2014; Micelli, 2011).

Furthermore, craft enterprises help maintain traditional practices and expertise, creating a valuable repository of knowledge that supports specific sectors, notably luxury markets and experiential tourism. This preservation not only enhances economic opportunities but also positions cities as unique destinations attracting high-value visitors, thus sustaining economic vibrancy and growth.

CRAFT ENTERPRISES AS DRIVERS OF GENERATIVE LOCAL COMMUNITIES

The influence of craft enterprises extends beyond economic aspects, profoundly impacting social and cultural dynamics. These businesses play a central role in preserving and transmitting traditional knowledge and skills cultivated within local vocational practices, actively contributing to the continuation and evolution of cultural heritage (Manfredi Latilla et al., 2019). Through their operations, craft enterprises foster cultural enrichment within communities by disseminating innovative practices, products, and technologies.

Moreover, these businesses often create communal spaces that promote social revitalization. They foster greater social cohesion, strengthen social bonds, and enhance residents' sense of belonging and identity. This social rejuvenation directly contributes to elevating community well-being and encourages active citizen participation in local cultural initiatives (Sepe & Di Trapani, 2010).

Craft enterprises can establish and sustain competitive advantages by effectively leveraging their unique cultural and traditional assets. The strategic use of cultural heritage within business models enables these enterprises to differentiate themselves in increasingly competitive markets. This differentiation is particularly relevant in sectors such as luxury goods and creative tourism, where the uniqueness and authenticity of products and experiences are paramount (Bettiol & Micelli, 2014). An illustrative case is the recent increased focus on craft skills and local heritage, driven by a demand from sophisticated consumer segments looking for unique and personalized products and services. By aligning their offerings with these trends, craft enterprises can significantly enhance their market position and profitability, contributing directly to urban economic resilience and competitiveness.

Craft businesses serve as vital elements within the socio-economic fabric of local communities. Existing literature highlights the importance of communities as dynamic systems characterized by identity, place, and shared spaces (Smith & Robinson, 2006). The active participation of community members in cultural and economic initiatives significantly supports urban regeneration efforts, ensuring their long-term success and sustainability (Li et al., 2020; Ostanel, 2017).

In conclusion, craft enterprises often act as catalysts for innovation and social connectivity. They not only maintain existing social networks but also foster the development of new relationships within communities. This generative role is essential for enhancing social cohesion, community resilience, and local pride. Furthermore, by incorporating community-based practices, these enterprises reinforce social capital and facilitate collaborative innovation, thereby creating the conditions for a sustainable urban regeneration.

TOURISM AND CRAFT: FROM CONFLICT TO OPPORTUNITY

Tourism has a dual impact on local communities, often fueling conflict and disease while generating economic benefits. On the one hand, the surge in visitor numbers can strain urban life. Italy, for example, recorded 458.4 million tourist presences in 2024, an all-time high (Confcommercio, 2024). In many art cities, residents have lamented what experts term overtourism, described as a phenomenon that leads to alienated residents, a degraded tourist experience, overloaded infrastructure, damage to nature, or threats to culture and heritage (McKinsey & Company & World Travel & Tourism Council, 2017).

According to a study on Managing Tourism Growth in Europe (Jordan et al., 2018), overtourism can be driven by factors such as the accessibility and affordability of travel, the traditional policy focused on promoting volume, an increase in international arrivals, the urbanization pressure, the gentrification and increasing prices in city centers and new neighborhoods, the proliferation of unregulated tourist accommodations, and the concentration of large groups of tourists. These factors can indeed lead to increased congestion, pressure on infrastructure, pollution and environmental degradation, living costs for residents, damage to historical sites and monuments, and loss of identity and authenticity (Jordan et al., 2018).

To control this situation, local authorities in Italy have resorted to drastic measures which span from the turnstiles at the Trevi Fountain to the crowd control in the center of Venice. These measures have led to an increase in the negative perception that tourism wears out cities and even leads to displacement of residents (Confcommercio Firenze, 2017). Such feelings are not unique to Italy; cities like Barcelona and Berlin, other than Venice and Milan, suffer the same over tourism complaints. Social diseases associated with the phenomenon and testified by residents include noise complaints, housing cost inflation due to short-term rentals, congestion, commercialization and privatization of public spaces, and environmental deterioration, including waste, air, and water quality issues (Peeters et al., 2018), thus confirming the findings of the study conducted by Jordan et al. (2018).

These common negative perceptions of tourism frame it as a force that, if not regulated, undermines the quality of life of residents and local identity (Laudiero, 2020). However, it is necessary not to forget that tourism also creates jobs and wealth before causing malaise (Confcommercio Firenze, 2017). This paradox sets the stage for reimagining tourism not as an inevitable source of conflict, but as an opportunity for positive community development, transforming tourism into a catalyst for local benefit rather than a source of tension.

Counterbalancing these issues can be significantly addressed by the rising trend in tourist preferences demanding authentic and immersive experiences. Many travelers today seek to "live like a local" and engage meaningfully with the places they visit, rather than just consume superficial sights (Paulauskaite et al., 2017). This trend has been conceptualized as creative tourism, defined by Richards and Wilson (2006) as tourism that emphasizes active learning and participation in the host culture. Tourists increasingly crave activities that allow personal connection, self-development, and cultural exchange, be it learning a traditional craft, cooking a regional recipe, or participating in local festivals (Hsia, 2020).

Importantly, authenticity-seeking tourists often explicitly value crafts and folk culture. In a bibliometric review of crafts and development, Bellver et al. (2023) found that "craft itself, most of the time, [is] a motivation for tourism development." Visitors are drawn to destinations where they can witness and even partake in traditional craftsmanship, for example, observing a master potter at work or taking a ceramics workshop. Such activities provide a richer narrative than passive sightseeing; they cater to the desire for experiential travel where memories are formed through doing and learning.

The convergence of overtourism challenges and the quest for authenticity points to a potential opportunity: craft-based heritage experiences as a bridge between visitors and locals. Crafts, encompassing artisan skills, handmade products, and traditional know-how, embody local identity and offer exactly the kind of genuine encounter many travelers seek. When tourism and crafts are deliberately linked, a win-win scenario can emerge, fostering sustainable local development while satisfying tourist expectations. Recent literature affirms that tourists' interest in "local traditional crafts" not only generates income for artisans but also "promot[e]s heritage conservation… and employment creation" in the community (Bellver et al., 2023, p. 4). In other words, an influx of visitors specifically drawn by crafts can help keep those very traditions alive, both culturally and economically. This intersection can create a virtuous cycle as it enables crafts to be more economically sustainable, to strengthen identity and pride, and tighten social cohesion. When tourism is built around these principles, it becomes an opportunity for growth for everyone.

EXPERIENTIAL TOURISM: A CRITICAL OVERVIEW OF EXISTING INITIATIVES

A number of successful projects have been launched in the recent past to provide tourists with unique and culturally sophisticated experiences. A prominent example of a top-down approach to experiential tourism is Airbnb Experiences, launched by the globally dominant home-sharing platform Airbnb. This service, introduced in 2016, allows hosts to offer curated activities to visitors, effectively leveraging Airbnb's vast user base to market local experiences. The offerings span many categories: an Italian guide in Airbnb Experiences highlights traditional culinary experiences, historic and cultural tours, and creative and artisanal workshops among the options. The concept has undoubted merits. It officially launched the idea of immersive travel on a large scale, leveraging on the growing interest toward creative tourism, and provided a platform for local enterprises (including craft practitioners and SMEs) to connect with a paying audience. By 2017, as Airbnb Experiences rolled out in cities like Milan and Rome, commentators noted that the platform was tapping into travelers' curiosity and desire to find a complicity with locals. Airbnb's massive reach and brand recognition gave experiential tourism a boost on a scale that few grassroots projects could achieve alone.

However, significant limitations accompany this top-down, platform-mediated model. The first limitation is the potential for standardization and commodification of experiences. While marketed as "unique" and "handcrafted" activities, many Airbnb Experiences tend to gravitate toward a narrow band of popular themes (e.g., food and wine tours, generic craft classes that appeal to a broad audience). The emphasis on scalable experiences that earn high ratings can lead to a degree of formulaic repetition across destinations.

A second limitation concerns the visibility and accessibility for local artisans. Despite Airbnb's global reach, the process of becoming an Experience host requires digital literacy, language skills (the ability to present the experience in English or other major languages), and meeting Airbnb's guidelines for host quality. Many small craft entrepreneurs or masters, especially older artisans, may lack these capacities, often leading many local artisans to remain invisible on the platforms.

Another critique is the question of genuine community benefit. Airbnb Experiences is a for-profit service that charges a fee to hosts; its priority is the satisfaction of paying customers (tourists), which may not always align with community priorities. The impact on craftspeople's income is also unclear. Hosts might earn extra revenue, but a significant cut goes to the platform. Moreover, there is no built-in mechanism to channel any of the profits into broader community projects or craft preservation funds.

These last limitations are strongly related to the nature of the platform itself. Airbnb, indeed, like the other sharing economy platforms, such as Uber, tends to concentrate economic and political power, disrupting both local policies and financial flows (Peeters et al., 2018). Additionally, although this initiative can lead tourists to choose non-conventional travel experiences, it may nudge them toward already-crowded sites, given their ability to quickly check and navigate reviews, and to contribute to the overtourism of the most popular places (McKinsey & Company & World Travel & Tourism Council, 2017). In this sense, the virtuousness of the collaboration can be limited by the corporate framework. Without community governance or profit-sharing, Airbnb's model remains transactional.

At the other end of the spectrum, there are bottom-up initiatives driven by local communities, artisan networks, and small enterprises. Throughout the world, there are numerous examples of grassroots efforts to link crafts and tourism: from local craft markets and open-studio trails to community-run workshops for visitors, to cooperative galleries featuring handmade goods. Often, cultural associations and third-sector organizations spearhead these initiatives, recognizing crafts as a vehicle for local development (Laudiero, 2020). Such bottom-up approaches have clear strengths. They are usually embedded in the local context, which means they can draw upon genuine community participation and ensure that benefits stay localized. Moreover, these initiatives can highlight very specific heritage skills that outsiders might overlook, and participants (both hosts and visitors) often report a high degree of satisfaction due to the personal, authentic, and intimate nature of the interactions.

However, bottom-up initiatives face significant visibility and scalability challenges. The very fact that they are local and independent means they often struggle to reach potential tourists who are not already on-site. This acknowledgment encapsulates the visibility gap: even when rich opportunities exist for tourists to experience crafts, the lack of a unifying promotion or easy discovery mechanism means demand doesn't fully meet supply. In Italy, a similar pattern exists. Small artisans in places off the main tourist circuit often rely on serendipity or word-of-mouth, but attracting international visitors is difficult without digital exposure.

Another challenge is that grassroots initiatives may lack professionalization or consistency, which can limit tourist satisfaction or trust. Some local initiatives have overcome this by forming networks or labels to assure visitors of a certain standard. For example, in the UK and Italy, "open studios" events create a circuit of trusted artisan visits. But without broader recognition, these remain niche (European Training Foundation, 2024). Even when bottom-up projects succeed in drawing visitors, they often depend on supportive policy and partnerships to survive. Without them, they risk remaining isolated experiments.

THE NEED FOR SUSTAINABLE TERRITORIAL ECOSYSTEMS

Both models in their pure version show visible limits. Platforms tend to quickly become merely extractive, while, on the other hand, bottom-up initiatives are characterized by financial and visibility constraints. To truly harness the virtuous synergy between crafts and sustainable tourism, a strategic and integrated approach is needed. This approach should combine the strengths of digital innovation with thoughtful management and governance strategies.

Digital technologies are indeed fundamental tools for scaling up craft-based tourism experiences and gaining visibility and recognition. However, their presence alone does not ensure the success of the experiences promoted. They must be accompanied by a strategic management guide that ensures quality, genuine buy-in from local stakeholders, continuous monitoring of outcomes and support, able to guarantee positive and sustainable impact on the territory and community engagement.

A clear example of the effectiveness of this model is well represented by Entreprise et Découverte, a national association that has been fully committed to promoting cultural heritage and local know-how. They have been able to not only provide tours among trustworthy craft artisans for tourists but also support in designing and managing these experiences for craftsmen. In this way, the association allows all the member artisans and entrepreneurs to be recognized as excellent and quality product and experiences providers and tourists to be easily guided among the authentic and creative experiences they are looking for, generating positive externalities both for the social and entrepreneurial fabric of the territory and for the overall satisfaction of the tourist demand. These achievements have been possible thanks to the creation of a well-managed ecosystem that combined digital presence with a strong brand identity and an on-the-ground and capillary network.

AN EMERGING MODEL IN THE VENETIAN CONTEXT

The venetian context represents an interesting case study to evaluate and measure the key features of an increasingly integrated territorial ecosystem, intended as a multi-level system of actors, resources, and relationships, in which coordination and value co-creation support sustainable development and competitiveness within a specific territory (Troisi et al., 2019).

In the historical center of Venice analysts observed an improved entrepreneurial attitude by local craft in shaping innovative experiences. At the same time, social entrepreneurs have been able to launch network projects that increased connectivity and promoted knowledge sharing. As regards these relevant craft initiatives to promote unique experiences, a selective process was applied to identify those most representative of the city's evolving relationship between craftsmanship and tourism. Martina Vidal Venezia, Orsoni 1888, and Lunardelli Venezia emerged from this process as emblematic case studies. These enterprises were chosen for their consolidated presence in the territory, their historical significance, and the national and international recognition they have received for their cultural and creative contributions (Comune di

Venezia, 2021; Fondazione Cologni Mestieri d'Arte, Foreman, 2017; Homo Faber Guide; ITP Italian Travel Press, 2024; Moledini, 2022; Molteni, 2023; Wallpaper magazine, 2019).

Each of them demonstrates a sustained capacity for renewal and innovation while remaining firmly embedded in the local context. In addition, particular attention was given to ensuring sectoral diversity, ranging from fashion to furniture, in order to highlight varied approaches to the integration of immersive and experiential practices within artisanal spaces. This selection thus reflects a deliberate effort to focus on those actors who best exemplify the potential of craft enterprises to reimagine tradition through contemporary engagement strategies.

The results clearly underline the transformative impact of framing experiences, combining digital technologies with strategic management. In conclusion of this paragraph, active network projects uniting dispersed local actors will be described, emphasizing the synergies of new technologies and traditional management tools to support local communities of practice.

MARTINA VIDAL VENEZIA

Martina Vidal Venezia is a family-run craft enterprise based on the island of Burano, Venice, that has upheld the renowned tradition of Burano lacemaking through four generations, specializing in luxury home linens, personalized embroidery, lace, lingerie, and accessories such as cashmere scarves. Recognizing the growing importance of experiential tourism, Martina Vidal Venezia has proactively developed an immersive visitor experience grounded in storytelling that emphasizes the company's historical linkage and commitment to traditional craftsmanship.

The firm has indeed established a family-operated museum within their atelier, showcasing antique lacework dating from the 17th to the 20th centuries, thereby reinforcing the narrative of cultural authenticity and heritage. Additionally, the firm offers educational courses at multiple proficiency levels, complementing the activities the museum offers and actively involving visitors and locals alike, thus fostering cultural transmission and community engagement.

The integration of advanced digital technologies for the effective promotion of the events and the workshops held on-site has significantly amplified visibility and accessibility of the company to an international audience. Additionally, Martina Vidal has recently integrated virtual reality technology into its offerings to enrich visitor experiences, allowing tourists and visitors to digitally engage with traditional lace-making processes both on-site and remotely.

Further enhancing its commitment to cultural sustainability and transmission of traditional skills, Martina Vidal Venezia has actively participated in the "Mano a Mano" project, an initiative realized in collaboration with the Fondazione "The Place of Wonder" and the Londra Palace Hotel in Venice aimed at preserving and promoting Venetian craftsmanship through dedicated training and mentorship for emerging artisans. Through this involvement, the company not only contributes to safeguarding the legacy of Burano lace-making but also actively supports the continuity and revitalization of Venice's artisanal heritage.

These strategic efforts in digital innovation and community engagement align with contemporary scholarly insights (Richards, 2021), which advocate for adapting traditional crafts to appeal to new generations, thereby ensuring cultural and economic sustainability.

ORSONI VENEZIA 1888

Orsoni Venezia 1888 is the only furnace that maintains the traditional art of handcrafting mosaic tesserae within the island of Venice. It is renowned globally for its exceptional quality and vast palette, exceeding 3,500 colors and including 24-carat gold leaf mosaics. Orsoni's legacy dates to 1888 when the founder, Angelo Orsoni, exhibited mosaic techniques at the Universal Exhibition in Paris, and continued subsequently with the contribution of Orsoni to monumental artistic works such as Gaudí's Sagrada Familia in Spain and San Marco's Basilica in Venice.

To enhance visitor engagement, Orsoni offers regular complimentary guided tours known as "The Wednesday Cultural Visits," enabling visitors to witness artisans at work and explore the "Library of Colours," a comprehensive archive showcasing the range of mosaic hues produced. Collaborations, such as the one with D20 Art Lab at Ca' Foscari University, have resulted in innovative, immersive installations like "Sounds from the Color Library," which employs Hyper Sonic Sound technology to narrate poetic interpretations of colors, significantly enhancing the sensory and emotional visitor experience.

Additionally, to further underline its intimate connection with art and culture, Orsoni actively engage in strategic collaborations and hosts an artist residency thanks to which the company has given life to various cultural and exhibition projects, such as "Phototaxis" by Paolo Pretolani, "Becoming with" by Luisa Eugeni and "La Joie de Vivre," created in collaboration with the School of Decorative Arts in Paris. All these projects are designed to allow visitors to experience mosaics in an innovative and contemporary way and to strengthen Orsoni's reputation as a leading cultural and artisanal heritage ambassador.

LUNARDELLI VENEZIA

Lunardelli Venezia, originating from Lunardelli est. 1967, is renowned for its mastery in woodworking, creating bespoke design pieces that encapsulate the multifaceted essence of Venice through the innovative combination of wood and other noble, traditional materials. A distinctive sustainable practice involves utilizing recycled wood from Venetian *bricole*, the iconic poles marking water routes in the lagoon, thus enhancing product authenticity while addressing environmental concerns.

Beyond its artisanal excellence, this company has evolved into a pivotal cultural hub within Venice, hosting, organizing, and participating in many artistic and cultural events that enrich the local community and promote public engagement. The company in fact participates prominently in high-profile cultural events like Venice Fashion Week and Homo Faber and organizes atelier exhibitions, conducts press tours to effectively communicate its narrative and processes, participates as panelist in conferences on the relationship between craft and tourism, participates in projects with students from Ca' Foscari University of Venice, and collaborates with both established and emerging local and international designers such as Jacopo Ascari, Alberto Lago, and Marco Zito, to reinterpret the historical knowledge of the island, enhance its potential by adopting a contemporary perspective, and encourage a dialogue with an international perspective.

Additionally, in collaboration with the Fondazione "The Place of Wonders" and the "Londra Palace Hotel" in Venice, Lunardelli contributed to the "Mano a Mano" project, aimed at preserving and promoting Venetian high craftsmanship. By participating as a "Wonder" artisan, Lunardelli engaged in training young artisans, thereby ensuring the transmission of invaluable woodworking skills to future generations.

Even though many of the events are organized within programs not necessarily run by Lunardelli, year after year the site venue has become a meeting point for the Venetian citizens and passionate alike. Through these multifaceted initiatives, Lunardelli Venezia exemplifies the role of a cultural mediator, bridging historical craftsmanship with contemporary design and societal engagement and reinforcing its status within Venice's prestigious artisan community.

UNIFYING PROJECTS: VENEZIADAVIVERE.COM, HOMO FABER ECONOMY, AND UPSKILL VENEZIA

The activities described in the previous paragraph illustrate the transformative impact of immersive experiences and their positive business outcomes. The three case studies, and others that deserve research attention, shed light on an interconnected community and a vibrant territorial ecosystem. The relevance of these initiatives helps craft enterprises differentiate themselves by effectively leveraging cultural heritage and artisanal know-how to foster creative and innovative experiences.

The visibility and the coherence of these experimentations largely rely on a number of well-structured and managed networks that contributed to innovation and knowledge sharing at a local level. Among these, Venezia da Vivere operates prominently as a media enterprise dedicated to unifying, representing, and enhancing Venice's living cultural and creative initiatives. Its strategic effort amplifies the visibility of local artisans through carefully curated events such as the Venice Fashion Week and Venice Biennale Experience. Additionally, Venezia da Vivere contributed to the promotion and transmission of traditional know-how thanks to the design and the implementation of the Mano a Mano project. All together, these initiatives effectively facilitate the dialogue between artisans, designers, and broader audiences, enhancing public engagement, strengthening local cultural identity and giving rise to a vibrant and active community.

Another important project, Upskill Venezia, developed in collaboration with Fondazione di Venezia, aimed at increasing the competitiveness of Venetian craft enterprises by encouraging technological innovation and digitalization. Through the managerial support of Upskill 4.0, a spin-off of Ca Foscari University of Venice, companies have been guided in rethinking their strategic positioning, branding, and communication strategies to reach a broader and more diverse international audience effectively. The process has implied an intense cooperation with the University students in order to foster digital innovation while preserving the authenticity of Venetian heritage.

Lastly, Homo Faber Economy, funded by the Veneto Region and realized by Ca' Foscari University in collaboration with several private foundations, firms, and public entities, specifically addresses the regeneration of Venice entrepreneurial and social fabric. This ambitious initiative focuses on nurturing new digital capabilities and managerial competencies among artisans, aligning their practices with contemporary market dynamics. Core objectives include the promotion of skills development to adapt to evolving consumer preferences and the establishment of a cohesive artisan community positioned as a distinctive strategic asset for Venice.

Collectively, these unifying projects represent critical facilitators of dynamic, generative communities and meaningful exchanges. They set the foundations for coherent and sustainable innovation, providing strategic managerial support, fostering cultural dialogue, and enabling positive impact measurement to drive effective long-term development and cultural sustainability in the Venetian context.

CONCLUSIONS

The analysis presented underscores the essential role of craft enterprises as catalysts for urban regeneration, highlighting their capacity to generate significant economic, social, and cultural benefits within urban communities. Through strategic management, community engagement, and the integration of digital technologies, craft enterprises can effectively leverage tourism to meet the growing global demand for authentic, immersive cultural experiences. Additionally, the analysis highlights the importance of combining two complementary trajectories: on the one hand, the impulse of bottom-up craft-based projects empowered by digital and managerial skills; on the other hand, the impact of top-down communication and coordination initiatives focused on the promotion of a consistent and authentic narrative of Venice.

The successful examples of Martina Vidal Venezia, Orsoni Venezia 1888, and Lunardelli Venezia demonstrate how artisanal tradition, when thoughtfully modernized and effectively communicated, can serve as a powerful driver for local development and cultural and heritage promotion. Unifying communication projects such as Venezia da Vivere, and managerial initiatives, such as Upskill Venezia or Homo Faber Economy, helped Venetian craft to develop a more distinctive international visibility by amplifying individual firms' efforts. The result is a robust, interconnected ecosystem that fosters ongoing innovation and competitive distinction. Ultimately, this comprehensive approach to cultural preservation and economic revitalization offers a replicable model for other historical urban contexts aiming to balance heritage conservation with contemporary market demands.

REFERENCES

Bellver, D. F., Prados-Peña, M. B., García-López, A. M., & Molina-Moreno, V. (2023). Crafts as a key factor in local development: A bibliometric analysis. *Heliyon*, 9(1), e13039.

Bettiol, M., Di Maria, E., & Micelli, S. (2020). *Knowledge management and Industry 4.0: New paradigms for value creation.* Springer.

Bettiol, M., & Micelli, S. (2014). The hidden side of design: The relevance of artisanship. *Design Issues, 30*(1), 7–18.

Cancellieri, A., & Ostanel, E. (2014). Ri-pubblicizzare la città: Pratiche spaziali, culture e istituzioni. *Territorio, 46–49.*

Comune di Venezia. (2021, December 15). *25 Marzo 2021: 1600 anni di Venezia – Progetto scuole, ludoteche e mosaico.* https://live.comune. venezia.it/it/2021/12/25-marzo-2021-1600-anni-di-venezia-progetto-scuole-ludoteche-e-mosaico-conferenza-stampa-di

Confcommercio. (2024). *Indagini, dati e informazioni sul settore del turismo in Italia.* https://www.confcommercio.it/-/turismo-in-italia

Confcommercio Firenze. (2017, July 20). *Il turismo uccide le città? Forum su overtourism a Firenze.* https://www.confcommercio.firenze.it/news/ eventi-progetti/il-turismo-uccide-le-citt%C3%A0-firenze-il-20-luglio-forum-su-over-tourism-e

Fondazione Cologni Mestieri d'Arte. (n.d.). *Martina Vidal: Dove la tradizione del merletto di Burano diventa esperienza da vivere.* https://www. fondazionecologni.it/it/interviste/ar/martina-vidal

Foreman, L. (2017, November 30). *When Venetian luxury ruled the world of fashion.* BBC Culture. https://www.bbc.com/culture/article/20171130-venetian-luxury-once-ruled-the-world-of-fashion?utm_source=chatgpt.com

Homo Faber Guide. (n.d.). *Lunardelli Venezia.* https://www.homofaber.com/ it/discover/lunardelli-venezia-woodwork-italy

Homo Faber Guide. (n.d.). *Martina Vidal.* https://www.homofaber.com/en/ discover/martina-vidal-lacemaking-italy

Hsia, C. (2020). Art intervention in the community context: Community-based art practice as an inspiration for creative tourism. In P. Mura, K. K. H. Tan & C. W. Choy (Eds.), *Contemporary Asian artistic expressions and tourism* (pp. 127–146). Springer. http://dx.doi.org/10.1007/978-981-15-4335-7_6

ITP Italian Travel Press. (2024). *Gaudì scelse la Fornace Orsoni per rivestire la Sagrada Familia: L'azienda che a Venezia produce mosaici a foglia d'oro.* https://www.italiantravelpress.it/gaudi-scelse-la-fornace-orsoni-per-rivestire-la-sagrada-familia-e-lazienda-che-a-venezia-produce-mosaici-a-foglia-doro/

Jordan, P., Pastras, P., & Psarros, M. (2018). *Managing tourism growth in Europe: The ECM toolbox.* https://www.ucm.es/data/cont/media/www/pag-107272/2018-Managing%20Tourism%20Growth%20in%20Europe%20The%20ECM%20Toolbox

Laudiero, A. (2020). Cultural third sector organizations and local development: New actors and tools for urban regeneration in deprived contexts. *Journal of Entrepreneurial and Organizational Diversity, 9*(2), 1–22.

Li, J., Krishnamurthy, S., Pereira Roders, A., & van Wesemael, P. (2020). Community participation in cultural heritage management: A systematic literature review comparing Chinese and international practices. *Cities, 96,* 102476. https://doi.org/10.1016/j.cities.2019.102476

Lusiani, M., & Panozzo, F. (2016). Culture on top: Beyond museification and culture-led regeneration of industrial heritage. *SSRN Electronic Journal.*

Manfredi Latilla, V., Frattini, F., Messeni Petruzzelli, A., & Berner, M. (2019). Knowledge management and knowledge transfer in arts and crafts organizations: Evidence from an exploratory multiple case-study analysis. *Journal of Knowledge Management, 23*(7), 1335–1354.

McKinsey & Company, & World Travel & Tourism Council. (2017). *Coping with success: Managing overcrowding in tourism destinations.* https://wttc.org/Research/Insights/Coping-with-Success-Managing-Overcrowding-in-Tourism-Destinations

Micelli, S. (2011). *Futuro artigiano: L'innovazione nelle mani degli italiani.* Marsilio Editori.

Moledini, R. F. (2022). Lunardelli: Gli arredi che raccontano Venezia. *The Ducker Magazine.* https://www.theducker.com/maestri-e-mestieri-d-arte/lunardelli-gli-arredi-che-raccontano-venezia/

Molteni&C. (2023). *Orsoni Venezia 1888: Art meets design.* https://www.molteni.it/us/news/event-at-fornace-orsoni-venezia-1888

Ostanel, E. (2017). Urban regeneration and social innovation: The role of community-based organisations in the railway station area in Padua, Italy. *Journal of Urban Regeneration and Renewal, 11*(1), 79–91.

Paulauskaite, D., Powell, R., Coca-Stefaniak, J. A., & Morrison, A. M. (2017). Living like a local: Authentic tourism experiences and the sharing economy. *International Journal of Tourism Research, 19*(6), 619–628.

Peeters, P. M., et al. (2018). *Overtourism: Impact and possible policy responses*. European Parliament. https://www.europarl.europa.eu/RegData/etudes/STUD/2018/629184/IPOL_STU(2018)629184_EN.pdf

Richards, G. (2021). Developing craft as a creative industry through tourism. *Brazilian Creative Industries Journal, 1,* 03-22. 10.25112/bcij.v1i1.2671.

Richards, G., & Wilson, J. (2006). Developing creativity in tourist experiences: A solution to the serial reproduction of culture? *Tourism Management, 27*(6), 1209–1223.

Sepe, M., & Di Trapani, G. (2010). Cultural tourism and creative regeneration: Two case studies. *International Journal of Culture, Tourism and Hospitality Research, 4*(3), 214–227.

Smith, M. K., & Robinson, M. (2006). *Cultural tourism in a changing world: Politics, participation and (re)presentation*. Channel View Publications.

Troisi, O., et al. (2019). Meta-management for sustainability in territorial ecosystems: The case of Libera's social reuse of territory. *Land Use Policy, 84,* 138–153.

Wallpaper Magazine. (2019). *A walking tour of Venice through art and design*. https://www.wallpaper.com/design/venice-art-design-tour

Part V

CONCLUSION

10

SUSTAINING IMPACT: LOOKING AHEAD IN TOURISM, CULTURAL, AND CREATIVE SECTORS

MARIA DELLA LUCIAᵃ, ERICA SANTINIᵃ, ANDREA CAPUTOᵃ
AND FABRIZIO PANOZZOᵇ

ᵃUniversity of Trento, Italy
ᵇCa' Foscari University of Venice, Italy

ABSTRACT

Sustainable Business Models in tourism, cultural, and creative sectors within the Italian Northeastern innovation ecosystem offer an exploratory and practice-oriented pathway for rethinking business models in complex, place-based industries. The metaphor of a transformational journey reflects the evolving nature of these business models in contexts where economic value creation intersects with cultural preservation, community well-being, and environmental regeneration. This metaphor also underscores the need to sustain and scale impact across multiple levels. This chapter synthesizes recurring patterns emerging from the book's four thematic sections and explores their implications for sustaining long-term impact from an ecosystem perspective. For regional innovation ecosystems to thrive, sustainable business models must act as cognitive and institutional vehicles that integrate digital technologies, data analytics, and narrative strategies to enable continuous learning, cross-sector experimentation, and the integration of diverse local knowledge. Fostering academic collaboration across disciplinary boundaries, cultivating long-term partnerships between universities and policy actors, and nurturing new forms of engagement between research and entrepreneurship are crucial for deeper ecosystemic engagement.

Keywords: Sustainable business models; tourism; cultural and creative industries; multi-level perspective; transformative journey; impact

INTRODUCTION

Sustainable Business Models in tourism, cultural, and creative sectors within the Italian Northeastern innovation ecosystem operate within a highly diverse and complex landscape, where sustainability is both a challenge and a necessity. Insights from practice reveal a dynamic, context-sensitive ecosystem shaped by place-specific characteristics, cultural heritage, and socio-economic diversity. This chapter adopts the metaphor of a transformational journey to reflect the evolving nature of these business models in contexts where economic value creation intersects with cultural preservation, community well-being, and environmental regeneration. This metaphor also underscores the need to sustain and scale impact across multiple levels.

This chapter synthesizes recurring patterns emerging from the book's four thematic sections and explores their implications for sustaining long-term impact from an ecosystem perspective. For regional innovation ecosystems to thrive, sustainable business models must master a delicate balance between coherence, ensuring aligned purpose and shared goals, and openness. In doing so, they act as cognitive and institutional vehicles that integrate digital technologies, data analytics, and narrative strategies to enable continuous learning, cross-sector experimentation, and the integration of diverse local knowledge. Universities are identified as key anchor institutions in this process, providing cognitive, infrastructural, and relational capacities to translate research into action. The chapter concludes with a threefold call for deeper ecosystemic engagement.

RETHINKING SUSTAINABLE BUSINESS MODELS: EMERGING PATTERNS THROUGH THE JOURNEY

Insights from the practice of SBMs in North-East Italy reveal several distinctive patterns that challenge conventional business model thinking and offer valuable lessons for advancing sustainability in tourism, cultural, and creative sectors. As detailed in the following sections, SBM practice demonstrates a growing shift toward flexible and adaptive organizational structures, a pragmatic integration of market dynamics with cultural and social values, a strong emphasis on place-based identity and community engagement, and an increasing focus on regenerative and inclusive practices.

FLEXIBILITY OF ORGANIZATIONAL STRUCTURES

A striking pattern emerges across the examined case studies regarding how tourism, cultural, and creative enterprises structure themselves to achieve sustainability. Rather than adopting conventional models characterized by formal hierarchies, fixed structures, and linear growth trajectories, these enterprises often operate through temporary, lightweight, and adaptive organizational structures tailored to specific projects and evolving circumstances. In Vanoy Valley, for instance, the community cooperative intentionally began as an informal association, recognizing that while "the cooperative has a production structure," the association provides the necessary space to "give a direction" to the initiative before committing to more formalized governance. Similarly, in Venice, artistic interventions such as *Souvenir, Venezia Africa,* and *TOTEM* demonstrate project-based organizational logics. These initiatives mobilize specific collaborators for defined periods, disbanding upon project completion and reassembling as needed.

Such organizational fluidity offers clear advantages, particularly in resource-constrained or uncertain environments. By minimizing fixed costs and administrative burdens, these structures enhance agility, allowing cultural producers to respond swiftly to emerging opportunities and challenges (Bocken et al., 2014; Boons & Lüdeke-Freund, 2013). Networks, temporary collaborations, and informal arrangements emerge as a primary operational logic, rather than exceptions or transitional phases. As artists involved in Venice-based initiatives explain, they rely on "informal networks rather than hierarchical organizations," activating "continuous professional and personal ties" when specific projects demand collective effort.

These models fundamentally challenge conventional assumptions within business model theory, which often equate success with organizational scaling and formal consolidation (Osterwalder & Pigneur, 2010; Teece, 2010). Instead, these enterprises embrace what Glasbeek (2024) terms *bricolage,* a distinctive mode of strategic improvisation in which resources, relationships, and symbolic capital are pragmatically assembled under conditions of uncertainty and chronic constraint. This pattern suggests that in tourism, cultural, and creative contexts, particularly those aligned with sustainable and regenerative development, organizational fluidity and adaptive creativity are not merely survival mechanisms. They represent deliberate, strategic resources that foster resilience, innovation, and long-term viability in complex and volatile environments.

STRATEGIC PRAGMATISM IN MARKET ENGAGEMENT

A nuanced relationship emerges between autonomy and market engagement, illustrating how tourism and cultural entrepreneurs navigate commercial pressures while safeguarding their core values. For instance, in Venice, artistic interventions such as *Souvenir*, *Venezia Africa*, and *TOTEM* exemplify what researchers describe as "a pragmatic, often ethical engagement with external demand" rather than an ideological submission to market forces. These practitioners adopt what can be termed *situated pragmatism*, strategically employing entrepreneurial behaviors as a flexible toolkit to navigate structural constraints while preserving their creative integrity (Beverland, 2005; Glasbeek, 2024). For instance, Ginko Film leverages private commissions to cross-subsidize its documentary projects, ensuring artistic priorities are maintained despite financial pressures. Other initiatives use commercial work as a vehicle for conceptual experimentation within client-defined boundaries, transforming economic necessity into a platform for innovation.

This delicate balancing act is also evident among craft and tourism enterprises. Within Venice's historic artisan economy, many artisans have developed immersive visitor experiences that generate essential revenue while simultaneously preserving traditional skills and techniques (Bettiol & Micelli, 2014; Jones et al., 2021). These cultural producers "pursue meaningful collaborations, often turning down projects that do not align with their ethical or creative standards." In Vanoi, the community-based enterprise's market engagement is pragmatically designed to deliver goods and services with the lowest possible environmental impact, showing a commitment to both sustainability and community integration alongside revenue generation. Rather than adhering to formalized business strategies typical of mainstream entrepreneurship (Osterwalder & Pigneur, 2010; Teece, 2010), these enterprises engage in what Glasbeek (2024) defines as *strategic improvisation*, a distinctive form of bricolage. Under conditions of uncertainty and chronic constraint, resources, networks, and symbolic capital are pragmatically combined and recombined in an ongoing process of adaptation (Baker & Nelson, 2005; Bastian & Zucchella, 2023).

This pattern highlights business models enabling a "continuous translation, resource combination, and adaptive improvisation", allowing tourism and cultural entrepreneurs to maintain creative autonomy, pursue sustainability, and secure livelihood opportunities, without compromising their cultural or ethical foundations.

EMBEDDEDNESS IN PLACE AND COMMUNITY

Across the examined case studies, place and community emerge as foundational elements in sustainable business models rather than merely contextual factors. Tourism and cultural and creative enterprises demonstrate that long-term viability is inseparable from meaningful, place-based engagement. The "modes of weaving coherence in place" illustrate this embeddedness as "embroidering," creating relationships with people on a territory grounded on shared values and common cultural heritage. In Castel Campo in Trentino, the deep connection between the estate and its surrounding territory demonstrates how place-based entrepreneurship fosters authenticity and shared value through a "deep ongoing relationship with Castel Campo's living natural and cultural heritage." The family's approach to stewardship reflects a distinct "sensitivity to sensing, listening to, understanding, and reinterpreting the place," creating a form of authenticity that is inherently local. Similarly, the evolution of the community cooperative in the Vanoi Valley shows how the community is both a beneficiary and co-creator of value. As one cooperative member explains, "the economic value of the cooperative returns to the members. It does not have to generate profit - the benefits must be invested in the community." Business practices from Venice show how craft-based experiences are fundamentally embedded within the urban fabric and local community.

This logic is also visible in Trentino's cultural festivals, where organizations intentionally build "collaborative linkages with citizens, volunteers, and local associations, who represent the social capital of the place." The importance of social capital and community embeddedness is particularly evident in rural contexts like the Cembra Valley. Here, the Contavalle Festival fosters participation through theater, storytelling, and decision-making processes that unfold year-round. Artists conduct "listening sessions with locals to incorporate their experiences and stories into performances," reinforcing cultural identity while strengthening local ownership.

This pattern of deep-rooted engagement reflects what craft researchers describe as "coherence through place" (Bettiol & Micelli, 2014; Jones et al., 2021), where enterprises do not extract value from communities but co-create

it with them. These authentic, place-based connections simultaneously reinforce the resilience of both the business model and the social fabric, offering
a replicable pattern for sustainable development.

REGENERATION AND INCLUSION

A defining pattern across the examined case studies is the dual emphasis
on *regeneration* of both environmental resources and cultural heritage, and
inclusion, understood as enhancing accessibility and fostering meaningful
participation. Together, these priorities reflect an expanded, integrated understanding of sustainability, encompassing active revitalization and equitable
participation. This regenerative and inclusive approach manifests in diverse
ways across contexts, sectors, and scales.

In rural areas, historic sites such as Castel Campo or community-based
enterprises become catalysts for local economic, social, and cultural vitality. These cases exemplify how stewardship of tangible and intangible heritage generates shared value through place-sensitive entrepreneurship (Della
Lucia & Trunfio, 2018; Herman et al., 2023). In tourism and hospitality,
the circular economy's regenerative models provide pathways for revalor-
izing waste streams, such as transforming used cooking oil into new products, thereby reducing environmental impact while creating economic value
(Bocken et al., 2014; Kirchherr, 2022).

Meanwhile, in urban settings like Venice, craft-based experiences revitalize communities by strengthening the social fabric and fostering authentic
engagement between residents and visitors. "Artisans act as custodians of traditional knowledge and skills," yet also invite visitors to "experience the city
beyond its iconic landmarks" (Bettiol & Micelli, 2014). Importantly, these
dynamics extend to digital environments, like TripAdvisor forums. Designing
tourism and cultural experiences that are accessible to all enables greater participation by travelers with disabilities or other vulnerabilities, ensuring more
equitable access to cultural and leisure experiences.

The strength of this integrated pattern lies in its capacity to foster holistic,
resilient, and inclusive development. Regenerative practices enhance community adaptability, reduce environmental pressures, and unlock new economic
opportunities rooted in existing resources and heritage (Bellato et al., 2022).
At the same time, a commitment to inclusion ensures that the benefits of
regeneration are equitably shared, broadening participation and reinforcing
social capital. Taken together, regeneration and inclusion offer a promising

framework for reimagining sustainability, not only as environmental steward-ship but as a path toward greater justice, accessibility, and community well-being deeply anchored in place and culture.

SUSTAINING IMPACT AT MULTIPLE LEVELS

The emerging patterns across the case studies provide actionable insights for sustaining the long-term impact of SBMs in tourism, culture, and the creative industries. These insights operate across multiple levels, from individual enter-prises to broader ecosystems and policy frameworks.

TOURISM, CULTURAL, AND CREATIVE ENTREPRENEURSHIP

Tourism, cultural, and creative entrepreneurs can benefit from embracing *bricolage* as a legitimate and strategic logic, particularly suited to their sec-tors (Baker & Nelson, 2005; Glasbeek, 2024). As evidenced in the Venetian case studies, bricolage enables entrepreneurs to operate effectively under chronic resource constraints by improvising, repurposing existing assets, and adapting to evolving opportunities. Entrepreneurs should leverage the flexibility and experimentation inherent in bricolage to generate place-based value.

Developing hybrid revenue models is equally critical. By combining income streams, such as workshops, educational offerings, digital content, and tra-ditional product sales, entrepreneurs can achieve greater financial stability while safeguarding artistic integrity and autonomy (Bettiol & Micelli, 2014; Beverland, 2005). The examples of Martina Vidal Venezia, Orsoni 1888, and Lunardelli Venezia illustrate how craft enterprises can successfully integrate experiential tourism with artisanal production without compromising their creative vision.

Moreover, cultivating collaborative networks emerges as a strategic neces-sity within precarious creative economies. Participation in platforms such as *Venezia da Vivere* or *Homo Faber Economy* enables entrepreneurs to access shared resources, knowledge, and visibility otherwise unattainable at an individual level (Jones et al., 2021). These networks, often informal and trust-based, function as dynamic ecosystems fostering care, innovation, and resilience at the intersection of tourism, cultural production, and local development.

ECOSYSTEM-LEVEL: SUSTAINABLE VALUE CREATION

Place managers must fundamentally realign priorities to place residents' needs before tourism development, acknowledging that sustainable tourism is contingent upon thriving, resilient communities. The Vanoi Valley exemplifies this approach, where the initial focus on tourism as an economic driver evolved into a broader agenda for community well-being, emphasizing essential services and stable resident populations as prerequisites for tourism sustainability. This agenda requires destination managers to invest in basic infrastructure, housing accessibility, and community services that primarily serve residents while creating the foundation for authentic visitor experiences.

Managers should simultaneously design tourism experiences that generate reciprocal benefits for local communities rather than extracting value from them (Courage et al., 2021). The artistic interventions in Venice demonstrate how cultural production can resist heritage commodification by authentically engaging with local artisans, traditions, and narratives. Projects like *Souvenir* illustrate how tourism, when thoughtfully curated, can contribute to cultural resilience by documenting traditional knowledge and fostering meaningful exchanges between visitors and residents.

Furthermore, ecosystem-wide value creation can be amplified by fostering direct connections between visitors and local producers through platforms that integrate cultural production, sustainability, and tourism. The circular economy model for repurposing waste cooking oil within tourism exemplifies how place-based production, environmental stewardship, and visitor engagement can be aligned to create regenerative and inclusive value chains (Bocken et al., 2014).

POLICY AND FUNDING FOR SUSTAINABLE INNOVATION

Policymakers and funding bodies operating at the intersection of tourism, cultural heritage, and the creative industries must reassess conventional success metrics rooted in growth, formalization, and linear development (Boons & Lüdeke-Freund, 2013; Foss & Saebi, 2018). As illustrated across the case studies, cultural and creative production and tourism experiences often thrive through adaptive capacity, embeddedness in place, and resilience rather than through expansion or rigid structures.

Moreover, there is a pressing need to legitimize informal, network-based cultural production, recognizing fluid collaborations, project-based structures, and non-hierarchical arrangements as strategic adaptations to systemic constraints, not signs of organizational underdevelopment (Gandini & Gerosa, 2025; Kroezen et al., 2021). Case studies of Trentino festivals and Venice's artistic initiatives highlight how flexibility, informal partnerships, and project-specific configurations enable cost-efficiency and creative autonomy.

Finally, funding mechanisms should evolve to accommodate non-linear, iterative development trajectories, recognizing bricolage and strategic improvisation as core components of sustainable business models. This entails flexible grant structures, staged investments decoupled from continuous growth expectations, and evaluation frameworks that value resource recombination, local knowledge integration, and adaptability. By supporting these alternative organizational logics, policymakers can foster a more diverse, resilient, and locally embedded cultural ecosystem that contributes meaningfully to sustainable tourism development while preserving the distinctive character of creative production.

THE JOURNEY AHEAD

In navigating the transformational journey toward the long-term impact of SBMs within the broader Italian Northeastern innovation ecosystem, the true progress is forged not in isolation but through interdependencies, dynamic feedback loops, and shared infrastructures. For this regional innovation ecosystem to successfully continue its journey, it must balance coherence with openness. Coherence, in this context, refers to the alignment of purpose, the shared understanding of systemic goals, and the integration of efforts that provide a stable trajectory for innovation. Openness, conversely, demands continuous effort to support the integration of diverse local knowledge, encourage cross-sector experimentation, and enable continuous learning across institutional boundaries, ensuring the ecosystem remains receptive to new ideas and adaptive to change. These key design principles serve as a foundation for any effective ecosystem framework that emphasizes trust building, infrastructure accumulation, and networked governance (Pidorycheva et al., 2020).

Sustainable business models emerge as critical enablers of this transformational journey by navigating the inherent tension and synergy between coherence and openness. They function as a bridge connecting system-level aspirations with organizational practice, aligning policy goals with entrepreneurial agency and community values. As contemporary studies on business model innovation unequivocally assert, SBMs must remain inherently flexible yet unwaveringly principled, to mediate between existing structures (coherence) and emergent opportunities (openness), and between the granular realities of local contexts and the sweeping forces of systemic transformation (Chesbrough, 2010; Foss & Saebi, 2018; Wirtz & Lovelock, 2016).

SBMs can drive, steer, and adapt to the demands of this complex and living regional system through their deeper, synergistic engagement with digital technologies, data analytics, and narrative strategies championed by the other research streams of the thematic network on tourism, culture, and creative industries (Spoke 6). Their interplay reflects the mutualistic logic that defines mature regional ecosystems, where diverse actors synergistically create collective value through coordinated efforts and strategic specialization (Guzman et al., 2024).

SUSTAINABLE BUSINESS MODELS AND DIGITAL TECHNOLOGIES

The digital transformation of tourism, culture, and creative sectors, while often portrayed as a technological imperative, can be understood as a process of business model reconfiguration. Technologies do not innovate on their own; instead, they become meaningful when embedded in practices that reshape how value is created, delivered, and experienced (Massi et al., 2020). It is through the lens of SBMs that digital change acquires its strategic direction and impact. The Spoke 6 research stream on digital technologies highlights how innovation emerges through the creative use of digital tools, platform development, and redefinition of the user experience. These developments are not merely operational improvements; their success is inherently tied to questions of inclusion, access, and community participation. This underscores how digital infrastructures, as they become more pervasive, intersect with the values, constraints, and identities that business models are designed to encode and express (Ammirato et al., 2022).

This interdependence is particularly evident in cultural heritage, where immersive technologies and augmented experiences necessitate new value propositions. SBMs must proactively adapt not only to accommodate evolving user expectations but also to address ethical challenges concerning authenticity, data use, and representational integrity (Russo-Spena et al., 2022). In this critical context, SBMs serve as platforms for alignment, connecting cultural institutions, creative professionals, and technology providers in the co-creation of meaningful experiences.

Recent work on digital business models within hospitality ecosystems further reinforces the necessity of a systemic approach, where innovation is increasingly driven by the co-creation of digital value within open and adaptive configurations of actors (Troisi et al., 2023). The diverse digital model configurations seen in the travel industry, stemming from the interplay of platforms, intermediaries, and user communities (Perelygina et al., 2022), compellingly illustrate that the success of digital transformation hinges less on mere technological capacity and more on the organizational ability to strategically adjust roles, processes, and partnerships around evolving digital opportunities – a core function of sustainable business model innovation.

Crucially, in this light, SBMs transcend being mere recipients of digital innovation; they become active agents shaping its direction and meaning. The fundamental challenge lies not simply in incorporating digital tools but in fundamentally realigning value logic around principles of participation, equity, and cultural relevance. By doing so, the sustainable business model transforms into a powerful infrastructure for embedding digital transformation within deeply rooted socially and culturally grounded innovation strategies, ensuring long-term positive impact.

SUSTAINABLE BUSINESS MODELS AND DATA ANALYTICS

Data has unequivocally become a defining asset in contemporary tourism and culture. However, its true value is not inherent; it critically depends on how it is interpreted, mobilized, and, crucially, embedded within SBMs. As the research stream on data analytics demonstrates, data is never neutral; it inherently reflects specific assumptions, priorities, and underlying power relations. Thus, the pivotal challenge for SBMs is to ensure that data use actively enhances sustainability, inclusion, and resilience, rather than merely driving efficiency.

Sustainable business models must proactively engage with data not only for operational optimization but also for shaping demonstrably more just and adaptive value creation processes. Analytics, when integrated thoughtfully, can illuminate underrepresented audiences, monitor socio-environmental impacts, and support collaborative decision-making among diverse stakeholders. When coupled with participatory governance and embedded local knowledge, data transcends its technical nature, becoming a tool for democratic sense-making rather than a mechanism for top-down control (Troisi et al., 2023).

Tourism SMEs, often constrained in their data capabilities, face both risks and opportunities in this landscape. Emerging research indicates that big data can either disrupt traditional business models or reinforce extractive dynamics, unless actors intentionally redesign their models to incorporate transparency, reciprocity, and mutual learning (Zwiegelaar & Stylos, 2025).

The ability to harness data responsibly requires new organizational capacities and new roles of intermediation by platforms, cooperatives, and hybrid actors within regional innovation ecosystems.

From the SBMs' perspective, data integration must be guided by questions of purpose and ethics. Critical inquiries arise: Who benefits from the data collected? What narratives are enabled, or silenced, by the design of analytic infrastructures? What indicators are used to define success in a sustainable context? Addressing these questions is paramount for developing models that incorporate data within the broader context of sustainability and cultural sensitivity. Moreover, data flows should be understood as part of value co-creation processes, where metrics are collaboratively produced with users, communities, and institutions.

Data also enable new forms of feedback that allow for business model iteration and adaptation. In ecosystems where conditions are volatile, rapidly changing, or contested, the ability to learn from data in real time supports resilience. However, such learning must go beyond technical indicators and incorporate qualitative, narrative, and situated insights to ensure that business models remain grounded in context and responsive to lived realities. Ultimately, sustainable business models must function not just as passive consumers of data but as active curators and discerning translators of meaning. Their role is to channel data toward actionable insight while aligning it unequivocally with participatory values and a holistic ecosystemic logic.

SUSTAINABLE BUSINESS MODELS AND NARRATIVE STRATEGIES

Narrative strategies shape how organizations define their purpose, engage with communities, and construct meaning. In tourism and cultural and creative sectors, storytelling plays a central role in articulating value, anchoring identity, and creating emotional resonance. As the research stream on communication strategies illustrates, narratives are part of the infrastructure through which SBMs operate and evolve. Storytelling serves as a way to embed values into business design. Instead of appealing only to consumers, narratives connect with a broader array of stakeholders – citizens, institutions, visitors, and entrepreneurs – around shared visions and long-term commitments. This storytelling ability is especially relevant in place-based and heritage-focused SBMs, where authenticity, memory, and care are intrinsic to the value proposition itself (Echavarria et al., 2022). Furthermore, community engagement through narrative also enhances cultural democracy. These processes are not only expressive but also strategic, feeding into the design of business models that reflect community priorities and social capital.

SBMs that integrate narrative strategies are better equipped to support cultural regeneration and resilience. This includes developing new formats for interpretation, such as interactive installations, digital guides, and story-driven apps. Such tools require collaborative governance and content co-production, fostering partnerships between curators, designers, residents, and entrepreneurs (Gatelier et al., 2022). In such settings, narrative becomes both a design principle and a platform for negotiation among diverse actors.

Recent scholarships also show that narrative value propositions can enable sustainable differentiation. Through approaches like "slow storytelling," firms are reconfiguring their models around emotional engagement, ecological depth, and cultural continuity (Gasparin & Mitussis, 2022). These models respond to the growing demand for meaningful experiences that go beyond mere consumption and foster long-term relational value. Therefore, narrative is not a mere supplement to SBMs but a fundamental mechanism of innovation and strategic alignment. Narrative is, therefore, not a supplement to sustainable business models but a fundamental mechanism of innovation and alignment. It links business strategy with lived experience, facilitates inclusive governance, and supports collective imaginaries of transformation. Within an innovation ecosystem, storytelling acts as a shared language that allows diverse actors to coordinate their actions and co-create a shared future.

CONCLUDING REFLECTIONS AND ECOSYSTEMIC DIRECTIONS

This volume has advanced a multidimensional understanding of SBMs within tourism, cultural, and creative sectors. These models, as we have argued, are far more than mere instruments of enterprise; they serve as critical connective infrastructures for aligning diverse societal needs, local identities, and cutting-edge research capabilities. From a theoretical standpoint, the contributions in this book extend the boundaries of business model innovation, introducing plural logics of value creation, such as place-based storytelling, cultural embeddedness, community engagement, and informal innovation ecosystems (Foss & Saebi, 2018; Gasparin & Mitussis, 2022). In practice, the cases discussed illuminate how small-scale actors, including cooperatives, rural networks, and heritage ventures, create innovation through adaptive, ethical, and locally meaningful arrangements (Dias et al., 2023; Gatelier et al., 2022).

These reflections are integral to a broader, ongoing shift toward research-driven regional innovation ecosystems, which aim to address complex territorial challenges through novel forms of collaboration among universities, industry, government, and civil society. However, this emerging model raises open questions about its long-term sustainability, systemic impact, and institutional viability. Ecosystems are not self-sustaining; their enduring success relies on the deliberate cultivation of legitimacy, the articulation of shared goals, and the development of agile, adaptive governance structures over time. Universities are increasingly recognized not only as knowledge producers but also as anchor institutions that provide cognitive, infrastructural, and relational capacities to their regions (Reichert, 2019). This role encompasses facilitating connections among diverse actors, shaping shared development trajectories, and translating cutting-edge research into tangible action through mission-oriented engagement (Asheim & Grillitsch, 2024). To fulfill this multifaceted function, universities must embrace collaborative leadership, proactive foresight, and embedded experimentation, as well as develop internal capacities that legitimize diverse forms of impact beyond commercial or technological indicators (Reichert, 2019).

Several mechanisms can support this ecosystemic evolution. Locally anchored spaces for experimentation, such as "lab villages" or collaborative hubs, can provide structured environments for co-design and situated innovation. Digital platforms can facilitate the circulation of knowledge, enable the mapping of shared opportunities, and foster transparency between stakeholders. Furthermore, entrepreneurial infrastructures, such as spin-off programs or mission-aligned venture studios, can support the translation of academic knowledge into regionally embedded and socially valuable entrepreneurship.

However, the effectiveness of these instruments depends on enabling institutional conditions. These include supportive and forward-looking policy frameworks, the availability of long-term funding, organizational agility, and the existence of multi-level governance models that ensure horizontal engagement and vertical policy alignment (Reichert, 2019). The co-alignment of university missions with regional innovation strategies is particularly vital and cannot be assumed without institutional incentives, trust-building, and cultural change within academia itself (Asheim & Grillitsch, 2024).

Within this broader horizon, sustainable business models represent strategic relational assets. They are frameworks for organizing collaborative value creation across diverse actors, varying temporalities, and complex resource systems. In the tourism and cultural and creative sectors, they function as infrastructures for translating intangible cultural values into concrete development strategies, while remaining responsive to social, environmental, and place-based needs.

This integrated understanding leads us to a call for deeper ecosystemic engagement. First, academic collaboration must transcend disciplinary boundaries and cultivate shared problem framings. Ecosystem-building requires the articulation of transversal capabilities, shared platforms for experimentation, and prospective thinking can help generate them (Massi et al., 2020; Troisi et al., 2023). Second, long-term partnerships between universities and policy actors must be fostered through mutual trust and a commitment to public value. Especially in culturally sensitive or tourism-rich regions, academia can play a strategic role in aligning development objectives with local identities and community needs (Mariani & Baggio, 2021; Sigala, 2018). Third, new forms of engagement between research and entrepreneurship must be cultivated. By embedding societal missions into business design and venture creation, sustainable business models can serve as relational infrastructures that support innovation grounded in place and meaning (Ammirato et al., 2022; Zwiegelaar & Stylos, 2025).

Ultimately, sustainable business models are more than strategic tools. They are cognitive and institutional vehicles for organizing collective futures. When embedded within long-term, mission-oriented regional innovation ecosystems, they play a crucial role in shaping knowledge practices that are not only effective but also inclusive, situated, and publicly legitimate.

REFERENCES

Ammirato, S., Felicetti, A. M., Linzalone, R., & Carlucci, D. (2022). Digital business models in cultural tourism. *International Journal of Entrepreneurial Behavior & Research*, 28(7), 1735–1762.

Asheim, B. T., & Grillitsch, M. (2024). *Universities as anchor institutions: Regional engagement and innovation systems in the context of mission-oriented innovation.* European Planning Studies.

Baker, T., & Nelson, R. E. (2005). Creating something from nothing: Resource construction through entrepreneurial bricolage. *Administrative Science Quarterly*, 50(3), 329–366.

Bastian, B., & Zucchella, A. (2023). Nascent entrepreneurs during start-up competitions: Between beauty contests and co-created problematization. *Journal of Business Venturing Insights*, 20, e00391.

Bellato, L., Frantzeskaki, N., & Nygaard, C. A. (2022). Regenerative tourism: A conceptual framework leveraging theory and practice. *Tourism Geographies*, 1–21.

Bettiol, M., & Micelli, S. (2014). The hidden side of design: The relevance of artisanship. *Design Issues, 30*(1), 7–18.

Beverland, M. B. (2005). Crafting brand authenticity: The case of luxury wines. *Journal of Management Studies, 42*(5), 1003–1029.

Bocken, N. M. P., Short, S. W., Rana, P., & Evans, S. (2014). A literature and practice review to develop sustainable business model archetypes. *Journal of Cleaner Production, 65*, 42–56.

Boons, F., & Lüdeke-Freund, F. (2013). Business models for sustainable innovation: State-of-the-art and steps towards a research agenda. *Journal of Cleaner Production, 45*, 9–19.

Chesbrough, H. (2010). *Open services innovation: Rethinking your business to grow and compete in a new era.* Jossey-Bass.

Courage, C., Bason, C., & Hillgren, P.-A. (2021). Co-design and the new landscapes of design. *She Ji: The Journal of Design, Economics, and Innovation, 7*(2), 178–197.

Della Lucia, M., & Trunfio, M. (2018). The role of the private actor in cultural regeneration: Hybridizing cultural heritage with creativity in the city. *Cities, 82*, 35–44.

Dias, J., Sampaio, M. P., & Matos, M. (2023). Rural tourism business models and sustainability: A systematic literature review. *Journal of Rural Studies, 103*, 103024.

Echavarria, D. J., Saiz-Álvarez, J. M., & Saiz-Fernandez, J. (2022). Sustainable business models and cultural heritage: A systematic review. *Sustainability, 14*(18), 11480.

Foss, N. J., & Saebi, T. (2018). Business models and business model innovation: Between wicked and paradigmatic problems. *Long Range Planning, 51*(1), 9–21.

Gandini, A., & Gerosa, A. (2025). What is 'neo-craft'work, and why it matters. *Organization Studies, 46*(4), 577–595.

Gasparin, M., & Mitussis, D. (2022). Slow storytelling: Narratives of value and meaningfulness in sustainable fashion. *Journal of Business Ethics, 175*(3), 577–590.

Gatelier, A., Deffains, G., & Dugué, L. (2022). Co-designing innovative solutions for cultural heritage. *Journal of Cultural Heritage Management and Sustainable Development, 12*(4), 629–644.

Glasbeek, L. (2024). Bricolage and its strategic connotations: A study of Greek social entrepreneurs in times of crisis. *British Journal of Management*, *0*, 1–20.

Guzman, J., Murray, F., Stern, S., & Williams, H. (2024). Accelerating innovation ecosystems: The promise and challenges of regional innovation engines. *Entrepreneurship and Innovation Policy and the Economy*, *3*(1), 9–75.

Herman, K., Szromek, A., & Naramski, M. (2023). Examining the utility of a sustainable business model for post-industrial tourism attractions: The case of the European Route of Industrial Heritage. *Journal of Heritage Tourism*, *18*(1), 36–55.

Jones, K. E., Van Assche, K., & Parkins, J. R. (2021). Reimagining craft for community development. *Local Environment*, *26*(7), 908–920.

Kirchherr, J. (2022). The circular economy: A new sustainability paradigm or just empty rhetoric? *Resources, Conservation and Recycling*, *176*, 105965.

Kroezen, J., Ravasi, D., Sasaki, I., Żebrowska, M., & Suddaby, R. (2021). Configurations of craft: Alternative models for organizing work. *Academy of Management Annals*, *15*(2), 502–536.

Mariani, M. M., & Baggio, R. (2021). The digital transformation of tourism ecosystems. *Annals of Tourism Research*, *87*, 103132.

Massi, M., Harrison, P., & Ciulli, F. (2020). How do digital innovations become part of an ecosystem? Introducing a multi-layer framework. *Journal of Business Research*, *122*, 1–12.

Osterwalder, A., & Pigneur, Y. (2010). *Business model generation: A handbook for visionaries, game changers, and challengers*. John Wiley & Sons.

Perelygina, M., Kucukusta, D., & Law, R. (2022). Digital business model configurations in the travel industry. *Tourism Management*, *88*, Article 104408.

Pidorycheva, I., Shevtsova, H., Antonyuk, V., Shvets, N., & Pchelynska, H. (2020). A conceptual framework for developing regional innovation ecosystems. *European Journal of Sustainable Development*, *9*(3), 626.

Reichert, S. (2019). *The changing role of universities in regional innovation ecosystems: A review of the literature*. European University Association.

Russo-Spena, T., Tregua, M., D'Auria, A., & Bifulco, F. (2022). A digital business model: An illustrated framework from the cultural heritage business.

International Journal of Entrepreneurial Behavior & Research, 28(8), 2000–2023.

Sigala, M. (2018). New technologies and smart tourism. *Journal of Hospitality and Tourism Technology*, 9(3), 295–300.

Teece, D. J. (2010). Business models, business strategy, and innovation. *Long Range Planning*, 43(2–3), 172–194.

Troisi, O., Visvizi, A., & Grimaldi, M. (2023). Digitalizing business models in hospitality ecosystems: Toward data-driven innovation. *European Journal of Innovation Management*, 26(7), 242–277.

Wirtz, J., & Lovelock, C. (2016). *Services marketing: People, technology, strategy* (8th ed.). World Scientific Publishing.

Zwiegelaar, B., & Stylos, N. (2025). The impact of big data on tourism business models: A systematic literature review and future research agenda. *Journal of Business Research*, 170, 114251.

www.ingramcontent.com/pod-product-compliance
Lightning Source LLC
Chambersburg PA
CBHW072013230526
45468CB00021B/1247